"To serve well and faithfully"

"To serve well and faithfully"

Labor and indentured servants in Pennsylvania, 1682–1800

SHARON V. SALINGER

UNIVERSITY OF CALIFORNIA, RIVERSIDE

The right of the
University of Cambridge
to print and sell
all manner of books
was granted by
Henry VIII in 1534.
The University has printed
and published continuously
since 1584.

CAMBRIDGE UNIVERSITY PRESS

CAMBRIDGE
NEW YORK   NEW ROCHELLE   MELBOURNE   SYDNEY

Published by the Press Syndicate of the University of Cambridge
The Pitt Building, Trumpington Street, Cambridge CB2 1RP
32 East 57th Street, New York, NY 10022, USA
10 Stamford Road, Oakleigh, Melbourne 3166, Australia

First published 1987

Printed in the United States of America

Library of Congress Cataloging-in-Publication Data
Salinger, Sharon V. (Sharon Vineberg)
"To serve well and faithfully".
Includes index.
1. Indentured servants–Pennsylvania–History.
2. Slave labor–Pennsylvania–History. I. Title.
HD4875.U5S25   1987   306'.363'09748   87–852

British Library Cataloguing in Publication Data
Salinger, Sharon V.
"To serve well and faithfully": Labor
and indentured servants in Pennsylvania,
1682–1800.
1. Indentured servants–Pennsylvania
–History
I. Title
331.6'2'09748   HD4875.U5

ISBN 0 521 33442 X

In memory of my mother
ANNA SHERMAN VINEBERG
and of GEORGE AGRON

Contents

Acknowledgments

INDENTURED SERVITUDE has always seemed to me an absolutely perfect topic. Who else studying early American history could claim to share experiences with people who lived almost three hundred years ago? My status, first as a graduate student and then junior faculty member, has given me a personal window into their world and has enabled me to understand firsthand the operations of the institution of indentured labor. Surely some striking differences exist between my indenture and that of the individuals who served in the seventeenth and eighteenth centuries. Most obviously, my term has gone on far longer than the standard colonial contract of three to four years. And my freedom dues have consisted neither of farm tools nor of one new and one used suit of clothes.

My debts have accumulated over the course of this project. Early on, Professor Richard S. Dunn and Professor Mary M. Dunn, directors of the Philadelphia Center for Early American Studies at the University of Pennsylvania, demonstrated their faith in my ability with a predoctoral fellowship, and I owe them a great deal of thanks. Their help was not merely financial. I profited immensely from seminars at the center and from interaction with the other fellows, especially Carole Shammas and Tom Doerflinger. In addition, a postdoctoral fellowship from the Regional Economic History Research Center at the Hagley Museum and Library, directed by Glenn Porter, enabled me to broaden the scope of the dissertation. Much of the research was conducted at the Historical Society of Pennsylvania and the Philadelphia City Archives. The staffs at both institutions were extremely helpful. Linda Stanley, head of the manuscript division at HSP, never seemed the slightest bit perturbed by my unannounced arrivals, endless questions, infinite number of call slips, and frantic long-distance telephone calls. The reference and interlibrary loan librarians at the University of California, Riverside, library, especially Nancy Huling, worked magic.

Chapter 1 turned into a team sport – one side encouraged the original historiographic debate, whereas the other thought it had no place in the manuscript. Mary Yeager of the University of California, Los Angeles, was on the winning side, and her influence pushed her team to the top. Most important, she implored me to think like an economic historian. Cindy Shelton not only entered the Chapter 1 fray, she joined the Melville Street Salon, Philadelphia. The salon broadened its focus on early American history by incorporating jogging around Clark Park, co-op dinners, and late-night discussions into its program.

At UCR, my colleagues have been wonderful. Arch Getty took time away from his study of Stalinist Russia to provide me with a schedule of purging and retention of text. Alice Wexler shared her historical skills and editing talents. I hope that some of her gifts as a writer rubbed off. Lou Masur took bad paragraphs into his own skillful hands and transformed them. John Phillips provided emergency sentences. Charles Wetherell not only critiqued the manuscript, but helped enormously with the tables. I even took most of his suggestions. Roger Ransom and Carl Strikwerda both played in the Chapter 1 game. Jacquelyn Haywood rescued me from embarrassing errors. Working with Edwin Gaustad has been marvelous. I interrupt him so often during the course of a day that a path has been worn between my office and his. However, he always appears not to mind yet another conversation about indentured servants or Education at Home, our favorite University of California program. Although this traditionally should mark the spot where I absolve the aforementioned scholars from responsibility for remaining errors, why would I have consulted such an august group if I had wanted to carry the burden alone?

Steven Hahn, from the University of California, San Diego, read the dissertation many years ago, and although he has not seen this manuscript, I am indebted to him. His recommendations for revising greatly affected my conceptualization of the book.

For fear of jeopardizing my future in the Department of History, I must also thank the wonderful staff–Clare Washington, Susan Braddock, Diane Sanford, and Connie Young–for their humor and good cheer. Connie cannot be flustered no matter how many times you jam the printer or overdraw your account.

Some institutions helped in very concrete ways. A National Endowment for the Humanities Summer Fellowship and generous grants from the Academic Senate of UCR provided research and travel funds. With these I was able to hire student research assistants, Xiao Hong Shen, Barbara Wallace, and Aimée Myers. Emily Teipe located the advertisements displayed on the cover. All worked through their own indentures admirably. Finally, a UCR Junior Faculty Development Award enabled me to devote a summer to the project.

I am deeply grateful for all of the help from Cambridge University Press. Two critics, one anonymous, provided extensive and helpful comments.

Acknowledgments

Both readers should recognize their marks on the finished product. Frank Smith, the editor, has truly eased the way.

Material from three journal articles of mine is used here by permission of the original publishers, to whom I extend my thanks: *Labor History*, for "Colonial Labor in Transition: The Decline of Indentured Servitude in Late Eighteenth-Century Philadelphia," vol. 22 (Spring 1981), 165–91; the *Pennsylvania Magazine of History & Biography*, for "'Send No More Women': Female Servants in Eighteenth-Century Philadelphia," vol. 107, no. 1 (January 1983), 29–48; and the *William & Mary Quarterly*, for "Artisans, Journeymen, and the Transformation of Labor in Late Eighteenth-Century Philadelphia," 3d ser., vol. 40 (January 1983), 62–84.

My greatest debt is to Gary B. Nash, who supervised the dissertation, the core of this book. He has been involved in the entire project from its inception in his graduate seminar to its completion. The flow from his red pen was so heavy at times, my chapters looked as if they had been involved in horrible traffic accidents. Through countless drafts, over a long period of time, Gary combined a balance of criticism and support for my work while setting a stunning example of the historian's craft with his own.

I must also acknowledge my cousins Murray and Alta Rudomin. They did not help directly with the book, but for years their constant refrain was "Is it finished yet?" Rather than continue to suffer this embarrassment, I spent less time with them than I would have otherwise, no doubt speeding up the process of completion. Frieda Agron, who will only occasionally admit to being related, lured me to Berkeley each summer, located a place to plug in the PC, and has always been there for everything.

A special thanks goes to my son Aaron. I suspect he won't find out what the book is about unless Bill Cosby presents it on television. And spending time with Aaron slowed the progress of this work considerably. But the delay was worth it. In the process, he helped me to clarify what is truly important in my life.

Finally, my mother had hoped to see this project completed. Although they did not meet her, the people at Cambridge University Press will experience her loss as well. She would have been a self-appointed book purchaser and distributor, no doubt boosting sales well above expectations. And that would have been just like her. She rarely judged; just offered support. This is only a small part of why I dedicate this book to her.

Abbreviations used in the notes

HSP	Historical Society of Pennsylvania, Philadelphia
JAH	*Journal of American History*
JEH	*Journal of Economic History*
JIH	*Journal of Interdisciplinary History*
JSH	*Journal of Social History*
Pa. Arch.	*Pennsylvania Archives*
PGM	*Pennsylvania Genealogical Magazine*
PGSP	*Pennsylvania German Society Proceedings*
PMHB	*Pennsylvania Magazine of History and Biography*
PRO	Public Record Office, Kew Gardens, London
WMQ	*William & Mary Quarterly*

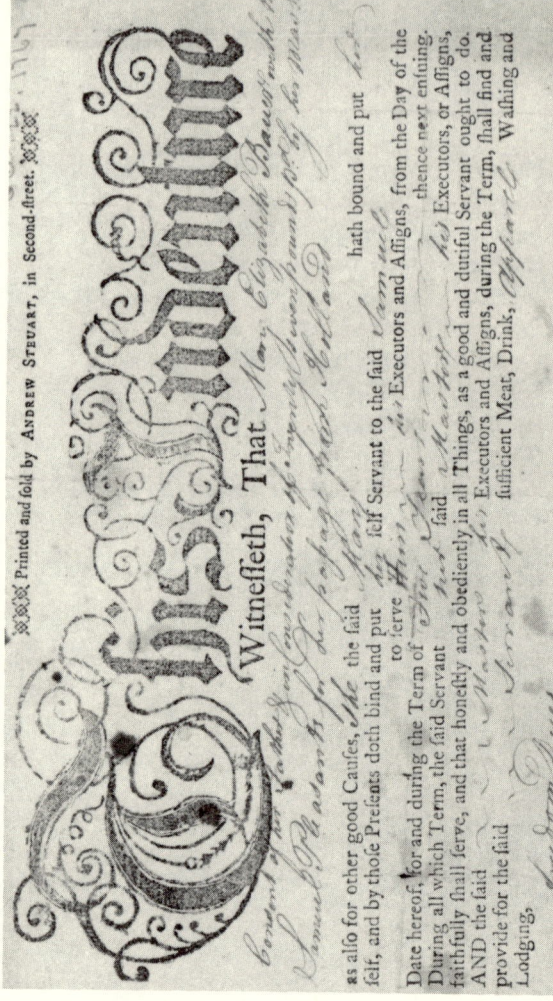

Introduction

GENERATIONS OF HISTORIANS have been fascinated by the history of unfree labor in early America. This has been especially true with the study of slavery – its relation to other forms of labor, its role in agricultural production, its effect on economic growth, and the world of slaves. Although less space has been devoted to studies of indentured servants, this literature is expanding as well. Bound servants played a key role in the development of the colonies, and we understand much about the origins and kinds of people who emigrated as servants, the operation of the system, the legal aspects of servitude, and the distribution of servants within the colonies. However, although we have gained considerable insight into the workings of the institution, we understand little about how indentured servitude functioned in specific colonies or how the institution changed over time. In addition, the servants themselves have remained elusive – the motivations that drew them to sign indentures, the kind of work they performed, the relationship between servants and masters, the role servants played in the labor force, and their experiences after they served their time.

This book begins with the notion that the institution of indentured servitude played a central role in the labor history of colonial Pennsylvania. However, within this role were two functions: one from the standpoint of masters and society, the other from the vantage point of the servants themselves. Colonial masters hoped that servitude would secure adequate numbers of laborers. Servants sought a means of transportation to the New World and dreamed of more prosperous futures. Both aspects of indentured labor – the institutional and the personal – are continuing threads in this analysis. The demand for servants, the reasons for the existence of the institution, the development and decline of unfree labor are explored alongside the changing experiences of the servants themselves.

The supply of free labor was unreliable and expensive to various degrees in all of the American colonies. In order to solve the problems caused by the shortage of free workers, colonies like Pennsylvania imported a large number of indentured servants. However, indentured servitude cannot be studied as an isolated labor institution. It played a vital role in the larger system of colonial labor that included both free and unfree, European and African workers. This study examines the history of indentured servitude within the larger context of slavery and free labor, from the inception of the colony through the course of the eighteenth century.

Thousands of individuals crossed the Atlantic to labor as bound workers in the Quaker colony. They came with little more than vague promises that servitude would propel them toward a future that would enable them to lead independent lives. What motivated them to take the chance? How did they experience such a potentially exploitative labor system? What work did they perform? And what became of them after they had served their time? These are some of the questions this study seeks to answer.

My approach is to trace the origins and development of unfree labor in Pennsylvania. The analysis combines both traditional, from the perspective of the institution of indentured labor, and social history, from the "bottom up." This strategy has made it possible to filter down to the most basic level of the institution, its role within the household economy, as well as to study bound labor from the experiences of individuals involved.

Pennsylvania labor passed through three major stages from the founding of the colony until the turn of the nineteenth century.[1] I present each phase chronologically, first emphasizing the changing contours of the institution of unfree labor and then exploring those changes as they affected servant experience. The first stage of indentured servitude began with the founding of Pennsylvania in 1682 and lasted until the 1720s, when immigration into the colony accelerated. Like all Pennsylvania servants, the individuals who were bound owed the first four to seven years of their labor to their masters and had few choices about their lives until they had served their time. However, throughout this initial phase, indentured labor in Pennsylvania was a personal institution. Servants, like their masters, emigrated over-whelmingly from England and often possessed skills. For many masters, indentured servitude was a means of helping poorer relatives and friends make the journey to Pennsylvania. Bound laborers were occasionally related to or at least acquainted with their masters before they left the Old World and in many cases found themselves on board the same ships as they traveled to the New World. As a result, these first servants were bound by

[1] Throughout this work, I use the concept of historical stages as defined by Immanuel Wallerstein. For Wallerstein, stages are not fixed historical entities that can be dated and described as finite units. Rather, they are "continuous" and "coexist" in reality. The stages in the labor history of eighteenth-century Pennsylvania include the development of the institutions of unfree labor and, later, the transformation from a predominantly unfree to free labor system. No attempt has been made to assign precise dates or to create concrete boundaries for these stages; that would be both undesirable and useless. Rather, they are seen as part of the whole social system within the "minisystems" of the economy. *The Capitalist World-Economy: Essays* (Cambridge, Eng., 1979), 3–5.

more than their labor contracts and tended to serve people they knew personally or who were known to their families. They toiled primarily in the rural areas of the colony, because in the unspecialized early economy farmers had the greatest demand for labor. During this initial stage, recognizable qualities of indentured servitude had been imported from England and indentured labor was a benign and paternalistic institution. It not only provided servants with tickets to the New World but launched them on postservitude careers that, although not uniformly successful, were better than those that future servants would experience.

By the middle of the eighteenth century a second stage had been reached, and it was at this time that the colony of Pennsylvania imprinted its own stamp on the system. English servants no longer emigrated to Pennsylvania in significant numbers, but a great influx of German and unskilled Scots-Irish swelled the servant population. The indenturing process became impersonal, and servants came to be thought of as valuable commodities in a lucrative transatlantic transportation business. Only rarely did masters utilize indentured servitude to bring friends and family to the New World. Rather, the institution became another means for merchants to stuff their pockets with specie and masters to satisfy their needs for workers. The market replaced familial contacts. In addition, as the Philadelphia population grew and the city became the commercial center of the Delaware River Valley, the demand for labor became most intense among urban artisans and merchants. By the mid–eighteenth century, a shrinking proportion of unfree laborers worked in agriculture. Most Pennsylvania servants arrived in the Quaker capital and remained there. Pennsylvania masters sought fewer gardeners and mowers; they now required workers for a host of urban jobs, from clerks and carters to carpenters and stevedores. As unfree labor became a vital part of the city work force, social tensions mounted, manifesting primarily in the form of servant runaways. Paternalism remained, but the marks of exploitation ran deep and were etched from the moment the servant boarded the ship. Clearly the institution had changed and so had the ability of former servants to succeed in the eighteenth-century economy.

The final stage in the history of indentured labor began after the middle of the eighteenth century, when the bound labor system began to wither. By the end of the eighteenth century, the organization of Philadelphia labor had been transformed from a dependence on unfree workers to a reliance on wage labor. Indentured servitude did not die, however, without a last gasp. The disruption of European transportation during the Revolution sapped the institution's vitality. However, indentured labor had a brief rebirth after the war in a peculiar form when hundreds of blacks, manumitted by masters who were complying with the 1780 Gradual Abolition Law, were indentured. Former slaves of all ages served long terms of indenture until this supply of unfree laborers also dried up; by the second decade of the nineteenth century, the institution was no longer viable.

The key to the transition from unfree to free labor was a shift from a situation of labor scarcity, which had characterized the colonial economy until the close of the Seven Years' War, to a situation of labor surplus. The postwar depression created a pool of excess laborers in Philadelphia. A few years later the American Revolution completed the transformation of the labor market as displaced workers used their newly found political power to demand their rights as workers. The issue in late-eighteenth-century Philadelphia labor history was no longer whether indentured servants could succeed in the colonial economy after achieving freedom, since few indentured servants remained in the mid-Atlantic states. Rather, the question concerned how labor relations would adapt to changes in production.

The labor surplus of the late eighteenth century was a product of unstable household economies; specifically, the immiseration of a substantial number of journeymen and master artisans fractured the once cohesive community of craftsmen. Successful master craftsmen gradually assumed the role of merchandisers and overseers of production that was increasingly organized away from the household; as this occurred journeymen and former masters were forced to enter a more impersonal labor market.

Unfree labor fulfilled its promise to masters and provided them with a fairly reliable quantity of servants and slaves at a time when free workers were expensive and in short supply. The perspective of the individuals who served, however, was quite different. After achieving their long-awaited freedom they found themselves still bound by a lack of opportunity. Independence remained elusive, and the hopes for bettering their lives receded. For historians, the reliance on unfree labor is more than just a small piece from the broader puzzle of labor history; it serves also to guide our perception of the transition from unfree to free labor. The change from a labor force with a significant proportion of unfree workers to one in which the vast majority of laborers worked for a wage was hardly a smooth, orderly process. However, by the end of the eighteenth century, pressure from the new labor relations had grown markedly. Wage workers, removed from the means of production, struggled to maintain some control over their lives.

I Models of unfree labor

"HELP IS NOT TO BE HAD at any rate" was the cry from North America throughout most of the colonial period. In 1680 Governor Leete of Connecticut reported to the Committee for Trade and Plantations that "there is seldom any want relief; because labor is deare." "Province wants workmen, workmen want not work; here are no beggars" came the message from Maryland in 1699. Samuel Sewell observed from New England that "help is scarce and hard to get, difficult to please, uncertain, etc." A 1694 report proclaimed that laborers in New England received wages six times greater than in Sweden and Denmark. And William Byrd II explained that he had abandoned his plans for introducing hemp into the Chesapeake because "Labour being much dearer than in Muscovy, as well as Freight, we can make no Earnings of it." The same chorus resounded from the middle colonies. Gabriel Thomas, the energetic promoter of emigration to Pennsylvania, urged that "Poor Labouring Men, Women and Children in England" make the journey to the Quaker colony, for "no beggars to be seen . . . nor indeed have any here the least Occasion or Temptation to take up that Scandalous Lazy Life."[1]

These accounts may exaggerate the favorable conditions for laborers in English North America, but the perceived scarcity of labor was a problem to be reckoned with in each of the colonies. Potential employers complained about the chronic shortage of free laborers, crying that the supply was unpredictable and wages too high. In the seventeenth century, a New England master was forced to sell cattle in order to pay his servant and soon discovered that in spite of this ploy, which provided temporary relief, he would have to let his servant go. John Winthrop recorded that the workman admonished his employer to "sell more cattle." "But how shall I do when all my cattle are gone?" queried the master. "You shall then serve me, and so you may have your cattle again" came the unsympathetic response.[2] In

1 Quotations are from Richard B. Morris, *Government and Labor in Early America* (New York, 1946), 44–6.
2 James Kendall Hosmer, ed., *Winthrop's Journal: History of New England* (New York, 1908; reprint, New York, 1966), 2:228.

1639 a writer from Maine predicted that, if the wage rates continued at their present rate, "the servants will be masters and the masters servants."[3]

Contemporaries identified the abundance of land as the most likely cause of the scarcity of free workers. Individuals did not need to work for others, these accounts claimed, because land was so inexpensive and plentiful. As the surveyor general of New York explained in 1723, "Every one is able to procure a piece of land at an inconsiderable rate and therefore is fond to set up for himself rather than work for hire."[4] Since free laborers were in short supply and commanded high wages, those who needed labor turned to unfree workers.

Colonial American society had three distinct types of unfree laborers: apprentices, indentured servants, and slaves. All three forms of unfree labor were utilized to various degrees in each of the colonies. However, the nature of each system and the degree of exploitation varied. Slavery occupied one extreme and apprenticeship the other. Only slavery demanded service for life and reduced the laborer to the status of chattel. Only apprenticeship combined education and labor with the promise of eventual self-employment.

The system of slavery, like indentured servitude, provided colonists with workers, and historians now concur that slavery was an important institution in most of the colonies and not just the "peculiar institution" of the South. Because only a small number of blacks were present in the early years of each colony, it is not clear whether a distinction existed between servitude and slavery.[5] The first blacks were bound out much like servants, for a specified number of years.[6] Gradually, colonists passed laws that bound blacks for life, and later the condition of slavery was passed on to the slave's descendants. Slaves were used extensively throughout the colonial period by the Quakers in Pennsylvania, as well as the Dutch and English in New York, and provided merchants with a lucrative trade in New England, where their numbers were relatively few.

Apprenticeship differed from indentured servitude and slavery in a number of ways. Apprentices were bound to a master for a period of years, and in exchange for obedience and work, the master provided food, clothing, lodging, and training in the "art and mysteries" of the master's

---

3 Quoted in Morris, *Government and Labor*, 45.

4 Quoted in Sung Bok Kim, *Landlord and Tenant in Colonial New York Manorial Society, 1664–1775* (Chapel Hill, N.C., 1978), 134.

5 Edmund S. Morgan, *American Slavery, American Freedom: The Ordeal of Colonial Virginia* (New York, 1975); Winthrop Jordan, *White over Black* (Chapel Hill, N.C., 1968), 44.

6 Philip S. Foner, *History of Black Americans: From Africa to the Emergence of the Cotton Kingdom* (Westport, Conn., 1975), 243. Winthrop Jordan argues that the evidence does not allow him to say with any assurance whether blacks and whites were treated differently in early America. After 1660, the differences in legal status are clear. *White over Black*, 44.

trade. The colonial apprentice system was borrowed from England, where it was designed to provide society with skilled labor as well as relieve the community of the burden of supporting orphaned or other poor or dependent children. The legal basis for apprenticeship in England had been recorded in the 1562 Statute of Artificers, which imposed a minimum of seven years of service for all persons entering an industrial calling and specified that the apprenticeship was not to expire before the worker reached the age of twenty-four. The statute placed restrictions on masters, too, by stipulating that only masters in certain occupations could take apprentices other than their own sons unless the parents of the apprentice possessed a freehold worth forty shillings.[7] By the seventeenth century, the English system had softened. For example, seven-year terms were required only in trades that continued to operate under the guild system.[8]

Although the system of apprenticeship was formal in nature — for example, the indenture was recorded on printed forms — by the late seventeenth century ties of kinship and community often determined the colonial apprentice-master relationship. Apprentices most often served in their locale, contracted to a family that they or their parents knew, and were incorporated into the family pattern. Except in cases where the apprentice was an orphan or the child of paupers, consent of the parents or legal guardian was required and probably served to protect the apprentice against arbitrary indenture. In Pennsylvania the law required that the apprentice enter into the agreement of his or her free will.

Apprenticeship did little to relieve the labor shortage in the colonies. Unlike servants and slaves, apprentices were drawn primarily from the native-born population. Also, apprentices started their service at a young age and thus performed tasks that reflected their immaturity rather than their future skills. As young children they ran errands, swept floors, started and maintained fires, and did other odd jobs.[9] Older apprentices gained the skills that would enable them to participate more fully in the labor force. Apprenticeship was not intended to supply the colonies with labor. Rather, as a colonial institution it was designed to secure places for orphans or children of paupers and to provide training, primarily to artisans, and to enable each craft to control the number of its members. Although artisans utilized the institution most often, a large range of occupations passed on

7 Morris, *Government and Labor*, 363–5.
8 Ibid., 365.
9 Both Abbot Smith and Richard Morris include apprentices under the heading of child labor in the indexes of their monographs. Abbot E. Smith, *Colonists in Bondage: White Servitude and Convict Labor in America, 1607–1776* (Chapel Hill, N.C., 1947; reprint, New York, 1971); Morris, *Government and Labor*. Also, in his biography of Thomas Paine, Eric Foner includes apprentices in the work force. *Tom Paine and Revolutionary America* (New York, 1976), 43–4.

skills through the system, from clerks and lawyers to seamstresses and doctors.

Apprenticeship differed in a more subtle way from indentured servitude – its closest unfree labor relative. Although designed to pass on skills, apprenticeship also reaffirmed the structure of society. Masters within the most desirable trades could command a payment to take on an apprentice. Thus the children of humble parents were unlikely to apprentice in trades that would have moved them up the status ladder. Sons were confined by the limits of their fathers' economic positions. George Robert Twelves Hewes of Boston apprenticed to a shoemaker, one of the most humble colonial trades, because he had no economic choice.[10] Benjamin Franklin is the most famous example of someone who experienced this system; his father chose not to apprentice young Franklin to a cutler "because of the high fee that was demanded."[11] Apprenticeship, unlike servitude, was a means to acquire skills, not to move upward.

Indentured servitude colored labor relations in each of the colonies. According to various estimates, between one-half and two-thirds of white immigrants from Great Britain and continental Europe came to the colonies as indentured servants.[12] The Virginia Company of London was responsible for introducing this labor system into the American colonies. "That individuals were bound by legal contracts was not strange, since apprenticeship was a familiar institution," writes Abbot Smith, the best historian of the institution, but the novel characteristic of the Virginia version of bound labor was the practice of "selling" servants. Servants were sent to Virginia by the hundreds by the Virginia Company and sold to resident planters.[13] Two additional innovations characterized the American version. First was the standardization of contracts. Although contracts were traditional for apprentices in England, the terms of service were defined by custom and contracts tended to be verbal rather than written. In addition, English agricultural servants, the group that most resembled colonial servants, left home after the age of ten and worked for a number of different households. They moved frequently, often annually.[14] Colonial servants

10 Alfred F. Young, "George Robert Twelves Hewes (1742–1840): A Boston Shoemaker and the Memory of the American Revolution," *WMQ*, 3d ser., 38 (October 1981), 561–623.
11 Morris, *Government and Labor*, 370. See also Franklin's comment about the apprenticeship in *The Autobiography of Benjamin Franklin*, Airmont Publishing House edition (New York, 1965), 19.
12 Smith, *Colonists in Bondage*, 3–4. For a more recent estimate that confirms that of Smith, see Richard S. Dunn, "Servants and Slaves: The Recruitment and Employment of Labor," in *Colonial British America: Essays in the New History of the Early Modern Era*, ed. Jack P. Greene and J. R. Pole (Baltimore, Md., 1984), 159.
13 Smith, *Colonists in Bondage*, 8–9.
14 David Galenson, *White Servitude in Colonial America: An Economic Analysis* (Cambridge, Eng., 1981), 6–8. Although they do not specifically mention the length of service, Louise

worked both in the agricultural sector, especially in the Chesapeake, and in the urban centers, and even though some of their situations were highly unstable, it was not unusual to serve an entire indenture with just one or two masters.

The legal framework of transatlantic indentured servitude grew in response to the trafficking in servants by "spirits." The English "spirit" was a familiar figure in seventeenth-century London folklore. He was a shadowy character who was either hired by merchants to gather a servant cargo or worked independently and sold individuals to shipmasters. Spirits won the dubious honor for leading thousands of English people to the New World through notorious recruitment methods. Roaming the streets of London in search of human cargo and armed with sweets and strong drink, the spirits coaxed unsuspecting children and adults onto ships bound for the colonies. The unwilling captives were then transported to the colonies and sold into servitude. In 1670 William Haverland, a convicted spirit, vividly described the activities of his compatriots. Haverland claimed that John Stewart, a fellow spirit, had in the previous twelve years delivered more than 500 persons annually for sale in the colonies. Stewart paid twenty-five shillings to anyone who would bring him victims and then sold them to a merchant for forty shillings. Haverland also told of a shoemaker who procured more than 830 individuals for transportation in one year and of another spirit who made his entire living trading in humans. In 1664 Lady Yarborough begged for assistance in finding "a poor boy of whom she had care [who] was stoled [sic] away by spirits, as they call them, who convey such boys to ships for New England or Barbadoes."[15]

The English government first attempted to curb these practices in 1645. A parliamentary ordinance required all officers and ministers of justice to "be very diligent in apprehending all such persons as are faulty in this kind, either stealing, selling, buying . . . or receiving Children so stolne [sic], and to keep them in safe imprisonment, till they may be brought to severe and exemplary punishment." Port officials were ordered to search all vessels for kidnapped children and to register all passengers embarking for foreign ports. In 1647 the order was repeated and gave further instructions to colonial governors to record the names of all persons entering the colony. Most likely, these injunctions elicited little response. No lists have survived, nor was there any decrease in the number of complaints about spiriting.[16]

Petitions to the king and council continued to address the issue of spiriting through the second half of the century. In 1664 the Council of

Tilly and Joan Scott do discuss the importance of servants in both the rural and urban setting. *Women, Work, and Family* (New York, 1978), 13, 14, 18, 20, and 22.
15 Smith, *Colonists in Bondage*, 74; *Calendar of State Papers, Colonial Series, America and West Indies, 1722–1773* (London, 1934), 5:221.
16 Smith, *Colonists in Bondage*, 71.

Foreign Plantations recommended that Parliament authorize an official registry office. In that year an office was established and a director appointed. In order to control the spirits' activities, servants were to declare their willingness to be transported, and the parents of minors had to grant permission.[17] The registry office identified two classes of servants: black and white. Black servants were to be "bought by way of trade," were to be sold at about twenty pounds per head, and were designated perpetual servants. White servants were to be procured primarily from England, with a few Irish or Scottish "felons condemned to death, sturdy beggars, gipsies, and other incorrigible rogues, poor and idle debauched persons."[18] These servants were also to be transported to the colonies at a rate of sixteen pounds per head, to be free after a specified period of time, and to receive ten pounds at the end of their service. Because no penalties were imposed on the violators of these orders and no systematic records from the registry office exist, it is not clear how effective the office was in curbing the activities of the spirits.[19] However, during this period, contracts were issued to record the individual's indenture. Virtually all servants who were bound in England had their indentures recorded on these forms.

The most common form of indenture in the continental colonies stipulated that the servant serve a master "well and faithfully [in] such employments as the master might assign" for a given length of time, usually three to four years, and often in a specific locale.[20] In return, the master agreed to pay the passage of the servant to the colonies, provide food, drink, clothing, and shelter during the term of indenture, and, depending on the individual transaction, provide some form of freedom dues upon completion of service. The terms of indentures varied widely, however. Skilled workers occasionally received wages, or clauses were included in their contracts to permit them to work outside the master's domain when the master had no work. German servants often insisted that they be taught English. Occasionally, servants were to be taught skills in exchange for additional years of service. Freedom dues also varied greatly, including anything from money and land to tools, clothes, animals, or seeds.[21]

The indenture served as a valuable document for the protection of the servant, for it was the only place where the length of service and the provisions for freedom were enumerated. At the end of service the docu-

17 Ibid., 73.

18 *Calendar of State Papers*, 5:229.

19 Smith, *Colonists in Bondage*, 73.

20 Ibid., 16–17. For an analysis of the variables involved in the length of indenture, see David W. Galenson, "Immigration and the Colonial Labor System: An Analysis of the Length of Indenture," *Explorations in Economic History* 14 (1977), 360–77.

21 Lawrence W. Towner, "A Good Master Well Served: A Social History of Servitude in Massachusetts, 1620–1750," (Ph.D. diss., Northwestern University, 1955), 30.

ment was the only proof an individual had that she or he was free. In 1656 pamphleteer John Hammond strongly urged all servants to make their contracts before leaving England. He also advised servants to take special care to guard the document in order to avoid any problems when the term of service had been completed.[22]

About the beginning of the eighteenth century, a variation of indentured servitude appeared. The redemptioner system transported thousands of German and Swiss families to the New World. Families often traveled down the Rhine River seeking passage to the colonies, only to find their financial resources depleted and insufficient to finance the entire journey. Ship captains took whatever money was left, put all of the family members on board a ship bound for the colonies, and upon arrival in the New World gave the passengers a period of time, usually fourteen days, to secure the balance of the payment. If the individuals were unable to accumulate the remaining cost of the transportation, they were sold into indentured servitude for a period sufficient to satisfy their indebtedness.[23]

Indentured servitude helped to relieve the colonial labor shortage during the seventeenth and eighteenth centuries and, as promised, provided servants with passage to the colonies. Individuals or families would exchange the price of a ticket to the New World for a three- to four-year work contract and the hope of a more prosperous future. Although the conditions of servitude varied from colony to colony, the servants' labor was always owned by the master for a specified period of time, their work was scrutinized closely, and they enjoyed only rare liberties. Opportunities would be available to them only when the terms of their service had been satisfied. Servitude and slavery shared characteristics as labor institutions, but the effect on the individuals bound is not comparable. In servitude, most individuals traveled voluntarily to the colonies, and the future looked hopeful. In slavery, transportation to the New World was involuntary, and the future dismal. Apprenticeship, indentured servitude, and slavery constituted, then, the range of unfree labor systems open to the colonial master. But understanding the options is not the same as explaining the development of unfree labor and the variation in its form from one time and place to another.

When I began the study of unfree labor in Pennsylvania, I assumed that the existing body of labor theory would help me to describe and predict the extent of unfree labor, the relationship between free and unfree workers, the transformation from unfree to free labor, and the experiences of bound workers both during and after servitude. I was only partially correct. Two basic themes with variations are used by economists and historians to

22 Smith, *Colonists in Bondage*, 19.
23 Ibid., 20–1.

explain the use of unfree labor. The first, developed from the neoclassical economic model, stresses the importance of abundant lands and a free market. The second utilizes Marxist economic theory and focuses on the means of production.

The theory, more than two centuries old, based on unlimited lands, argues that unfree labor is feasible only where resources are abundant relative to population. Individual colonists acquired more land than they could cultivate on their own and thus turned to slavery in an effort to utilize the land and maximize production and profitability.[24] Variations of the free-land hypothesis add important correctives. For example, it is argued that abundant land by itself cannot dictate a need for unfree labor; the fundamental requirement for a slave system must include the production of a surplus.[25]

Another variation of the classical model, the staple theory, seeks to identify how colonial societies generated the surplus to invest in labor. This

24 Adam Smith is the best known proponent of the effects of widely available land on labor organization. Adam Smith, *An Inquiry into the Nature and Causes of the Wealth of Nations* (London, 1776; reprint, New York, 1937), 532. Smith's model is powerful and it has informed the work of Cheesman Herrick, Abbot Smith, and Richard Morris. Cheesman A. Herrick, *White Servitude in Pennsylvania: Indentured and Redemption Labor in the Colony and Commonwealth* (Freeport, N.Y., 1926; reprint, Freeport, N.Y., 1970), 1–2. Abbot Smith implicitly concurred that indentured labor was utilized predominantly in agricultural production. Even when an occasional artisan emigrated as an indentured servant, he too was employed as a farmhand. Smith admitted that skilled servants could be exempted from "toil in the ground," but this dispensation had to be worked out before they left England and noted specifically in the indenture. Smith, *Colonists in Bondage*, 3–5, 257-8.

Adam Smith's legacy is also evident in Richard Morris's encyclopedic study of government and labor. Morris described the limited use of unfree labor in New England and equated it with intensive agriculture that required few servants. He noted too, however, the relatively small pool of non-English unfree laborers throughout New England. He was not surprised to discover an extensive bound labor force in the middle colonies because of the large population of non-English people. Finally, because the Chesapeake and the southern colonies produced staple crops for export, they began with the labor of indentured servants and then switched to black slaves. Morris seemed intuitively aware that bound laborers existed in the colonial cities, but he was discouraged in analyzing them by what he felt to be an insurmountable problem of gathering appropriate data. *Government and Labor*, 310–14.

25 Evesy Domar focused on the labor of Eastern Europe. He argued that land alone was neither a necessary nor a sufficient condition. Domar's point is that, when land is plentiful, rent on land falls to zero, which encourages landowners to seek ways of getting the equivalent of rent from unfree labor. When a marketable surplus can be generated, sufficient capital and incentive exist to invest in unfree labor. "The Causes of Slavery or Serfdom: A Hypothesis," *JEH* 30 (1970), 21–2. See also Orlando Patterson, "The Structural Origins of Slavery: A Critique of the Nieboer-Domar Hypothesis from a Comparative Perspective," in *Comparative Perspectives on Slavery in New World Plantation Societies*, ed. Vera Rubin and Arthur Tuden, Annals of the New York Academy of Science (New York, 1977), 292:12.

model relates the process of colonial development to the production of natural resources.[26] It matters little whether these resources are cultivated, like tobacco or sugar, or indigenous, like timber and fish; in either case, the products become the marketable surplus of a region and thus the area's staple commodity. In a refinement of the staple theory the cultivation requirements of the particular staple product dictate the choice of labor system. The labor intensity of tobacco cultivation, for example, as compared with that of wheat, makes it well suited to slave labor.[27]

Finally, in the most recent application of the staple theory, the focus shifts to the labor market. In this model the geographic distribution of indentured servants on the eastern shores of the Atlantic was based, to a great extent, on the freedom that servants enjoyed to contract the best possible indenture.[28]

26 In this model two key regions exist: the metropolis and the colonies. In the metropolis the economy is diversified, produces all types of agricultural and industrial commodities, is well supplied with capital and labor, but is dependent on the colonies for the supply of raw materials. The colonies have the opposite advantages, for they have abundant natural resources but lack capital and labor. Through colonization the metropolis transfers its capital and labor to capture the abundant colonial resources. However, the availability of land exacerbates the colonial labor shortage, and as a result wages remain high and the incentives to use unfree labor grow. David Galenson and Russell Menard, "Approaches to the Analysis of Economic Growth in Colonial British America," *Historical Methods* 13 (1980) 3–18.

27 Carville Earle argues that tobacco requires frequent tending throughout the growing season, whereas grains demand labor only at sporadic times. Thus they lend themselves to cultivation by free labor that can be hired and discharged seasonally. "A Staple Interpretation of Slavery and Free Labor," *Geographical Review* 68 (1978), 51, 54–6, 57. Max Schumacher writes that an average family of seven people could plant twenty to thirty acres of wheat, but they could not depend on harvesting the crop successfully without additional labor. *The Northern Farmer and His Markets During the Late Colonial Period* (Berkeley, Calif., 1948), 41.

H. A. Gemery and Jan Hogendorn reject a model based on resources, availability of land, and staple crop production. Such a model, they argue, focuses more attention on the demand for workers than on their supply. In this theory, the supply of laborers – free workers, indentured servants, and slaves – is the most critical factor in shaping the colonial labor force. Free labor tended to be relatively inelastic except at high costs, whereas both indentured servants and slaves were part of an elastic labor supply. "The Atlantic Slave Trade: A Tentative Economic Model," *Journal of African History* 15 (1974), 223–46.

28 In David Galenson's model, servants selected their colonial destinations on the basis of a complex relationship of variables. The older, skilled, and literate servants negotiated shorter terms of service than unskilled, younger servants, and the former opted primarily for the West Indies whereas the latter chose the Chesapeake. The geographic distribution of indentured labor was based largely on the potential servant's assessment of the presence or absence of opportunity. *White Servitude.* Oscar Handlin suggested this approach in a review of Abbot Smith's book *Colonists in Bondage* (*WMQ*, 3d ser., 5 [1948], 110). Galenson goes overboard in assuming that servants knew the labor market well enough to shop around for the best indenture, which in turn reflected their maximum productivity. The variation caused by skill level is less than one-tenth of a year. This perspective reflects,

Models that emphasize productive relations rather than classical economic theory offer some useful insights as well. Such theories argue that each mode of labor is best suited to a particular kind of production. According to one presentation, for example, slavery dominated the labor in regions where labor was unskilled, where the market was large and increasing, and where production was monocultural. In contrast, free labor was found where towns flourished, where the population density was higher, and where the occupational range was complex and "the trend [was] toward variety and specialization."[29]

These labor theories provide considerable insight into unfree labor in early America. They clarify the heavy reliance on bound workers in the colonial Chesapeake and at the same time account for the minimal use of servants and slaves in New England. Throughout the first five decades or so after settlement in Virginia, fertile land was abundant and easily acquired.[30] When planters discovered that tobacco grew extremely well and was profitable, all that restricted their production was the size of the labor force. The more hands available, the more "brown gold" that could be planted, tended, harvested, and sold. Free laborers were scarce and expensive, so Virginians lured unfree workers by encouraging immigration. Indentured servants were transported to the colony at the expense of the Virginia Company and were promised land in exchange for seven years of their labor. For the first fifty years of the colony, the tobacco economy was sustained and at times flourished with the labor of indentured servants.

Toward the end of the seventeenth century, the unfree labor force in Virginia gradually shifted from servants to slaves. This shift occurred for a number of reasons. In part, the supply of English indentured servants dwindled while the demand for labor continued to increase. In addition,

as Joyce Appleby has written, a propensity like that of Adam Smith, who "was able to assume that human beings possessed an innate commercial mentality." *Economic Thought and Ideology in Seventeenth-Century England* (Princeton, N.J., 1978), ix. See also Lewis C. Gray, *History of Agriculture in the Southern United States* (Washington, D. C., 1933), 350. Gary B. Nash believes that servants played only a minor role in determining their colonial destinations. *The Urban Crucible: Social Change, Political Consciousness, and the Origins of the American Revolution* (Cambridge, Mass., 1979), 111.

29 Immanuel Wallerstein, *The Modern-World-System: Capitalist Agriculture and the Origins of the European World-Economy in the Sixteenth Century* (New York, 1976), 100–1; Wallerstein, *The Capitalist World-Economy: Essays* (Cambridge, Eng., 1979), 38, 87–102. The debate over Wallerstein's theories of capitalist formation is still raging. However, this does not mitigate the value of his insights regarding the centrality of productive relations to unfree labor. Wallerstein, *The Modern World System*, esp. 87–102. Marcus Rediker, in "'Good Hands, Stout Heart, and Fast Feet': The History and Culture of Working People in Early America," *Labour/Travail* 10 (Autumn 1982), 123–44, does a superb job of placing the experiences, practices, and ideas of laborers in the context of labor systems.

30 The following section relies heavily on Edmund S. Morgan, *American Slavery, American Freedom* (New York, 1975). See also Dunn, "Servants and Slaves," 159.

fifty years after Virginia was founded, the rate of mortality dropped. Slaves became relatively cheaper, both because the risk from early death diminished and the Royal Africa Company's monopoly on the slave trade ended in 1698. The decreasing supply of servants rendered them too expensive. Planters switched to the less expensive African slaves.[31]

Colonial New England, in contrast to the Chesapeake, relied only minimally on unfree labor. The largest concentration of unfree labor in the Northeast could be found in the commercial centers. Although land was plentiful during the first two generations after settlement, no profitable staple crop was exploited, nor did a plantation system dominate the economy. Rather, the economic organization was based on the family farm. When additional laborers were required, employers hired on a casual basis.

These contrasting examples reveal a picture of unfree labor that was predominantly rural, that was involved in the production of a highly labor intensive staple crop, and in which labor changed from servitude to slavery. The difficulty arises, however, in trying to mold this pattern to the labor history of Pennsylvania. Abundant lands, high wages, labor scarcity, and staple crop production contributed, but only indirectly. When institutions of unfree labor reached their height in the Quaker colony, the demand for unfree workers was felt most keenly by artisans. Initially, unfree labor was utilized in the rural sector but not in a staple crop economy; by the second decade of the eighteenth century, unfree labor had shifted to the urban sector. The city was geared toward the market, but it was a commercial center – a locus of exchange rather than production. Those involved in production were producing primarily for local rather than colonial or international markets.

In addition, the Pennsylvania system of unfree labor did not change from one consisting primarily of servants to one of slaves. Throughout the history of the colony, servants and slaves were members of interchangeable labor forces. Although the Quaker residents preferred the labor of white servants, the proportion of servants and slaves depended on supply. When servants were unavailable, the colonists turned to African slaves. Finally, unfree labor died of natural causes. Although legislation ended slavery by 1780, the conditions of labor scarcity that encouraged Philadelphia masters to buy bound workers no longer existed. By the late eighteenth century, urban labor had been transformed from one that depended heavily on unfree workers to one in which free labor dominated.

It is not surprising that we know most about unfree labor in the rural sector. Although evident in all of the colonies, unfree labor was critical in regions of staple crop production, especially when the staple crops were

31 Russell Menard, "From Servants to Slaves: The Transformation of the Chesapeake Labor System," *Southern Studies* 16 (1977), 375; Dunn, "Servants and Slaves," 162.

labor intensive. In addition, agricultural production dominated the early American economy – more than three-fourths of the colonial population worked the land for their livings. However, the history of unfree labor and the exclusive focus on the rural economy have constrained attempts to describe unfree labor or to develop a general theory of labor.

The case of Pennsylvania allows us to build on some of the techniques and theories used by economists and historians. For example, issues such as the supply of particular kinds of bound labor are critical to understanding why masters would prefer one type of unfree labor over another. Conversely, labor demand must be assessed. The relative costs of free labor should be considered. In the urban context, abundant lands and high wages were important not because they required unfree labor, but because they drained off free workers and affected demand. Finally, the role of the individual must be considered. Clearly, African slaves had no choice about where they might serve. However, for most of its history, servitude was a voluntary system and the decisions servants made about where to emigrate affected supply.

The history of unfree labor in Pennsylvania raises new questions in part because it does not conform to the general pattern presented by economists and historians. Clearly, staple crop production cannot account for the heavy reliance on unfree labor in the urban economy.[32] Admittedly, colonial Pennsylvania, like the rest of early America, was overwhelmingly rural; only about 10 percent of the population resided in the colony's one city.[33] However, each of the colonial port towns played a far greater role in the economic growth and political development of the colonies than its relative size would predict. Each of the three northern port towns, Philadelphia,

32 Galenson and Menard discuss urbanization, but not in terms of requirements for unfree labor. "Approaches to the Analysis of Economic Growth," 15. Urban slavery has not been totally neglected. In 1964, Richard Wade published his important book *Slavery in the Cities: The South 1820–1860* (New York, 1964). Wade emphasized that urban slavery was quite unlike the bondage in agricultural production, for city life provided slaves with greater freedoms. Wade argued that urban slavery suffered from an internal contradiction. It was necessary to relax the restrictions on slaves to ensure more efficient production. However, these freedoms generated fear in the minds of white urbanites, making the urban setting incompatible with a slave system.

   More recently, Claudia Goldin reversed Wade's conclusions. In *Urban Slavery in the American South, 1820–1860* (Chicago, 1976) she argues that the city slave market responded not only to local demand and supply but also to the workings of the larger agricultural slave market. In contrast to Wade, Goldin found that "cities and slavery were not incompatible" (p. xiii). Goldin argued that the city's labor force was complex and could draw on different forms of labor. In addition, the impression that slavery and cities were incompatible was the result of an effective propaganda machine generated by urban tradesmen and artisans who resented the competition by black workers.

33 John J. McCusker and Russell R. Menard, *The Economy of British America: Needs and Opportunities for Study* (Chapel Hill, N.C., 1985), 250.

Boston, and New York, was tied to the region of staple production. Each city processed, transported, and marketed the products and was a significant consumer market as well.[34] Cities may have been tied to staple crop production, but urban labor was not bound by the cultivation requirements of a staple crop.

Finally, the labor transition in the Quaker colony did not conform to the pattern established in the Chesapeake. It has been argued that, before the shift from servitude to slavery in Virginia, servants were increasingly mistreated and servitude began to resemble slavery.[35] Indentured servitude in Pennsylvania passed through two phases as well. It began as a personal system with few constraints. As the population of the colony grew and the demand for labor intensified, an increasingly complex legal code punished each infraction by servants with harsher penalties. The law also addressed the growing inclination of masters to abuse their servants. However, these changes in the institution did not signal an end to servitude and the beginnings of slavery. Rather, servants and slaves were used interchangeably throughout the history of the colony, and when unfree labor disappeared it was replaced by free labor.

The primary productive unit in the colonies and the focus of this study is the household. It did not matter whether the productive activity was a craft or agriculture or whether it emerged in the northern, middle, or southern colonies, since almost all preindustrial work was organized around the household. The household also formed the center of the bound laborer's experience. Servants lived, worked, and had their views of freedom shaped by their productive environment. The household formation furnished one model of economic and social relationships that they hoped to emulate in freedom. By peering inside the household, this study seeks to uncover the meaning and consequences of servitude for servants. This personal side of the tale is the most difficult to recapture, but much can be wrung from intractable data.

The study of servitude raises many important questions. What was the relation of servant labor to slave labor and of unfree work to free? What was the character of servitude and how did it change over time? Why did unfree labor yield to free labor and what of those who experienced the transition? Answers to these questions provide a detailed picture of unfree labor in Pennsylvania and enable us to rescue from historical obscurity those who served well and faithfully.

34 McCusker and Menard include a fascinating discussion of the debate over the role of cities in population and economics, and conclude that we know very little about the topic. Ibid., 250–5.
35 Morgan, *American Slavery, American Freedom*, 215–34.

2 Labor and servants in early Pennsylvania

WHEN THE FIRST SHIPS brought passengers from England to Pennsylvania in December 1681, what greeted the arrivals did not inspire optimism. The initial land division was barely completed when the storms arrived and everyone had to scramble to prepare for winter.[1] Caves scattered along the Delaware River had to suffice as the first shelters. "They began to dig the cellars," Daniel Pastorius reported, "and build the huts, in which not without much hardship, they spent the first winter."[2] Philadelphia consisted of a sparse collection of cabins surrounded by forest and shrubs. Soon after settling in his new home, Pastorius lost his way "among the bushes" going from the riverbank "to the house of the baker Cornelius Bom a few streets off."[3] The new town was barely distinguishable from the surrounding countryside.

In addition to the uncertain beginning, an inadequate supply of laborers plagued Pennsylvania during most of the colonial period. As in the New England and Chesapeake colonies, Pennsylvanians could choose between two forms of labor: free and unfree. However, the Quaker colony suffered from a mixture of high wages and a chronic scarcity of free workers. In 1698 Governor Thomas explained the causes:

> The chief reason why Wages of Servants of all sorts is much higher here than there, arises from the great Fertility and Produce of this Place besides, if these Stipends were refused them, they would quickly set up for themselves, for they can have Provision very cheap, and Land for a very small matter, or next to nothing in comparison of the Purchase of Lands in England.[4]

---

1 L. O. Kuhns, *German and Swiss Settlements of Colonial Pennsylvania* (New York, 1901), 40; Gary B. Nash, *Quakers and Politics: Pennsylvania 1681–1726* (Princeton, N.J., 1968), 3.
2 Samuel Pennypacker, "The Settlements of Germantown, Pennsylvania," *PGSP* 9 (1898), 71.
3 Samuel Pennypacker, "Francis Daniel Pastorius," *PGSP* 9 (1898), 109.
4 Quoted in Albert C. Myers, *Narratives of Early Pennsylvania, West New Jersey, and Delaware, 1630–1707* (New York, 1912), 328.

With high wages and a shortage of labor, the inhabitants of the Quaker colony turned to unfree workers.

The Free Society of Traders, a joint stock company involved in the early planning and economic organization of Pennsylvania, included indentured servants and slaves in the original design for the development of the colony. The society intended to supply the colony with two hundred indentured servants and an unknown number of slaves[5] to serve as an agricultural labor force that would quickly produce commodity surpluses as well as participate in early manufacture.[6] In a letter urging his brother Norton to subscribe to the Free Society, James Claypoole waxed that "we are to send over 100 servants to build houses, to plant and improve the land, and for cattle and to set up a glass house for bottles, drinking glass and window glass to supply the Islands and continent of America."[7]

Claypoole also requested that some slaves be shipped from Barbados to Pennsylvania for his personal use. When the slaves had still not been sent by the time he arrived in the colony, Claypoole expressed disappointment to his brother: "If they had been sent, I should have taken it very kindly and have balanced account with thee in some reasonable time. Now my desire is that if thou dost not send them all, however, to send me a boy between 12 or 20 years."[8] Like Africans in the early history of other North American

5 Gary B. Nash, "The Free Society of Traders and the Early Politics of Pennsylvania," *PMHB* 89 (1965), 154. In his first published account of the plan to people the colony, William Penn included the lure of land. Persons who brought servants into the colony would receive fifty acres per servant, and at the end of the service, each servant could claim fifty acres. Penn's concern was population and indirectly labor. Cheesman A. Herrick, *White Servitude in Pennsylvania: Indentured and Redemption Labor in Colony and Commonwealth* (Freeport, N.Y., 1926; reprint, Freeport, N.Y., 1970), 32.

6 Nash, *Quakers and Politics*, 21.

7 James Claypoole to Norton Claypoole, July 14, 1682, in Marion Balderston ed., *James Claypoole Letter Book: London and Philadelphia, 1681–1684* (San Marino, Calif., 1967), 133.

8 James Claypoole to Edward Claypoole, December 2, 1683 in ibid., 223. Other examples of early slavery come from Cornelius Bom, who wrote in 1684 that he had a Negro servant, and in the same year, Herman Op der Graeff described how black men or Moors were held as slaves. Edward R. Turner, "Slavery in Colonial Pennsylvania," *PMHB* 35 (1911), 141; Darold D. Wax, "The Negro Slave Trade in Colonial Pennsylvania" (Ph.D. diss., University of Washington, 1962), 20; Richard Wright, The *Negro in Pennsylvania: A Study in Economic History* (New York, 1912; reprint, New York, 1969), 2.

Although there were no slaves in the Delaware region before Penn arrived, the origins of perpetual bondage for blacks in Pennsylvania remain a mystery. From the beginning blacks were treated separately by being forced to work more than twice as long as the average indenture for a white servant and then being required to give future production to the society. And yet Penn noted that the value of blacks was that they toiled for life. In 1685 a deed of sale for a Negro recorded that the master would own him "forever." See Edward R. Turner, *Negro in Pennsylvania: Slavery–Servitude–Freedom, 1639–1861* (New York, 1911; reprint, New York, 1969), 19.

No laws were passed during the seventeenth century to legalize slavery. However, slaves

colonies, the blacks included in the Free Society's scheme for colonial development initially had ambiguous status. The society stipulated that after fourteen years of service blacks were to receive their freedom and a parcel of land, provided they gave the society two-thirds of their production.[9] Penn, however, referred to blacks as slaves as if no ambiguity surrounded their status. In the charter to the society, Penn included a section on the treatment of Africans;[10] and in a letter to James Harrison, Penn made it clear that slaves served in perpetuity. Penn informed Harrison that he was sending a white servant gardener to train "two men and a boy in the art. It were better that they were blacks, for then, a man has them while they live."[11]

Pennsylvania's first indentured servants as well as the initial free immigrants came primarily from England. In the 1680s, the English Quakers responded to William Penn's vigorous campaign to people his newly chartered lands, and thousands left their homelands to participate in his "Holy Experiment." This movement of English to Pennsylvania brought more settlers than any other colonizing effort. James Claypoole was so impressed by the volume of immigrants that in January 1683 he reported, "There had been twenty-one sail ships arrived last summer."[12] A letter from Penn in December referred to the arrival of a total of twenty-three ships that brought two thousand immigrants to Pennsylvania.[13] Another two thousand people landed on the Delaware shores in 1683, about one thousand of whom came in one six-week period toward the end of the year.[14] So

were present in the colony. A 1700 statute differentiated between white servants and slaves in the crime of embezzlement. White servants served additional time, but blacks were to be publicly whipped. This implies that there was no way to extend the service of blacks, and thus they could be punished only by corporal treatment. Also in 1700, separate court systems were apparently established for blacks. Turner, *Negro in Pennsylvania*, 19–20, 23–30.

Only after 1725 did the law deal specifically with the issue of slavery. This law regulated a black person, whether slave or free, "because he was a Negro." Marriage and intercourse between whites and blacks was restricted. The only other aspect of slave life specifically addressed by the legal code was designed to compensate masters who suffered a loss of their slaves condemned to death for capital offenses. In 1725–6, this law specified that, when a slave was convicted, the justices would pay the master the value of the slave from funds collected from import duties. Turner, *Negro in Pennsylvania*, 26–8.

9 "Articles of the Free Society of Traders," *PMHB* 5 (1881), 37–50, Article 18.

10 Turner, "Slavery in Colonial Pennsylvania," 141.

11 Quoted in Wright, *Negro in Pennsylvania*, 6–7.

12 James Claypoole to Robert Turner, January 9, 1682–3, in Balderston, ed., *James Claypoole Letter Book*, 179.

13 Nash, *Quakers and Politics*, 49; Marion Balderston, "William Penn's Twenty-Three Ships," *PGM* 23 (1968), 27–67.

14 Marion Balderston, "Pennsylvania's 1683 Ships and Some of their Passengers," *PGM* 24 (1965), 69–114; and James Claypoole to Edward Claypoole, December 2, 1683, in

immense was the volume of immigration in 1684 that it stretched the colony's limited stores. Pastorius complained that "this province did not produce sufficient means of subsistence for such an influx, wherefore all food became rather dear."[15] The first wave of immigration had come to a close by the end of 1685 but not before fifty more ships had deposited an additional four thousand settlers.[16] By the 1690s, most of the eight thousand people in Pennsylvania were English.

A very small proportion of seventeenth-century immigration to Pennsylvania originated from Ireland and Germany. The first to venture to Pennsylvania from Ireland were Quakers.[17] The tide of emigration was low in 1683, but the floodgates opened in the eighteenth century. These Irish Friends had migrated from England during the disruptions of the English conquest and took over the lands from displaced Irish Catholics. With the reestablishment of Catholic control, the Friends came under a barrage of harassment and many chose to uproot themselves again. Fewer than fifty Irish Friends found their way to Pennsylvania in the seventeenth century.[18]

German settlers arrived in Pennsylvania from the founding of the colony. William Penn made several journeys to the Rhineland before the king granted Penn his charter. After he received his grant, Penn directed part of his recruiting effort toward Germany.[19] He established agents to spread the word about the unlimited opportunities in Pennsylvania and sold land to German merchants, urging them to find buyers among prospective immigrants. Germans did emigrate in the seventeenth century, but their number was small. Most of them followed Daniel Pastorius and were virtually all Quakers.[20] Some of those who did venture to Pennsylvania wrote letters home detailing the favorable circumstances of the new colony, and these accounts influenced future migration. In the eighteenth century, German immigrants would make Pennsylvania their primary destination.

The size of the unfree labor population in seventeenth-century Pennsylvania is difficult to determine. At least 196 servants arrived in the Quaker colony in the 1680s in addition to an unknown number arranged for by the

Balderson, ed., James *Claypoole Letter Bok*, 223–4.

15 Samuel Pennypacker, "Letters Home," *PGSP* 9 (1898), 138–9.
16 Nash, *Quakers and Politics*, 50.
17 Albert Cook Myers, *Immigration of the Irish Quakers into Pennsylvania, 1682–1750* (Swarthmore, Pa., 1902), 41–6; Dennis Clark, *The Irish in Philadelphia: Ten Generations of Urban Experience* (Philadelphia, 1973), 5–6.
18 Myers, *Immigration*, 83.
19 Farley Grubb, "Immigrants and Servants in the Colony and Commonwealth of Pennsylvania: A Quantitative and Economic Analysis" (Ph.D. diss., University of Chicago, 1984), 3–4.
20 John F. Watson, *Annals of Philadelphia and Pennsylvania in Olden Times* (Philadelphia, 1909), 1:19.

Free Society.[21] Surviving records show that at least 271 individuals were indentured to Pennsylvania owners during the 1680s. The size of the slave population of the young colony is equally elusive, since the society never specified how many they planned to import. One estimate places the number of slaves in the early decades between four hundred and five hundred.[22] By 1693 the Philadelphia slave population was sufficiently large that the Provincial Council "protested the tumultuous gathering of the Negroes in the town of Philadelphia on the first days of the week."[23]

Unfree labor was used more extensively in agriculture during the early stages of the colony than would be the case later, because establishing new farms required intensive labor. In addition to "taming the forests and providing subsistence," the farmer had to build shelter.[24] Farmers complained that neither tenants nor workers could be found. When farm laborers were available, they demanded "victuals in the bargain."[25] In 1682 James Claypoole clearly had agricultural labor in mind for his slaves: "Advise me in thy next, when I might have two Negroes for that they might be fit for cutting down trees, building, plowing or any sort of labor that is required in the first planting of a country."[26] In December 1684 an English mercantile house transported 150 African slaves to Philadelphia, where they were "eagerly purchased by Quaker settlers who were engaged in the difficult work of clearing trees and brush and erecting crude houses."[27] During the "first planting of the country" Pennsylvania was characterized by labor scarcity and high wages, and the highly intensive process of establishing new farms encouraged the use of unfree labor.

Rural Pennsylvania did not suffer from problems of labor scarcity for long. After farms were established, the broad economic orientation made a reliance on unfree labor unnecessary. The bulk of Pennsylvania agriculture was involved in the production of grains, crops that required intensive labor only for short periods of time during the planting and harvesting. The

---

21 Balderston, "William Penn's Ships," 23, 27–67; Balderston, "Pennsylvania's 1683 Ships," 24, 691–714; "A Partial List of the Families Who Arrived at Philadelphia Between 1682 and 1687 with the Dates of Their Arrival," *PMHB* 8 (1884), 328–40. No record indicates that the two hundred servants sent by the Free Society ever arrived in Pennsylvania.

22 Wax, "Negro Slave Trade," 24.

23 *Minutes of the Provincial Council, Colonial Records* (Philadelphia and Harrisburg, 1852–3), 1:38.

24 Clarence Danhoff, *Changes in Agriculture: The Northern United States, 1820–1870* (Cambridge, Mass., 1969), 15–16. Danhoff focuses on a later period than the one under discussion. However, the tasks involved in establishing farms changed very little. If anything, the differences would have been technological and should have minimized the problems in the nineteenth century.

25 Quoted in James T. Lemon, *The Best Poor Man's Country* (Baltimore, Md., 1972), 179.

26 Quoted in Wright, *Negro in Pennsylvania*, 6.

27 Quoted in Gary B. Nash, "Slaves and Slaveowners in Colonial Philadelphia," *WMQ*, 3d ser., 30 (1973), 225.

production of grains virtually began with colonization. As early as 1700 James Logan remarked that farmers in Pennsylvania depended on wheat. A German diarist wrote that "wheat bread was eaten in almost all places." In 1775 the picture was the same: "Wheat is the grand article of the province. They sow enormous quantities."[28] After 1740, the average Pennsylvania farm sold between one-third and one-half of its production. Perhaps 80 percent of the farms grew a surplus to sell.[29] Unlike their counterparts in the tobacco-producing colonies who were encouraged by increased production to utilize unfree labor, Pennsylvania farmers were not motivated by either high prices or high demand to invest in bound labor.

Theories of unfree labor would predict that the nature of the staple crop encouraged the hiring of free day laborers rather than the purchase of a servant or slave. In good times "tillage by hired laborers is cheap, the net gain greater," despite high wages.[30] The working conditions of an agricultural laborer were such that "a year in some farming states, such as Pennsylvania, is only eight months in duration, four months being lost to the laborer, who is turned away as a useless animal."[31]

However, the production requirements of grain do not alone account for Pennsylvania's tentative use of unfree labor in the agricultural sector. Virginia, after all, converted some of its agricultural production from tobacco to grain in the late eighteenth century. Although the shift did reduce the demand for slave labor it did not lead to its abandonment.[32] In 1860 Virginia still had the largest slave population in the United States.

The key to labor in seventeenth-century rural Pennsylvania lies in the nature of its agricultural economy. Although farmers cultivated grains for market, grain production allowed and encouraged more diversified production than was the case in the Chesapeake. Farm families in the middle colonies, though certainly not self-sufficient, were leaning in that direction, and the labor of family members and occasional day workers was sufficient.

Although it reflected the early labor scarcity in areas of agricultural production, the use of unfree labor also suggested the future urban orientation of the system. It has been possible to identify the residences of 117 of the colony's first servants. Fifty-two (44 percent) were bound to owners residing in Philadelphia; the others belonged to masters who were

28 Quoted in Lemon, *Best Poor Man's Country*, 154.
29 James T. Lemon, "Household Consumption in Eighteenth-Century America and Its Relationship to Production and Trade: The Situation Among Farmers of Southeastern Pennsylvania," *Agricultural History* 91 (1967), 60, 65–6.
30 Quoted in Lemon, *Best Poor Man's Country*, 179–80.
31 Quoted in Stanley Lebergott, "Change in Unemployment," in *The Reinterpretation of American Economic History*, ed. Robert Fogel and Stanley Engerman (New York, 1971), 75.
32 Paul G. E. Clemens, *The Atlantic Economy and Colonial Maryland's Eastern Shore: Tobacco to Grain*, (Ithaca, N.Y., 1980), 216–17.

scattered throughout the rural areas of the colony.[33] A list of owners' occupations supplemented with a description of servants' skills reveals that more than half of the servants arriving in the 1680s worked for masters with urban occupations. The 50 owners whose occupations could be identified account for 165 servants. Of these, 18 (35 percent) were husbandmen or yeomen; 76 servants (46 percent) labored for these owners. Within the first years of settlement, when Philadelphia had a population of approximately 1,250, there were 150 slaves and at least 86 servants residing in the city. In a community where about 430 free persons labored, 191, or about 30 percent, of the labor force was unfree.[34]

Although the town attracted a high proportion of servants from the beginning of settlement, the precise number of servants involved in agricultural labor was probably higher than these figures would indicate. Many of the colony's first purchasers, merchants like Robert Turner, owned a large number of servants. Although a few of Turner's bound workers remained in

33 The 196 individuals followed in this study include all servants indentured in the colony from 1681 to 1687 to owners residing originally in Philadelphia, Chester, and Bucks counties. Jack Pomfret credits the extraordinary growth of Philadelphia to the fact that a large number of early immigrants settled in "Penn's great city." "Indentured servants were transported by as many Quaker artisan-merchants to assist in inaugurating business," Pomfret explains, "as by substantial yeomen to assist in development of agricultural lands." "The First Purchasers of Pennsylvania, 1681–1700," *PMHB* 80 (1956), 154.

34 The free work force was calculated by increasing the number of the city's taxables by 20 percent. The city's tax lists included only 5 percent women as heads of household. We know very little about the role of women in the colonial urban labor force, but a 5 percent total seems too small to include all of the females who worked in some capacity outside the home. See Sharon V. Salinger and Charles Wetherell, "Wealth and Renting in Prerevolutionary Philadelphia," *JAH* 71 (1985), 835. Carl Bridenbaugh writes that "female craftsmen [*sic*] were found in the occupations of milliners, mantua-makers, dyers, menders, and scourers." He also notes that in Philadelphia the dressing and laying out of the dead and attendance at funerals were largely women's business. *Cities in Revolt: Urban Life in America, 1743–1776* (New York, 1955), 273–4. Women also performed menial tasks at the hospital. See Billy G. Smith, "The Best Poor Man's Country: Living Standards of the Lower Sort in Late Eighteenth-Century Philadelphia," Working Papers from the Regional History Research Center (Wilmington, Delaware, 1979), 2:42; Carole Shammas, "The Female Social Structure of Philadelphia in 1775," *PMHB* 107 (1983), 69–104; and Frances May Manges, "Women Shopkeepers, Tavernkeepers, and Artisans in Colonial Philadelphia" (Ph.D. diss., University of Pennsylvania, 1958). Philadelphia newspapers refer to women in the labor force. See especially the *Pennsylvania Gazette,* March 4, 1746; January 27, 1747; May 7, 1747; August 4, 1748; September 29, 1748; October 6, 1748. Also the *American Weekly Mercury* for July 15, 1742; November 25, 1742.

In addition, male heads of household were also missing from the tax rolls. Thus I have increased the number of taxables by 20 percent as a more accurate reflection of the work force. Although this figure may be high, it will make the proportion of unfree laborers in the city a conservative rather than inflated figure. Salinger and Wetherell, "Wealth and Renting," 835.

Philadelphia to help him establish his mercantile business, many of the others were employed on his thousand acres outside the city.

Life in seventeenth-century Pennsylvania was not easy. Servants exchanged long hours of hard work, six days per week, in a new country with few amenities, for food and lodging and the promise of a stake in society. Servant experiences varied according to the whim of their masters. Their terms could pass uneventfully, or they could be sold, punished, or made generally miserable.

"Paternalism" best describes the master–servant relationship in early Pennsylvania. Although the term is often criticized as being too vague to be useful, it implies a number of concrete yet potentially contradictory relationships. Inequality permeated the master–servant relationship, but this did not prevent the expression of mutual concern and human warmth.[35] Moreover, although servants were members of the master's household, the power relations were always clear. And while masters and servants worked side by side, masters controlled virtually every aspect of their servants' lives. The relationship between servant and master was different from that between employee and employer, for the lives of these people "were intertwined, for better or worse," and no doubt from the servants' perspective, it was often for the worse.[36] As Eugene Genovese has argued, the subordination of one group to another in a system of unfree labor renders it fundamentally a class relationship, although a complex and ambiguous one.[37] In slavery, paternalism undermines the relationship among the oppressed, linking them instead, as individuals, to their oppressors. Genovese's model cannot be adapted wholesale to the servant experience in Pennsylvania, but it does provide important insights into the master-servant relationship. Although early Pennsylvania society was organized around the household, it would be a mistake to assume that a family orientation replaced a class structure. Masters and servants worked and ate together, and often slept in the same room, but inherent in the relationship was the constant reminder of the vertical ordering of society.

Through the first two decades of the colony's history, indentured labor was marked by many of the elements of the English institution. Both male and female servants were a common feature in seventeenth-century English husbandry, and between one-quarter and one-third of English families had

35 E. P. Thompson, "Eighteenth-Century English Society: Class Struggle without Class?" *Social History* 3 (May 1978), 133–65.
36 Eric Hobsbawm and George Rudé, *Captain Swing* (New York, 1968), 38–9.
37 Eugene D. Genovese, *Roll, Jordan, Roll: The World the Slaves Made* (New York, 1972), 3. Obviously, Genovese is describing the world of slaves rather than servants, and racism is the dominant characteristic of the master-slave relationship. However, his other insights into the paternalistic relationship are relevant to servitude as well.

servants.[38] Women who left farming regions made their way to the cities to labor as domestic servants.[39] For agricultural and domestic servants, the system was defined by custom. Referred to as family, servants resided in the master's home, where they received room, board, and, occasionally, low wages. Servant contracts were more likely to be oral than written, and the terms of service tended to be short. Indeed, annual mobility was common, although some servants bound themselves for longer and shorter periods. But a substantial body of laws and a considerable amount of litigation, brought to the courts by both servants and masters, certifies that the terms were enforceable even though the contracts were oral.[40]

Without romanticizing the servant experiences, it can be said that indentured labor was a relatively benign system in the first period in Pennsylvania, in part because the English version of servitude survived – a distinctive colonial institution did not develop until the eighteenth century. From the outset, the terms of service in Pennsylvania were longer than in England, but seventeenth-century indentures were the shortest in the history of the colony's institution. In addition, servants were conveyed to the Quaker colony under a personal system and often traveled with their masters as part of the family. At times, servants were relatives or friends of people who had already emigrated. Although some servants had written indentures, for many the contracts remained informal. And within this potentially exploitative labor system, labor and social relations in seventeenth-century Pennsylvania were characterized by at least an outward calm.

Relationships between masters and servants that developed before emigration also imparted a character to indentured labor during the first decades of the colony. James Claypoole corresponded with his English servant Hugh Masland before their departure, informing him of their tentative travel schedule and each change in the plans.[41] The letter headings in the correspondence with Masland were in the form reserved for business letters, and their interaction minimized status differences. In fact, Claypoole trusted Masland sufficiently to rely on his judgment in the selection of a capable carpenter or joiner who might accompany them to Pennsylvania.[42]

Although they did not know each other before their arrival in Pennsylvania, Thomas Janney revealed the close relationship he had with his

38 David W. Galenson, *White Servitude in Colonial America: An Economic Analysis* (Cambridge, Eng., 1981), 6–7.

39 Sharon V. Salinger, "'Send No More Women': Female Servants in Eighteenth-Century Philadelphia," *PMHB* 107 (1983), 30.

40 Galenson, *White Servitude*, 6–8.

41 James Claypoole to Hugh Masland, London, February 14, 1683, and May 1, 1683, in Balderston, ed., *James Claypoole Letter Book*, 209, 210.

42 James Claypoole to Hugh Masland, February 14, 1683, in ibid., 209.

servant, John Nield, by going to court on Nield's behalf. Janney appeared as a trustee for his servant when Nield was unable to collect money owed to him. Nield worked for wages when his master did not have sufficient work to keep him occupied. When he was unable to collect his salary, Janney tried to help.[43] In some cases the complexion of the master-servant relationship was influenced by ties of kinship. For example, Frances Hough came to Pennsylvania from England in 1683 to serve his kinsman, Richard Hough, a Bucks County yeoman.[44]

When servants preceded their masters to Pennsylvania, they had sole responsibility for attending to the many necessary details before the arrival of the master and his family. Edward Cole, a brickmaker, was bound in England to James Claypoole and arrived in Pennsylvania some months before his master. Cole was instructed to build a house and have it completed and ready for the family's arrival. Claypoole requested that "if it be but a slight house like a barn, with one floor or two chambers and will hold us and our goods and keep us from the sun and weather, it may suffice."[45] In a letter to Cole, Claypoole urged that a cellar be included, for "I shall bring wines and other liquor that the heat may otherwise spoil."[46] Cole followed the directions so literally that he neglected to include a fireplace. Claypoole expressed his dismay over the omission and master and servant set to work immediately upon Claypoole's arrival to remedy the error before winter arrived.

The complexity of the master-servant relationship and the combination of exploitation and mutuality are evident in instances where conflicts did arise. Only five servants in this early group are known to have run away, but in cases where the details are available, ill treatment by the master appears to have been the primary cause. Richard Bestitraser traveled from England to Pennsylvania with his master John Holme. Three years later, a different master, James Stanfield, petitioned the Chester County Court to award him compensation for the trouble and expense incurred because Bestitraser and two other servants had run away. Not only had Bestitraser been sold once, but his new owner was sufficiently oppressive to inspire all three of his servants to abscond.[47] Joseph Chorley arrived from England in 1683 to serve two years with John Clows, a Bucks County husbandman. In 1684 Chorley petitioned the court for redress against his owner because Clows

---

43 *Records of the Courts of Quarter Sessions and Common Pleas of Bucks County, Pennsylvania, 1684–1700* (Meadville, Pa., 1943), 11, 284.

44 "Residents of Bucks County, Pennsylvania," *PMHB* 9 (1885), 226–7; "Families Who Arrived at Philadelphia," 331.

45 James Claypoole to John Goodson, July 21, 1682, in Balderston, ed., *James Claypoole Letter Book*, 150.

46 James Claypoole to Edward Cole, July 21, 1682, in ibid., 153.

47 *Records of the Courts of Chester County, Pennsylvania, 1681–1697* (Meadville, Pa., 1910), 178–9.

refused to pay for the treatment of a wound after he accidentally shot himself in the leg.[48]

Female servants were especially vulnerable. The deaths of Mary King and Ruth Birch appear attributable to abusive masters. In 1685 Henry Reynolds was bound before the Provincial Circular Court held at Chester. Reynolds was accused of wounding, beating, and causing the death of his late servant, Mary King. Since no one prosecuted, petitioned, or brought a complaint against Reynolds, he was freed.[49] Ruth Birch, on her deathbed, blamed her master and his wife for her condition.[50]

The type of labor servants performed affected the master-servant relationship. Agricultural labor was always arduous. Planting and harvesting accounted for only a small proportion of the tasks, since the land first had to be cleared of timber and rock, and buildings erected.[51] Daniel Pastorius found the effort of preparing the land so consuming that he felt compelled to write an account of the process, describing, among other details, the "massive oaks" that had to be felled. The trees had to be removed one by one, and Pennsylvania farmers employed the "Yankee system."[52] Each tree was chopped down; the trunk was trimmed and hauled away. Farmers then plowed around the stump. As much as a year of this back-breaking labor was required to prepare two to three acres for cultivation. No doubt, many of Pennsylvania's first servants spent their time in this way. A second never ending chore was supplying firewood. The family's requirement for fuel must have seemed endless, and many servants were occupied hour after hour with an ax and cart.

Labor in Philadelphia was no easier than in the country, and construction work was the first priority. Pastorius explained that "together with our servant [we] put up a little house one-half under the earth and half above, which is indeed only thirty feet long, and fifteen broad, but when the people from Crefeld were lodging with me, it could accommodate twenty persons."[53] Robert Turner's servant, Robert Salford, was employed early in 1684 to lay the foundation for Philadelphia's first brick house.[54] In some cases, after the work was completed, servants and masters occupied spaces that were not much larger than the initial cave dwellings.

---

48 *Records of the Courts of Bucks County,* 8.
49 Minutes of the Provincial Council, 1:158–9.
50 *The Burlington Court Book* (Washington, D.C., 1944), 95.
51 Pennypacker, "Letters Home," 145.
52 New England farmers employed the same system. By the alternative method, farmers cut through the sap layer, left the trees to dry out, and then burned them. Rowland Berthoff, *An Unsettled People* (New York, 1971), 36.
53 Pennypacker, "Letters Home," 144–45.
54 Hannah Benner Roach, "The Planting of Philadelphia: A Seventeenth-Century Real Estate Development," *PMHB* 92 (1968), 168, n. 47.

Considerable variation was evident in the terms of indenture for Pennsylvania's first servants. For the 196 who arrived in Pennsylvania from 1682 to 1687, more than 57 percent were indentured for four years. The rest served various terms, ranging from the one year Cornelius Netherwood owed Edmund Cutler, a Bucks County webster, to the nineteen years James Molinex was to serve John Cutler.[55] In six cases servants were promised annual salaries that ranged from three to eighty pounds. Included in this group was the special class of servants indentured to the Free Society of Traders. However, most of these were indentured only in the sense of being contract laborers; they were highly skilled craftsmen who reveal a class structure within the servant class. Not only did they receive substantial salaries, but they were housed in private lodging.[56] For example, Richard Townsend, an English carpenter, arrived in Pennsylvania with his wife and daughter in 1682 under indenture to the society. His contract stipulated that he would work for the society for five years at an annual salary of fifty pounds. Joshua Tittery, a glassmaker, came from England in 1683 and was also under contract to the society at a promised salary of more than eighty pounds per year. Even this seemingly ideal arrangement had its troubles. In December 1685 Tittery had to sue the faltering society for more than 160 pounds of unpaid salary.[57]

For the fourteen servants bound as married couples, the harshness of servant life may have been slightly tempered. The stresses caused by leaving one's homeland, traveling across the ocean, and embarking on an unknown course may have been eased by sharing the journey with family members and by living with a sympathetic partner in the same household. Even married people were sometimes vulnerable, however. Roger Bradbury and his family were unfortunately separated upon arrival. Roger and his daughters came to Pennsylvania and served Bucks County yeoman Randolph Blackshaw, whereas his wife Ellenor and their three sons were sold to a Maryland owner.[58] Not surprisingly, Roger Bradbury does not appear later in the Pennsylvania records as a freeman. Evidently, he left Pennsylvania after serving his time and was reunited with his family.

---

55 "Residents of Bucks County," 232–3.
56 If all servants had received salaries, the practice would have rendered indentured servitude untenable since the appeal of the institution was that it was less expensive than wage labor. During this period, unskilled laborers commanded "fourteen to fifteen pounds a year with their living." Day workmen got eighteen pence to half a crown for their keep. During harvest time, they received three to four shillings per day and food. Herrick, *White Servitude in Pennsylvania*, 37.
57 Samuel Pennypacker, *Pennsylvania Colonial Cases: The Administration of Law in Pennsylvania prior to AD 1700 as Shown in Cases Decided and in Court Proceedings* (Philadelphia, 1892), 86–8.
58 Balderston, "William Penn's Ships," 65.

For all of the exploitation inherent in a bound labor system, the institution of indentured servitude functioned with only minimal overt conflict in the early years. For the most part, Pennsylvania's seventeenth-century servants worked out their indentures uneventfully and entered society as free persons. At this point, indentured servitude had fulfilled its first promise – the men and women who served were provided with transportation to Pennsylvania. By signing an indenture, individuals expected to exchange their Old World poverty for more prosperous lives.

An examination of the economic statuses of former servants at even one point in their postservitude careers will provide some insight into their degree of economic mobility. In addition to sharing the experience of servitude, the men and women who traveled to the New World as indentured servants stood at the bottom of the social structure when they arrived.[59] Moreover, the majority were between the ages of eighteen and twenty-two, almost all were from England, and they began their careers as free persons within a few years of one another. The analysis of servant careers should yield valuable insights into the mobility of former servants, as well as clues to the fluidity of seventeenth-century Pennsylvania society.

Despite the appeal of a mobility study, it requires caution. Success in the form of rapid upward mobility may have had little significance for former servants.[60] However, it is clear that indentured servants demanded more

59 For a similar analysis of Maryland servants see Russell Menard, "From Servants to Freeholders: Status Mobility and Property Accumulation in Seventeenth-Century Maryland," *WMQ*, 3d ser., 30 (1973), 37–64. Menard's article serves as a model for the mobility study that follows. The appendix to Herrick's book contains a list of the laws involving servants and slaves. *White Servitude in Pennsylvania*, Appendix I.

A cohort analysis was used. With this technique one first identifies a group of individuals who experienced the identical event at the same time and then follows them through the rest of their lives to measure changes that occur. See Robert V. Wells, "On the Dangers of Constructing Artificial Cohorts in Times of Rapid Social Change," *JIH* 9 (1978), 103. In the present analysis, the common experience is servitude, which in turn includes a whole range of shared characteristics.

Owing to the nature of the sources, the difficulty of tracing names, and the general obscurity of many of the laboring classes, the results of this study and the study of eighteenth-century servants indicate minimum mobility; servants did at least as well as these results reveal. I included information on individuals only when I could be reasonably confident that I was following the correct person. When I encountered the same name many times in one tax list or other source, I dropped the name from the list. Also, easily transformed names like Dure, which became Dyer, or Dwyer, or Ottey, which became Ott or Otte, were excluded from the group.

60 E. P. Thompson found that, in industrializing England, even though social life was undergoing important alterations and mobility was becoming increasingly common, the horizons for each successive generation had not changed. "Eighteenth-Century English Society," Social History 3 (May 1978), 152. Also see James A. Henretta, *The Evolution of American Society, 1700–1815* (New York, 1973), 8; Henretta, "The Study of Social Mobility: Ideologies, Assumptions, and Conceptual Bias," *Labor History* 18 (1977),

from their futures than their Old World environment could provide. They committed themselves to labor for a minimum of four years, said goodbye to family and friends, and undertook an arduous migration to an unknown life in America. Moreover, once they had arrived in the New World, their Old World view may have been altered and replaced "by a fresh perception of the possibilities afforded by the new environment." Although "most artisans did not wish to become lawyers, merchants, or doctors, neither did they expect to become poor in colonial America."[61] In the Old World, these individuals dared not hope to own land. But in the New World, they witnessed the relative ease with which people had acquired property. Although they may not have reached for the top, they did expect to take a place in the society as independent, self-sustaining individuals.

Social and economic mobility for former servants was measured by their ability to gain a degree of economic independence and social status. If we are unable to plumb the subjective realities and aspirations of these individuals, we can at least measure the extent to which they succeeded in trading in their positions at the bottom of the economic ladder in the Old World for more comfortable lives in the New.

The categories used to measure the economic mobility of former servants are based on property accumulation and an assessment of economic success. Mobility is defined by the movement of these individuals from the propertyless and economically dependent category at the moment of freedom to property ownership or other indices of economic success at other points in their careers.[62] Three forms of analysis are employed. First, by examining tax assessments, deeds, and inventories of estate it is possible to measure the extent to which former servants held property or other tangible assets sufficient to suggest comfortable material conditions. Second, when possible, these data are compared with data for a control group consisting of men who were married during the years servants gained their freedom and were thus in approximately the same stage in the life cycle as servants and of roughly similar ages.[63] This method allows us to test whether servitude

165–79; Henretta, "Families and Farms: *Mentalité* in Pre-Industrial America," *WMQ*, 3d ser., 35 (1978), 3–32; and Gary B. Nash, "Up from the Bottom in Franklin's Philadelphia," *Past and Present*, no. 77 (1977), 59–60.

61 Nash, "Up from the Bottom," 60–1.

62 Quintile or decile classifications of taxables based on assessed wealth are the most common categories used to measure economic mobility. However, they are at best relative indices and obscure information concerning variations of income and life conditions of individuals. For this study, the ownership or nonownership of property was used as the strategy to determine mobility. See Salinger and Wetherell, "Wealth and Renting," 833.

63 I selected the control group by recording the names of all males who married from 1687 to 1692, when the majority of the servants attained freedom. My purpose was to select a group whose ages were comparable to those of freed servants, who were beginning their careers at about the same time and who experienced similar conditions within Pennsyl-

blocked economic mobility because some stigma was attached to the institution, or whether the fluidity of Pennsylvania society enabled all individuals to attain a "decent competency" during their lives. Finally, it is occasionally possible to compare Philadelphia's former servants and members of the control group with the port city's residents as a whole.

An early death or geographic mobility was the most salient element in the postservitude careers of many freed servants. Of the first 196 servants, who served between 1682 and 1686, 56 never appear in the records as free persons. It is likely that many missing former servants died during their service or shortly thereafter.[64] Only 10 of the 56 servants are known to have died before their terms of service were completed, but this figure is probably low since servants under indenture rarely had sufficient assets to justify a will. Moreover, the combination of the difficult transatlantic journey, the new disease environment, primitive lodging, and limited personal resources plus an occasional unsympathetic master suggests that early death may have been common.[65]

Even for servants who survived the rigors of servitude, a long life was not common. Dates of death are known for fifty-one servants; of these, twenty-one (41 percent) died before they reached their midthirties.[66] Six more servants (12 pecent of those whose date of death is known) died before reaching the age of forty. Compared with the known average mortality for adults reaching the age of twenty in contemporary areas of colonial America, servants experienced a high rate of early death.[67] Robert Salford

vania society. No doubt, some who married were widowers and therefore not of the same ages. However, the number of older men was probably no greater than the number of servants who were above the ages of eighteen to twenty-two years. The names were taken from William Montgomery Clemens, *American Marriage Records before 1699* (Pompton Lakes, N.J., 1926). Clemens compiled his data on Pennsylvania marriages from the records of the Society of Friends.

64 The mortality and geographic mobility are assumed to be higher than for the general population. However, it is almost impossible to calculate rates of death or migration for servants. Those known to have moved went either to other Pennsylvania counties or into West New Jersey or Maryland. Records from all of these areas made some tracing possible. Those servants who never appeared in any of these records died, moved very far away, went back to England, or were sold out of the area before their indentures were completed. Early sale is unlikely since these transactions would have been detected in the court records and only one was discovered. *The Records of the Courts of Bucks County* (p. 163) show that George Phillips was illegally sold out of the province.

65 One servant who died while serving his indenture left a will.

66 The ages for servants are not known in all cases. When unknown, they were calculated by assuming an average age of twenty years for servants serving a three- to four-year indenture. If the indenture was longer, age was estimated by subtracting the length of the indenture from twenty-one, the age of majority.

67 No mortality data are available for the early period in Pennsylvania history. Comparable data for New England indicate that, for those who survived to age twenty, long lives, well into the sixth and seventh decade, were the rule. See Philip J. Greven, Jr., *Four*

was typical of those who died young. He died in 1688, just one year after his indenture had been completed. He had accumulated nothing but debts during this brief time. He left no will, and his creditors gobbled up his limited assets.

Other servants disappear from the records because their masters moved or sold them to someone from another area, or the servants moved away after they had completed their indentures.[68] Hannah Falkener, for example, arrived in the Quaker capital from London in September 1683, and was bound for four years to Thomas Janeway, a Bucks County husbandman. On May 29, 1689, Falkener married Pascoe Chubb of Andover, Massachusetts.[69] They apparently moved there, since no further record can be found of either. Of the 196 servants who labored for their owners in Bucks, Philadelphia, or Chester counties, 34 are known to have left the area. Although a few of them moved as far away as Hannah Falkener, the majority of these mobile former servants seem to have settled in New Castle County or West New Jersey. Establishing a persistence rate for this early servant group is impossible, but Table 2.1 suggests considerable geographic movement. Philadelphia, Chester, and Bucks counties remained the most common places for freed servants to live, and Chester County increased in popularity. Proportionately more servants settled there than in any other area.

The residence patterns of Pennsylvania's first servants, both before and after they were granted freedom, support two important findings about the organization of labor in the early colony. First, from the very beginning of the colony's founding, the city drew a high proportion, more than 36 percent, of indentured servants. Second, the residence patterns of former servants show that, after attaining their freedom, the majority settled in the rural areas of the colony, Bucks, Chester, and Philadelphia counties, thus reducing the number of available laborers in the developing town. Of the servants who could be located within the first decade after gaining freedom, 64 percent resided in these three counties, with about one-quarter living in

Generations: Population, Land, and Family in Colonial Andover, Massachusetts (Ithaca, N.Y., 1970), 26–7; John Demos, "Notes on the Life in Plymouth Colony," *WMQ*, 3d ser., 22 (1965), 270–2; Kenneth Lockridge, "The Population of Dedham, Massachusetts, 1636–1736" *Economic History Review* 19 (1966), 332–3; Thomas Jefferson Wertenbacker, *The First Americans, 1607–1690* (New York, 1929), 184–6.

68 For some reason, a large number of the servants that were never found in the sources belonged to a few owners. For example, Jasper Farmer, who died before reaching Pennsylvania, owned nineteen servants. Most or all of these servants remained with his wife and son's families on their plantation in Chester County, but twelve of the nineteen never appeared again in the colonial records. It may be that the experience of working in gang-type agricultural labor had a deleterious effect on the servants, or the premature death of an owner or a move caused servants to fade from view.

69 Clemens, *American Marriage Records*, 87.

Table 2.1. *Residence patterns of masters and former servants indentured in selected periods, 1682–6*

	Owners		First decade after freedom		Second decade		Third decade	
Location	N	%	N	%	N	%	N	%
Philadelphia								
City	71	36.2	10	12.5	3	8.8	8	20.5
County	30	15.3	14	17.5	7	20.6	11	28.2
Chester County	17	8.7	14	17.5	13	38.2	12	30.8
Bucks County	78	39.8	23	28.8	6	17.6	6	15.4
Other								
Pennsylvania Co.	—	—	15	18.8	5	14.7	1	2.6
Other colonies	—	—	3	3.9	—	—	1	2.6
Total	196		80		34		39	

Above the "First decade after freedom", "Second decade" and "Third decade" columns is the heading **Former servants**.

Note: Decades are measured from the year the servant gained freedom. Although the years are dissimilar for each individual, the relative intervals after servitude are constant.

Sources: Philadelphia, Chester, Bucks, New Castle, Kent, Sussex County tax lists, 1693; New Castle and Philadelphia County tax lists, 1696; Philadelphia poor tax, 1709; Chester County tax lists, 1715, 1718, 1719, 1720, 1721, 1722, 1724, 1725, 1726, 1730; wills and inventories for Bucks, Chester, and Philadelphia counties; *Records of the Courts of Quarter Sessions and Common Pleas of Bucks County, Pennsylvania, 1684-1700* (Meadville, Pa., 1943); *Records of the Courts of Chester County, Pennsylvania, 1681-1697* (Meadville, Pa., 1910).

scattered Pennsylvania counties or outside the colony. Only 12 percent continued to live in Philadelphia. This pattern changed only slightly throughout the careers of these individuals, but at no time did a comparable number live in Philadelphia as had served there.

Precisely what drew these former servants away from the city is not clear. Those from agricultural areas in England may have preferred the rural life and perhaps the notion of abundant lands lured them. Although the majority of the colony's rural residents farmed, many were part-time farmers and the remainder artisans and laborers.[70] Perhaps the combination

70 Lemon, *Best Poor Man's Country,* 7–8.

of working for wages and the possibility of acquiring land made rural Pennsylvania desirable to former servants. In any case, the majority chose not to remain in the growing port town.

The economic climate in seventeenth-century Pennsylvania provided ample opportunity for the first generation of former servants. The colony experienced steady growth for the first half-century after its founding.[71] Only the depression years from 1722 to 1728 proved exceptions, and this downturn in the economy occurred late in the careers of these individuals. Many had already died or were at the end of their productive lives. Thus it appears that the new colony afforded reasonable opportunities for economic advancement.

Postservitude careers varied in part because the colony had an inconsistent land policy. Freedom land was the most important item included in freedom dues, but it was never promised on a regular basis. Soon after Penn received the charter for Pennsylvania, he wrote a pamphlet to advertise for settlers and to specify the terms of settlement. Penn revealed his desire to attract three types of people to the colony: land purchasers, renters, and servants.[72] In the original pamphlet, Penn wrote:

> To the third sort, to wit, servants that are carried over they shall have fifty acres after their time is expired: for I think it an unconscionable thing that those who are able to pay the passage of the servants should take up five hundred acres on that account, and make the poor men work like slaves, and when their four years are out to keep the five hundred acres to themselves, and let them have none.[73]

Penn thus stipulated that every one who purchased a mimimum of five hundred acres of land would be entitled to a ten-acre city site. In addition, each first purchaser was encouraged to transport servants with the promise of an additional fifty acres for each servant brought into the colony. Also, each servant, on completion of the terms of indenture, would receive a headright of fifty acres. Among the seventy-five servants for whom indenture terms are known, sixty-six (88 percent) were explicitly promised fifty acres of land upon completion of their indentures. Of these servants,

---

71 Nash, "Up from the Bottom," 60.
72 "Some Account of the Province of Pennsylvania" (London, 1681), in James E. Walsh, "William Penn Stops the Press," *Harvard Library Bulletin* 5 (1951), 94–9; Frank Ried Diffenderfer, *The German Immigration into Pennsylvania Through the Port of Philadelphia, 1700–1775* and *The Redemptioners* (part VII of *Pennsylvania: The German Influence in Its Settlement and Development: a Narrative and Critical History in the Pennsylvania-German Society Proceedings and Addresses*, vol. 10; reprint, Lancaster, Pa., 1900), 275; Herrick, *White Servitude in Pennsylvania, 32–3*.
73 Quoted in Walsh, "William Penn," 98.

including ten who were promised land and money, only forty-six servants were recorded as collecting their headright.[74]

Not all servants, however, benefited from Penn's liberal land policy. The agreement provided land only to those servants who were transported to the Quaker colony by their first-purchaser masters. More important, the promise of freedom land was never included in the statutes passed in Pennsylvania by the elected legislature and appears to have been abandoned within the first decade of settlement.[75]

Landownership was one path to success. Philip Howell arrived from England in 1683 to serve David Davis of Philadelphia County. After about a year, Howell bought the remainder of his four-year indenture.[76] On May 5, 1686, he married a widow, Jane Luffe,[77] and two years later he purchased a city lot. By 1693 Howell, a tailor by trade, had acquired a second lot on the riverbank and his total assessed wealth was one hundred pounds, putting him in the top 30 percent of Philadelphia's taxpayers. Ten years later, Howell applied to the commissioners of property to take up the headland of thirteen servants whose rights he had acquired.[78] Howell's wife died in 1697;[79] twenty years later, Howell died a wealthy man. His estate was valued at more than 800 pounds, placing it in the top 10 percent of Philadelphia inventories.[80] Howell's story reveals all of the ambiguities of

74 Ned C. Landsman found that very few of the Scottish servants who traveled to East New Jersey in the seventeenth century took up their headright. He suggests that many servants may not have identified landownership as a possibility. Landsman concludes that there was an ethnic bias against landownership among this class of Scottish immigrants. *Scotland and Its First American Colony, 1683–1765* (Princeton, N.J., 1985).

75 Diffenderfer, *German Immigration,* 275; Pomfret, "First Purchasers," 147; Herrick, *White Servitude in Pennsylvania,* 32–3; William R. Shepherd, "Land System of Provincial Pennsylvania," *Annual Report of the American Historical Society* (1895), 118; William R. Shepherd, *Proprietary Government in Pennsylvania* (New York, 1896), 18; Samuel Hazard, *Annals of Pennsylvania from the Discovery of the Delaware, 1609–1682* (Philadelphia, 1850), 510, 518.

The promise of headland, or freedom land, was never written into law, and no written statement indicating the cessation of the practice was found. Herrick suggests that the awarding of headland was withdrawn in 1700 owing to some abuses within the system, a growing scarcity of land, and a shift in the institution of servitude into a trade system. Thus servants were no longer being transported with land purchasers, the original stipulation in Penn's "Conditions and Concessions." *White Servitude in Pennsylvania,* 33.

76 Balderston, "Pennsylvania's 1683 Ships," 99.

77 Clemens, *American Marriage Records,* 146.

78 Warrants and Surveys, 1684–1749, HSP; "Minutes of the Board of Property of the Province of Pennsylvania," *Pa. Arch.,* 2d Ser., 19 (1890), 409, 229–30, 325; and Philadelphia County Taxables, 1693, HSP. This tax list is published in *PMHB* 8 (1884), 82–105.

79 Abstract of the Records of Death and Burials Kept by the Philadelphia Monthly Meeting, 1688–1826. The original is in the possession of the Hicksite Friends. I worked from a microfilm copy held by the Church of the Latter Day Saints, Los Angeles.

80 The Howell inventory is incomplete. Department of Wills, City Hall Annex, Philadel-

poor men who acquired land. For him, landownership provided the means to gain economic independence, but the picture was not as sanguine for the more than one-quarter of the former servants who sold him their headrights. The evidence suggests that their most immediate need was cash, and they were unable to hold onto the land.

For the servants who were promised fifty acres of freedom land and wanted to farm, the path to landownership should have been only as long as the trip to the deed office to claim the headright. Many servants, like Howell, succeeded in becoming landowners, but the system of freedom land by no means provided all of these servants with a freehold. Some servants never collected their freedom land,[81] and of those who did, many were unable to accept the land grant until almost ten years after their service had been completed. Edward Doyle traveled from Ireland to Pennsylvania in 1683 and served a four-year indenture to Joseph Fisher, a wealthy yeoman. Nine years after obtaining his freedom, Doyle was granted his fifty acres of land.[82] However, in that same year, Doyle petitioned the Bucks County court, "setting forth his want of reliefe."[83] In 1699 Doyle was again in financial distress, and the sheriff's deputy was called upon to summon a jury for his trial for debt.[84] He died in 1702 and left no inventory. In 1720 Thomas Rogers and his wife requested their hundred-acre headright. Rogers was allowed only one fifty-acre parcel since his wife had died and was unable to claim the allotment personally.[85]

Why many servants failed to claim their freedom land or did so only long after they had been granted their freedom is unclear. Most likely they lacked the capital or credit necessary to establish farms, and the interval between the attainment of freedom and the filing of a claim reflects the time it took to acquire the necessary capital. Funds were required not only to record the deed and pay clerks and surveyors, but also to purchase provisions, tools, seed, and livestock. To accumulate the capital or credit, former servants had to work for wages over a considerable period of time.[86] Since the servants

phia. In order to place the Howell inventory within the range of personal wealth in the city as a whole, I used the data presented in Gary B. Nash, "Urban Wealth and Poverty in Pre-Revolutionary America," *JIH* 9 (1976), 568, Table 8.

81 I traced landownership by first checking the list of servant names with the "Minutes of the Board of Property" to see if a servant claimed the rights to the headlands. Then I consulted all other lists that might yield information about landownership: "Blackwell's Rent Roll of 1693," *PGM* 23 (1963); John Reed, "An Explanation of the Map of the City of Philadelphia: The Date of Surveys of all Lots . . . 1689," *Pa. Arch.*, 3d ser., 3 (1894), 384–401; Warrants and Surveys, 1684–1749, HSP; and finally the deed records, City Hall, Philadelphia.

82 *Records of the Courts of Bucks County*, 305.

83 Ibid., 308.

84 Ibid., 391.

85 "Minutes of the Board of Property," 671–2.

86 See Menard's discussion, "From Servant to Freeholder," 50. Another possibility is that the

who obtained their headright did not need to purchase it, it is possible that they settled on the land, worked as day laborers until they had saved enough capital, and then registered the deed. It is revealing that, of six servants who received salaries while under indenture, those who took up their headrights did so within the first ten years after the completion of their indenture – a shorter lag time than that of the servant group as a whole. Some freed servants were never able to afford their freedom land, as suggested by the number who sold their rights for ready cash.

Sixty-eight former servants, about one-third of those located in the sources, acquired land. Table 2.2 reveals that of these, the majority remained small landholders. Almost half (46.6 percent) of the sixty-eight former servants who owned land never increased their holdings above the original 50 acres. Nine of these sold the rights to their headland, leaving them ultimately landless. Thirty-seven former servants farmed parcels ranging in size from 50 to 300 acres. Only four became large landowners, accumulating between 500 and 900 acres at one point in their lives.

Marriage and inheritance provided the most assured route to economic success and landownership. Andrew Heath became a rich man through his marriage to Elizabeth Venables, the widow of a wealthy Bucks County yeoman.[87] Heath received more than 600 acres, all of which he ultimately sold. Heath's wealth through marriage did not ensure an untroubled future, however. In 1698, he was arrested and accused of refusing to relinquish the land for which he had received payment. In 1701 Heath was indicted for adultery with his daughter-in-law, Frances Venables. He pleaded guilty, was fined, and paid the court costs. Ralph Cowgill married the daughter of his owner and through gifts and purchases came into possession of almost 700 acres of land, becoming the second largest landowner in this group of former servants.[88] Servant William Smith inherited land from his former owner, Francis Russell, a miller who owned 3 acres in Bucks County and an additional 25 acres in Bristol Township, where he erected his mill. Another parcel of land, beyond Wrightstown, was left to Smith by will.[89] Seven other servants, like Heath, Cowgill, and Smith, acquired property through marriage or inheritance in amounts ranging from the 600 acres of Heath to the city lot inherited by Joseph Mather from his father-in-law John Russell.

lag time reflects only the length of time it took to record the deed, not to settle. See Marc Egnal, "The Pennsylvania Economy, 1748–1762: An Analysis of Short-Run Fluctuations in the Context of Long-Run Changes in the Atlantic Trading Community" (Ph.D. diss., University of Wisconsin, 1974), 64.

87 *Records of the Courts of Bucks County*, 32; "Minutes of the Board of Property," 243, 261, 326; *Burlington Court Book*, 261–62.

88 Oliver Hough, "Atkinson Families of Bucks County, Pennsylvania," *PMHB* 30 (1906), 482; *Records of the Courts of Bucks* County, 292, 311; "Minutes of the Board of Property," 246.

89 Balderston, "Pennsylvania's 1683 Ships," 81.

Table 2.2. *Acquisition of land by servants indentured between 1682 and 1686 after attaining freedom and by age mates*

	Former servants					
Number of acres	1–10 years		11–30 years		Total	
	N	%	N	%	N	%
1–50	7	28.0	20	46.5	27	46.6
51–100	6	24.0	8	18.6	14	20.6
101–150	3	12.0	2	4.7	5	7.4
151–200	5	20.0	5	11.6	10	14.7
200+	4	16.0	8	18.6	12	17.7
Total (N = 196)	25		43		68	

	Age mates					
Number of acres	1–10 years after marriage		11–30 years after marriage		Total	
	N	%	N	%	N	%
1–50	1	3.3			1	2.7
51–100	2	6.7	1	14.3	3	8.1
101–150	8	26.7	1	14.3	9	24.3
151–200	4	13.3			4	10.8
201+	15	50.0	5	71.4	20	54.1
Total (N = 98)	30		7		37	

Note: For servants, the decades are timed after they gained their freedom; for the control group, from the year of marriage. Thus these are not the same dates represented in each period, but rather the same relative period.

Sources: "East and West New Jersey Deeds and Patents," *New Jersey Archives*, 1st ser., vol. 21 (Paterson, N.J., 1899); "Minutes of the Board of Property of the Province of Pennsylvania," *Pennsylvania Archives,* 2d ser., vol. 19 (Harrisburg, Pa., 1893); *Records of the Courts of Chester County, Pennsylvania, 1681–1697* (Meadville, Pa., 1910); *Records of the Courts of Quarter Sessions and Common Pleas of Bucks County* (Meadville, Pa., 1943); "Map of Philadelphia, . . . Grant for Surveying and Laying Out . . . ," Pennsylvania Archives, 2d ser., vol. 7 (Harrisburg, Pa., 1898), 186–92; wills and inventories; and deed books, City Archives, Philadelphia.

For female former servants, marriage was also the surest means of mobility. Of the sixteen women who served indentures and who could be traced through the colonial records, all but six married former servants. Hannah Mogridge and Cicely Wooley married servants from the Free Society of Traders; both couples were allowed to marry before their indentures had been completed.[90] Elizabeth Day and Jeremiah Osbourne served the same owner and married as soon as they were free.[91] Servants who married one another did have some advantages, for it was possible for them to begin married life with their combined headland of 100 acres. Alice Dickenson and Edmund McVeagh were married after completing their indentures, and they collected their 100 acres of headland. Although they sold the rights to the land to Philip Howell in 1703, they requested a survey on an additional 250 acres of land purchased in Dublin Township in the previous year.[92] James Sutton and Hannah Falkener received 100 acres of land, but in 1718 they were paying one penny sterling per acre on 45 acres. The Suttons appeared in the County Commissioner's Report as owing money; they had apparently run away with a debt of two shillings and six pence on their estate. Even with their 100 acres of combined freedom land, they had been unable to keep ahead of the bill collector and by 1728 had left the area, not to be found again in the Pennsylvania colonial records.[93]

The six women who did not marry former servants fared quite well. Jan Worral married Samuel Dark of the Middletown Quaker Meeting in December 1686, two months after she had achieved her freedom. Dark served as constable from Bucks County in 1686 and was later sent as a representative to the Provincial Assembly.[94] Elinor Barber arrived in Pennsylvania with her owner Griffith Jones in February 1681. In May 1689 she married Philadelphia merchant James Thomas, who, by 1701, owned at least 400 acres and paid tax on one of the highest assessments on the 1709 tax list.[95]

Landownership was not a sure route to economic independence for former servants, however, and it is difficult to reconcile the apparent economic expansiveness of early Pennsylvania with the unremarkable rate of land acquisition by these individuals. Although land was relatively accessible during the early years of settlement and more than one-third of these first servants were entitled to a fifty-acre headright, only 34 percent of

90 Clemens, *American Marriage Records,* 238.

91 "Minutes of the Board of Property," 318, 320, 409.

92 Balderston, "William Penn's Ships, 36; "Minutes of the Board of Property," 330, 409.

93 "Minutes of the Board of Property," 638; County Commissioners' Minutes, 1728, vol. 1, City Archives, Philadelphia.

94 Clemens, *American Marriage Records,* 238; *Records of the Courts of Bucks County,* 42; J. H. Battle, *History of Bucks County Pennsylvania Including an Account of Its Original Exploration* (Philadelphia, 1887), 682.

95 Clemens, *American Marriage Records,* 30; "Minutes of the Board of Property," 276, 286.

the indentured servants followed through the colonial records acquired any land. Of those who did receive freedom land, almost 40 percent (twenty-six individuals) never possessed more than fifty acres of land – a quantity that even with the most fertile soil conditions and efficient farming techniques would allow a family to scratch out only the barest of livings.[96] Penn's liberal land policy, implemented only briefly, did not rescue all of these free persons from subsistence. But whatever the cause of the low rate of land acquisition, it does not appear to have been related to the status of servitude. Former servants and members of the control cohort had virtually the same rate of landlessness. Sixty-five percent of the former servants and 62 percent of the control group failed to become freeholders.

Although the rate of landownership was the same for former servants and for the control group, members of the control group tended to accumulate more property. More than 40 percent of the control group who acquired land held 300 or more acres, whereas not quite 6 percent of the former servants owned that much acreage. Almost half of the latter had to survive on fifty or fewer acres; not quite 3 percent of the control group lived on such small acreage. Furthermore, the process of land acquisition took much longer for former servants. They were still taking up their first parcels of land twenty years after gaining freedom, whereas individuals in the control group acquired most of their land ten years into their careers.

Landownership and the agricultural life were not the only possibilities open to former servants in early Pennsylvania. Christopher Lobb traveled to Pennsylvania in 1686 from England, and settled with his owner, James Fox, in Plymouth Township in Philadelphia County. Soon after gaining freedom, Lobb married Isabel Cliff, also a former servant, and they lived out their lives in Philadelphia.[97] Lobb was assessed at the minimum tax in 1693,

---

96 In analyzing Maryland servants, Menard categorizes small landholders as those with 50 to 400 acres. "From Servant to Freeholder," 40. James T. Lemon notes that in Pennsylvania most land grants tended to range from 100 to 500 acres. Lemon writes that, in 1710, the average farm size in Chester County was 245 acres; the lowest quartile of owners held from 125 to 190 acres. During the later part of the eighteenth century, Lemon notes, even in "the fertile Lancaster Plain, farms of sixty to seventy-five acres would have been inadequate to sustain families." *Best Poor Man's Country*, 65, 88–91. Although these data are taken from a period eighty years after the first group of former servants took up their lands, no one argues that farming methods changed in ways that would have required less land for the earlier period. If anything, agricultural production should have gained in efficiency, thereby requiring less land. Also see Kenneth Lockridge, "Land, Population, and the Evolution of New England Society," *Past and Present* 39 (1968), 64–6. Percy Bidwell and John I. Falconer provide a rough estimate of landholding in early New England. *History of Agriculture in the Northern United States, 1620–1860* (Washington, D.C., 1925), 84–142. See also Charles Grant, *Democracy in the Connecticut Frontier of Kent* (New York, 1961), 36–8; Max Schumacher, *The Northern Farmer and His Markets During the Late Colonial Period* (Berkeley, Calif., 1948).

97 Balderston, "Pennsylvania's 1683 Ships," 93.

suggesting that he had no taxable property. By 1704 he had teams for hire in the city, although he was a woolcomber by trade.[98] Lobb left a small estate of ten pounds when he died in 1709, which placed him in the bottom 30 percent of Philadelphia inventoried decedents.

A number of skilled artisan-servants continued to work at their trades after they gained freedom. Robert Kent, an English shoemaker, arrived in Pennsylvania in 1685 to serve Philip Alford, also a shoemaker. Kent apparently served only one year, for in 1686 he married Margaret Thompson.[99] Three years later Kent was renting a city lot and house in Philadelphia. This probably served as the living quarters for Kent and his wife, as well as the space for his shoemaker's shop. Kent died that same year after accumulating personal property valued at 85 pounds, which places him in the middle third of decedents whose estates were inventoried in this period.[100] Samuel Bradshaw arrived from Ireland in 1683 to serve Philadelphia merchant Robert Turner. Bradshaw settled in Darby Township, Chester County, in 1712 and listed his occupation as a malster. He died in 1728 with a substantial estate valued at 373 pounds.[101] Although not a skilled worker, Joseph Chorley also earned his living outside agriculture. Chorley was listed in his will as a yeoman, but he was in charge of the ferry in Bucks County until complaints were issued against his mismanagement and the ferry was moved to Gilbert Wheeler's. After losing the rights to the ferry, Chorley requested and received a license to keep an ordinary. Although Chorley left an estate valued at more than 190 pounds in 1704, he had three separate court appearances for debts totaling 160 pounds in 1699.[102]

The tax lists provide only the barest glimpse of servant mobility and property accumulation. Only forty-one former servants (21 percent) could be located on the tax lists ten years after gaining freedom. As difficult as it was to find these individuals on the tax lists, the control group was more elusive; fewer than 10 percent could be located on Philadelphia tax lists ten years after their marriages in the same city. Table 2.3 reveals that, of the servants who were assessed, more than one-third never acquired taxable property and were rated at the minimum assessment. Another third had only minimal assets between twenty and fifty pounds. The record of the control group is so thin that it is difficult to draw useful conclusions. Almost

98 *Minutes of the Common Council, 1704–1776* (Philadelphia, 1847), 6.

99 Balderston, "William Penn's Ships," 50; Clemens, *American Marriage Records,* 134; "Record of Pennsylvania Marriages Prior to 1810," *Pa. Arch.,* 2d ser., 8:vi.

100 "Abstract of Wills," *PGSP* 1 (1889), 134; Abstract of the Records of Death and Burials Kept by the Philadelphia Monthly Meeting, 1688–1826.

101 "Families Who Arrived at Philadelphia," 334.

102 *Records of the Courts of Bucks County,* 321, 326, 329, 361, 362, 364, 366–7. The inventory is in the Department of Wills, City Hall Annex, Philadelphia.

Table 2.3. *Distribution of taxable wealth among former servants indentured between 1682 and 1686 and among age mates*

Assessment (pounds)	Totals			
	Servants		Age mates	
	N	%	N	%
Per head	22	37.9	—	—
1–50	20	34.5	7	33.3
51–100	9	15.5	11	52.4
100 +	7	12.1	3	14.3
Total	58		21	

Sources: Philadelphia, Chester, Bucks, New Castle, Kent County tax lists, 1693; Philadelphia, Bucks, Chester County tax lists, 1696; Philadelphia poor tax, 1709; Chester County tax, 1715, 1718, 1719, 1720, 1721, 1722, 1724, 1725, 1726, 1730.

half of those assessed were rated at a slightly higher level, with taxable property ranging from fifty to seventy-five pounds. On the Philadelphia 1693 assessment list, three-quarters of the servants fell within the bottom half of the city's taxpayers. Although servants were clustered more heavily in the lower assessment brackets, both groups had comparable proportions in the highest assessment levels, the top 70th to 100th percentile of the city's taxpayers. Only four servants had to send the collector away because they were too poor to pay their tax, and no members of the control group were found on the county commissioners' rolls, the lists of those who had to be excused from paying a tax.

Former servants accumulated so little property that only a small proportion of them left estates worthy of an inventory. The control group may have been slightly wealthier.[103] Only a scant number of inventories of estates exist – for thirty-six (18 percent) of the former servants and twenty-seven (28 percent) of the control group. Table 2.4 provides the inventory data and compares the inventories of individual former servants and control group members with all Philadelphia inventories for the period. Clearly, servants tended to leave smaller estates. More than half (52.8 percent) left personal property of less than 100 pounds. Sixty percent left estates of 150 pounds or less. More than 20 percent left estates valued at less than 50 pounds, an amount that suggests they led simple lives with meager

---

103 Gary Nash reports that less than half of all Boston heads of household and a smaller proportion of Philadelphians left inventories of estate. Thus servants left proportionately fewer inventories than the rest of the population. "Urban Wealth and Poverty," 548.

Table 2.4. *Distribution of inventoried wealth among former servants, age mates, and Philadelphia decedents, 1680–1720*

Value (pounds)	Former servants		Control group		Philadelphia 1680–1720	
	N	%	N	%	N	%
1–50	8	22.2	3	11.1	44	15.7
51–100	11	30.6	2	7.4	41	14.6
101–150	3	8.3	4	14.8	30	10.7
151–200	6	16.7	2	7.4	25	8.9
200+	8	22.2	16	59.3	141	50.1
Total	36		27		281	

Note: The Philadelphia data represent only those inventories filed from 1680 to 1720 in order to approximate the age range of the servant group and to ensure that these individuals spent their productive years during the corresponding period.

Sources: Inventories of estate for the inhabitants of Philadelphia, Chester, and Bucks counties during the first 20 years of the colony are located in the Department of Wills, City Hall Annex, Philadelphia. Beginning in the eighteenth century, Chester County inventories are located in the Department of Wills, Chester County Courthouse, West Chester, Pa; Bucks County wills are in the Department of Wills, Bucks County Courthouse, Doylestown, Pa. The Philadelphia data were provided by Gary B. Nash. I worked from a computer printout.

personal possessions. On the opposite end of the wealth spectrum fewer than 14 percent of the former servants left estates valued at more than 300 pounds. Yet more than one-third of the inventories filed in Philadelphia represented estates valued at greater than this amount. Although the record of the control group is again very thin, it appears that individuals who had not served indentures were more than three times as likely to achieve a substantial estate than former servants.

Colonial officeholding provides the final index of the mobility of former servants. Despite their long struggles to acquire land, twenty-five former servants advanced to positions in local or colonial government. The high degree of government participation suggests that political life in the new colony was relatively open, and there was ample room in the political system for those interested in serving. In addition, no stigma was attached to servitude that prevented a former servant from becoming an elected official. Admittedly, most of the offices held by former servants were petty positions, and their terms tended to be brief. Nine former servants served as

two worked as assessors. None of these jobs was repeated for more than two terms, except that of petty juror. However, three former servants served in the Provincial Assembly, the highest elected office in the colony. Of these, all served only one term, and only one, Henry Hollingsworth, held more than one governmental office. Hollingsworth ventured to Pennsylvania from Ireland in 1683 to serve merchant Robert Turner for two years. In 1688 he returned to Ireland to marry Lydia Atkinson. When he moved back to Pennsylvania in 1689, he settled in New Castle County. Hollingsworth served as deputy surveyor, sheriff, clerk of the courts, coroner, and surveyor, and in addition represented New Castle County in the Provincial Assembly.[104]

Available evidence strongly suggests that the opportunities for the men and women who entered Pennsylvania society as indentured servants in the late seventeenth century varied greatly. Of the 196 servants who served in the initial wave of settlement, 68, or almost one-third, acquired land. Of these 68, slightly more than one-third lived on parcels of fifty acres or less, an amount that would have barely provided subsistence. The rest lived on more substantial holdings, certainly adequate for comfortable lives. For the 18 percent who left inventories, tradesmen and husbandmen, serving a three- to four-year indenture in the Quaker colony provided an efficient route for ascent up the economic ladder. More than one-third of these former servants traveled an economic course that resembled the career patterns of age mates who had not served indentures. Fewer were as wealthy or accumulated their assets as quickly, but some, like Philip Howell and Christopher Lobb, managed to achieve a measure of economic mobility. For them, seventeenth-century Pennsylvania afforded opportunity for economic success. For Edward Doyle, however, serving a four-year indenture meant trying to stay one step ahead of his creditors. Even a fairly benign labor institution could launch no more than a fraction of indentured servants on successful careers.

In early Pennsylvania, life after servitude contrasted sharply with that of Maryland's first servants. About 90 percent of Maryland's former servants achieved landownership and typically "established themselves as small planters on leased land immediately after they had completed their terms."[105] The economy of early Maryland allowed a man who started at the bottom without special advantages to acquire a substantial estate and a responsible position. Maryland's former servants found it easier to claim their freedom lands than their counterparts in Pennsylvania. Although both

---

104 Myers, *Immigration*, 314, 332; George Smith, *History of Delaware County: from the Discovery of the Territory Included within Its Limits to the Present Time* . . . (Philadelphia, 1862), 469–70.
105 Menard, "From Servant to Freeholder," 52.

groups postponed claiming their lands, owing to limited capital, servants from the Chesapeake waited only a few years and only 10 percent failed to escape tenancy. In addition, Maryland's former servants had a wider range of economic options. Each colony enabled former servants to work for wages; but Maryland also offered the possibility of sharecropping and leaseholding, which during these early years not only enabled them to accumulate start-up capital but allowed them to continue earning after they had taken possession of their own lands. Both Pennsylvania and Maryland had fluid economies – land was plentiful and wages high – but Pennsylvania did not offer its former servants the same wide range of options.[106]

The outlook was mixed and uncertain for former Pennsylvania servants. Although many fared quite well as free persons, an equal number fought a continuous battle for economic security. For the large group hidden from historical view – for the servants who died prematurely, who had nothing to give the tax collector, or who grappled with a lifelong problem of debt – serving a four-year indenture was not a means of advancing up the economic ladder or achieving a "decent competency." Their very lack of visibility may reflect high geographic mobility – movement that in turn suggests a continuing search for economic well-being.

The economic problems servants faced after attaining freedom foreshadow the greater difficulties in the eighteenth century. In the new century, indentured labor evolved from a benign personal system based on English servitude to one that was increasingly harsh and formal with some aspects unique to Pennsylvania. Written indentures replaced oral contracts. The time had passed when servants shared space on the ship with their masters and traveled much like any other transatlantic passenger. They now crossed the Atlantic as cargo to be sold and traded like any valuable commodity. The terms of service became longer. And whereas former seventeenth-century servants tended to settle in rural areas of the colony even if they had served indentures in Philadelphia, freed servants in the eighteenth century would remain in the city. Such shifts would mark a new phase in the history of indentured labor in Philadelphia. The master-servant relationship, the level of social conflict, and the economic prospects of freed servants would change dramatically in the eighteenth century, and labor itself would be transformed.

106 Ibid., 54, 57.

3 Pennsylvania labor in the eighteenth century

On April 28, 1772, a familiar scene was enacted in Philadelphia. The brig *Patty* had arrived with indentured servants for sale.[1] Two days later a notice appeared in the *Pennsylvania Gazette* advertising about "100 servants and redemptioners, men, women, boys and girls . . . whose times are to be disposed of by the master."[2] Among these servants, John Kenny was bound for four years to Dr. James Graham. Dr. Graham paid the ship's captain, Robert Hardie, twenty pounds for Kenny's passage from Ireland. Peter Haldeman, having paid ten pounds to Captain Hardie, acquired John Bohilly until 1780. Mary Roche was to serve the printer Robert Aikin for four years, or three years "if she behaves well," at a cost of fourteen pounds and six shillings. And Jeffrey Connell purchased the labor of John Little for his first four years of life in the colony for seventeen pounds.[3]

Kenny, Bohilly, Roche, and Connell served their indentures in a very different setting than their seventeenth-century predecessors. The institution of unfree labor had grown dramatically. The growth of unfree labor in eighteenth-century Pennsylvania depended on a complex series of relations: the expansion and retraction of the economy, war and peace, and the supply of servants and slaves. Each of these variables interacted to affect unfree labor in definite ways. In the eighteenth century, the ethnic composition of the servant population, the locus of unfree labor, and the relationship between servants and slaves changed. Most of all, servitude was no longer governed by custom. Rather, it became truly distinct from its English precedent – rigid and formalized – and the demand for unfree labor produced a horrible transportation system.

By the mid–eighteenth century, Penn's "greene country town" had evolved into an urban center. The city landscape was dotted with the stately

1 *Pennsylvania Gazette*, April 20, 1772.
2 Ibid.
3 "List of Servants and Apprentices Bound and Assigned Before John Gibson, Mayor of Philadelphia, May 1771 to May 1773," manuscript, AM 3795, HSP.

Georgian homes of prosperous merchants and artisans, a well-known statehouse, and many grand churches. Penn's town had not yet filled the distance between the Delaware and the Schuylkill rivers, but it had stretched out along the Delaware.[4]

Philadelphia experienced growing pains as it changed from a country town into the largest city in British North America. In 1739 the Assembly considered a petition that complained of the "great annoyance arising from Slaughter Houses, Tan Yards, Skinner Lime Pits, &c. erected in the publick Dock, and streets."[5] The petitioners prayed that "for the Convenience and Reputation of the City, and the health of the Inhabitants, the Erecting of new Tan Yards, &c. within the City may be Restrained."[6] Slaughterhouses, tan yards, and skinner's lime pits might be housed within the borders of a small town, but they were hardly appropriate spectacles of a burgeoning port city.

The growth of Philadelphia took its toll on the health of its inhabitants. For the first time epidemic diseases swept through the city and mortality rose.[7] Nevertheless, the city showed signs of general prosperity: Taverns flourished, the upper class held balls and music recitals, advertisements for dancing instruction and French lessons appeared in the papers, and a theater was established. Two weekly newspapers kept the city informed about colonial and international news. A large range of imported goods were available, and Philadelphia boasted some of the finest craftsmen in all of North America. By 1750 the muddy streets were being paved and lighted, and open sewers were covered. As Franklin remarked in 1749, "In the settling of new countries, the first care of the planters must be to provide and secure the necessities of life." Franklin felt confident that Pennsylvania had passed through this stage of development and that many citizens enjoyed wealth and leisure.[8]

Demand for unfree labor was small after the first decade of settlement through the first three decades of the new century. The economic health of Philadelphia depended on trade, which oscillated between "bursts of activity and periods of recession." Wars accounted for some of the variation, since the health of trade depended on the control over ocean

---

4 Marc M. Egnal, "The Pennsylvania Economy, 1748–1762: An Analysis of Short-Run Fluctuations in the Context of Long-Run Changes in the Atlantic Trading Community," (Ph.D. diss., University of Wisconsin, 1974), 1.

5 *Votes and Proceedings of the House of Representatives of the Province of Pennsylvania,* Pa. Arch., 3:2487.

6 Ibid.

7 Billy G. Smith, "Death and Life in a Colonial Immigrant City: A Demographic Analysis of Philadelphia," *JEH* 37 (1977), 863–89.

8 "On the Need for an Academy" (August 24, 1749) in *The Papers of Benjamin Franklin,* ed. Leonard W. Labaree, Whitfield J. Bell, Jr., Helen Boatfield, and Helene H. Fineman (New Haven, Conn., 1959), 3:385–6.

routes between Pennsylvania, Britain, and the West Indian islands, where most of the colony's exports were marketed. During the first half of King William's War (1689–97) French privateers virtually ruined English shipping. As a result, Pennsylvania trade slumped badly. During the closing years of the war, the French were restrained and trade resumed and recovered.[9]

Queen Anne's War (1702–13) affected Philadelphia trade in the same way, and the demand for unfree laborers was small during the war as well as at its conclusion. The early years of the war were characterized by havoc on the seas, when once again the French badly disrupted North American shipping. As a result, the grain market virtually collapsed and the Pennsylvania economy suffered. Even the largest Philadelphia merchants were not immune. Samuel Carpenter had been a mercantile success in the late seventeenth century, but he too went bankrupt.[10] The demand for labor remained low. By 1706, economic conditions had improved, and by the end of the war, the Philadelphia economy had recovered. The halting growth of the economy resulted in only limited labor demand. A Philadelphia merchant wrote in 1715, "I must entreat you to send me no more Negroes for sale, for our people don't care to buy."[11] Philadelphia entered a brief phase of growth and prosperity that was too short to affect the demand for labor.[12]

Following the Peace of Utrecht, the colonies at long last entered a period of peace, but the first major depression descended upon Philadelphia in 1720. A precipitous drop in grain prices cut into farmers' fortunes, and the downturn in the areas of agriculture production adversely affected urban workers as well. According to the Assembly, work stopped in the city's shipyards, specie disappeared, and property values plummeted.[13] "How deplorable are the Lives of the Common People," moaned one pamphleteer in 1721. And late that same year Governor William Keith wrote, "The ship Builder & Carpenter starve for want of Employment."[14] In such circumstances the demand for unfree labor continued to be small. Few individuals had the excess capital to invest in unfree labor, and those who did could hire laborers since the stagnating economy created unemployment. Wars and an uneven economy reduced the demand for unfree workers in Pennsylvania.

9 Gary B. Nash, *The Urban Crucible: Social Change, Political Consciousness, and the Origins of the American Revolution* (Cambridge, Mass., 1979), 73.
10 Ibid.
11 Quoted in John F. Watson, *Annals of Philadelphia, and Pennsylvania* . . . (Philadelphia, 1857), 2:264.
12 Nash, *Urban Crucible*, 73.
13 Ibid., 119.
14 Quoted in ibid., 119.

Beginning in 1728, the economy grew steadily. The fertility of the land and rural proximity to the colonial markets, combined with an increasing demand for Pennsylvania products, primarily grain, supported a prosperous rural sector.[15] The growth of rural production had a positive effect on Philadelphia, too. Before 1730, the Philadelphia merchant community dealt primarily in a trading network with the British Isles and the West Indies. By the mid-1730s, however, merchants had expanded their trade to include southern Europe and coastal North America.[16] Agricultural production rose steadily to take advantage of the increased foreign demand for wheat, flour, and bread. The tonnage clearing the port of Philadelphia began to climb after 1726 and, except for a few years, rose steadily. Wheat demonstrated its strength as an export commodity, and iron and flax also showed steady increases.[17]

The city's rapid growth, closely tied to the prosperity of the commercial sector, increased the demand for labor. Most of the jobs in the Quaker city were related to overseas trade. As export commodities grew, local shipbuilding boomed. Merchants required larger vessels and began to use brigs, snows, and ships more consistently in the transatlantic trade. Twice as much shipping was built in 1726 as in any year before 1723. For a period of six and one-half years, 194 ocean-going vessels were built along the Delaware.[18] Apart from the labor requirements of industries directly involved in trade, other areas of the labor market were affected indirectly. Philadelphia had a sizable population involved in the building trades and in the manufacture of shoes, cloth, and furniture. The Pennsylvania boom created labor demand in all of these sectors. Since wages were still high and free workers scarce, Philadelphia residents turned to imported bound laborers.

Employment opportunities in the city remained high because the availability of inexpensive land drained off free laborers from the urban economy. Newly arrived immigrants, sons of craftsmen, and recently freed servants could live in the city; opportunities were good because day workers commanded high wages. But if an individual longed for the agricultural life, there was, as Peter Kalm wrote, such an amount of good land yet uncultivated "that a newly married man can, without difficulty, get a spot where he may subsist with his wife and children."[19] Franklin corroborated Kalm's observation in 1751: "Land being plenty in America, and so cheap as that a labouring Man, that understands Husbandry, can in short Time

15 James T. Lemon, *The Best Poor Man's Country* (Baltimore, Md., 1972), 194.
16 James G. Lydon, "Philadelphia Commercial Expansion, 1720–1739," *PMHB* 91 (1967), 403–4.
17 Ibid., 402–3.
18 Ibid., 403–5.
19 Quoted in Egnal, "Pennsylvania Economy," 15.

save money enough to purchase a Piece of New Land sufficient for a Plantation."[20] Opportunity in Pennsylvania seemed unlimited, and as Johann Christopher Sauer reported, "Scarcely had I arrived here when I was offered a vocation, as a foundry was to be constructed. . . . Because one may hold here as much property as one wishes, also pay for it when one desires, everybody hurries to take up some property."[21]

The Philadelphia economy expanded throughout the 1730s, and good times became boom times after England declared war on Spain in 1739.[22] The hostilities sparked demand for Pennsylvania products, and the prices of bread, flour, and meat rose as profits soared. Perhaps no index of the economic prosperity is as revealing as the small number of city poor. From 1730 to 1753 less than 1 percent of the city population was either too poor to pay a tax or required public assistance.[23] Throughout this period full employment was the norm. The peace-loving Quakers were never enthusiastic participants in colonial wars and this war was no exception, but they participated readily in the profitable provisioning of the British forces in the Caribbean. The war stimulated the Pennsylvania economy, and the demand for labor in the port city escalated.

Prosperity in Philadelphia was uneven during the 1740s and 1750s. The Quaker capital underwent its first major mobilization during the Anglo-French War of 1744–8. Merchants, once again, recorded their profits in their credit ledgers as demand for Pennsylvania produce remained high and merchants with capital took advantage of privateering opportunities. While prosperity characterized much of the Pennsylvania economy, the market for imported goods was sluggish from 1748 to 1749 and experienced a commercial downturn from 1750 to 1754. The end of the hostilities, announced in America in the summer of 1748, coincided with a strong demand for Pennsylvania produce from the West Indies. However, by the first months of 1749, flour prices had fallen and reached a low point in the spring of 1750. High grain production could not cushion the blow from low prices. Between 1750 and 1754, merchants' profits from the sale of manufactures declined and their secondary land and shipbuilding activities slumped.[24] One direct result of this business cycle was a reduction in the capital available in both the rural and urban sectors. From 1748 to 1752 the

---

20 *Papers of Benjamin Franklin,* 4:228.
21 "An Early Description of Pennsylvania, Letters of Christopher Sower, Written in 1724 . . ." *PMHB* 45 (1921), 247–51.
22 Nash, *Urban Crucible,* 120–3.
23 Nash calculated the number of poor by analyzing the number of individuals who could not pay their taxes and the number of persons receiving direct aid. I calculated the ratio of poor to population by using Nash's figures. Ibid., 127 and Appendix, Table 13, 407–8.
24 Egnal, "Pennsylvania Economy," 97–9.

demand for servants remained high, but Pennsylvanians had difficulties paying for their unfree workers.

By the middle of the eighteenth century, a healthy economy and a shortage of wage laborers further sparked the demand for unfree laborers. In addition to heightened demand, a steady stream of immigrant workers poured into Pennsylvania. Trading patterns within the expanding economy affected the supply of indentured labor as the number of vessels that traveled to the ports of servant embarkation increased. When bulky flax was exchanged in Ireland for more compact finished linen, space was available for servant cargoes.[25]

Conditions in Europe contributed to increased immigration. As a result, the ethnic composition of the servant population was altered from predominantly English in the seventeenth century to primarily Scots-Irish and German in the eighteenth. Economic circumstances in northern Ireland and Germany forced thousands of people from their homes; four- to five-year indentures served as their tickets to the New World. Throughout Britain, people left the scene of their economic hardship and made their way toward the cities, especially London, only to join thousands of others seeking a livelihood.[26] Lacking even the sum to pay for their passage, many of them were compelled to indenture themselves. Clinging to the hope that the New World would provide a fresh start and a fruitful future, they signed away several years of their lives in exchange for their voyage and set their sights on the western shores of the Atlantic. Throughout most of the eighteenth century, Scots-Irish and German emigrants undergirded indentured labor, and the Quaker colony welcomed the incoming tide of humanity.

First among the new groups were mainly Scots-Irish who had settled in Ulster at the invitation of James I. Although religious persecution provided the primary impetus for the early Quaker movement from Ireland, economic restrictions had the greater influence on driving the Scots-Irish from their homelands in the eighteenth century.[27] Five waves of emigration from northern Ireland crested during the first three-quarters of the eighteenth century. The first came in the wake of six years of insufficient rainfall, between 1715 and 1720, that "ruined crops, discouraged farmers and so curtailed the supply of flax that weavers of linen cloth were desperate."[28]

25 Ibid., 78.

26 Richard Hofstadter, *America at 1750: A Social Portrait* (New York, 1971), 34–5.

27 Albert Cook Myers, *Immigration of the Irish Quakers into Pennsylvania, 1682–1750* (Swarthmore, Pa., 1902), 46–9; Dennis Clark, *The Irish in Philadelphia: Ten Generations of Urban Experience* (Philadelphia, 1973), 6; R. J. Dickson, *Ulster Emigration to Colonial America, 1718–1775* (London, 1966), 10–14; Wayland F. Dunaway, *The Scotch-Irish of Colonial Pennsylvania* (Chapel Hill, N.C., 1944), 28.

28 Quoted in James G. Leyburn, *The Scotch-Irish: A Social History* (Chapel Hill, N.C., 1962), 164.

The prices of food rose far beyond the means of poor people, and rising rents exacerbated these difficulties.[29] Many leases expired in 1717, and landlords took the opportunity to increase rents. In 1717 more than five thousand northern Irish journeyed to the New World.[30]

Although it is impossible to know precisely how many Irish emigrated, the Quaker colony appears to have received the majority. In 1717 Jonathan Dickinson reported that "from ye north of Ireland many hundreds in about four months" had arrived in Philadelphia and during the summer "we have had 12 or 13 sayle of ships from the North of Ireland with a swarm of people."[31] Although the magnitude of the movement was small, the more important consequence was that the "flood gates of emigration were opened . . . as an outlet for the distressed and discontented."[32]

Famine led to the second wave of Irish emigration in 1728 and 1729.[33] The size of this movement alarmed members of the English Parliament, and a committee was appointed to investigate its causes. Archbishop Boulter wrote in 1728 that "the scarcity and dearness of provision still increase in the North. . . . The humor of going to America still continues, and the scarcity of provisions certainly makes many quit us." In July Boulter wrote that "we have hundreds of families, (all Protestants) removing out of the North to America and the least obstruction in the linen manufacture by which the North subsists, must occasion the greater number following." Finally, in November, Boulter described the three bad harvests and reported that "above 4,200 men, women, and children have been shipped off from home . . . above 3,100 this last summer."[34]

Although it is not possible to calculate the precise number of emigrants between 1725 and 1727, approximately 5,000 people came to America from Ireland. Eight or nine vessels transported close to 1,000 Irish to the port of New Castle alone in 1727. By 1727 it appears that the number of Irish arrivals was growing. In March, seven ships loaded passengers at Belfast. In July, twenty-five ships were to have left Londonderry for the

29 Dickson, *Ulster Emigration*, 29.
30 Ibid.; Leyburn, *Scotch-Irish*, 170.
31 Quoted in Leyburn, *Scotch-Irish*, 170.
32 Dickson, *Ulster Emigration*, 24.
33 Ibid., 42.
34 Quoted in Leyburn, *Scotch-Irish*, 171. Dickson writes that it is difficult to assess the relative importance of religious and economic factors in this second wave of emigration; but if shipping advertisements are a useful guide, rents and other economic hardships were most frequently mentioned. References to religious motivation were rare. Dickson argues, however, that it would be a mistake to exclude the issue of tithes as a major thrust toward emigration. Not only were Presbyterian farmers having to support a church whose services were of no value, but tithes were an expense they could ill afford. Already threatened by rising food costs and high rents, the paying of tithes was more than an irritant. *Ulster Emigration*, 38–41.

ports of the middle colonies with 3,500 emigrants. The number of Irish landing in Delaware River ports in 1729 most likely exceeded 4,000; "1,155 of the 1,708 immigrants who landed at Philadelphia in that year were Irish."[35]

The number of Scots-Irish who arrived in Pennsylvania was sufficient to elicit contemporary comment.[36] In 1729 the *Pennsylvania Gazette* reported that

> Poverty, Misery and Want are becoming almost universal among [the Irish] . . . that there is not corn enough raised for their subsistence one year with another the labouring People have little to do, and consequently are not able to purchase Bread at its present dear Rate . . . their griping avaricious landlords exercise over them the most merciless Racking Tyranny and Oppression. Hence it is that such swarms of them are driven over into America.[37]

James Logan, secretary of Pennsylvania, wrote, "It looks as if Ireland is to send all its inhabitants hither, for last week not less than six ships arrived, and every day two or three arrive also."[38]

The third period of large-scale Irish emigration occurred from 1731 to 1770.[39] R. J. Dickson claims that the migrants of the 1730s tended to be farmers hit with rising rents. In 1731 South Carolina offered a rich bounty for immigrants that enticed many Irish to embark for that colony. A burst of immigration occurred in 1740 in response to a short-lived famine. For the period after midcentury, it is possible to estimate the volume of Irish emigration to Pennsylvania by charting ship arrivals in the port of Philadelphia. From 1750 to 1770, an average of five ships per year brought settlers to Pennsylvania, and the stream barely slowed through the Seven Years' War. Forty-nine ships deposited more than 6,000 Irish from 1756 to 1763. From 1764 to 1770, the number of ships depositing Irish settlers averaged nine ships per year, bringing more than 1,300 persons annually to the port of Philadelphia.[40]

The climax of Irish emigration came in the fourth phase: 1770–5. This mass exodus was directly tied to the linen industry, which by 1773 "appeared to have collapsed into a 'drooping and almost ruined state.'" Linen had remained the primary industry in the North, and virtually no

35 Dickson, *Ulster Emigration*, 32–3. The total number of Irish who came to the continental colonies during the 1720s was approximately fifteen thousand.
36 Dickson, *Ulster Emigration*, 32.
37 *Pennsylvania Gazette*, November 20, 1729.
38 Leyburn, *Scotch-Irish*, 171.
39 Dickson admits that the periodization is due to the paucity of information. *Ulster Emigration*, 48.
40 Ibid., 51, 52, Appendix E.

families escaped the effects of a depressed trade. Added to these woes was a continued harassment from rack renting and high prices. As a contemporary explained:

> The deplorable state to which oppression has brought us to, by reason of heavy rents . . . are grievous to be born so that betwixt landlord and rectors, the very marrow is screwed out of our bones . . . they are rendered incapable to support their starving families with the common necessaries of life.

The cost of bread rose so high it approached famine prices. The "scarcity of food combined with the dininishing sales of linen reduced" the Irish to a new level of poverty and pushed the volume of emigration to a new high.[41] In 1771 alone, nineteen ships landed passengers in Philadelphia, and more than 8,000 Irish arrived in the Quaker colony in the years from 1771 to 1775.

Germany provided the second major source of immigrants to Pennsylvania. Individuals, families, and groups made their way down the Rhine and boarded ships bound for the New World. Although the causes for migration had been great in the seventeenth century, the reasons for the eighteenth-century movement from Germany were even more compelling. Pennsylvania was not involved in the earliest movement from Germany. In 1709 fourteen thousand Rhinelanders fled first to Holland and then to England. From England, they were transported to Ireland, New York, and the Carolinas; two thousand returned to Germany and many remained in England.[42]

By the second decade of the eighteenth century, the Quaker colony had become the most popular destination for Germans. The volume of immigrants to Pennsylvania was so large it aroused concern among the colony's English inhabitants. Governor Keith addressed the council in 1717 and warned that "the great number of foreigners from Germany" could have dangerous consequences for the colony. Keith recommended that non-English immigrants be required to take an oath of loyalty to the colony.[43]

Keith's recommendation did not become law until 1727, thus accurate estimates of the volume of German immigration are possible only after that year. However, German immigration into Pennsylvania was heavy for a decade before this. Not only did colonial officials become concerned as early as 1717, but in 1719 Jonathan Dickinson reported that "we are daily expecting ships from London, which bring over Palatines in number six or

41 Ibid., 69, 78, 79, Appendix E.
42 Farley Grubb, "Immigrants and Servants in the Colony and Commonwealth of Pennsylvania: A Quantitative and Economic Analysis" (Ph.D. diss., University of Chicago, 1984), 4.
43 *Colonial Records,* 1st Ser., 3:29.

seven thousand."[44] Dickinson may have exaggerated, but Germans were arriving in sufficient number to cause Pennsylvanians to take notice.

The volume of the German migration to Pennsylvania can be charted with some precision from 1727 to the end of the colonial period.[45] Ships bringing passengers from Germany arrived in Philadelphia almost monthly after 1727. The first peak was reached in 1732 and 1733, when eighteen ships deposited almost 3,500 passengers. The next high point came between 1738 and 1741, when forty ships brought more than 7,000 Palatines to Philadelphia. But the apogee of German immigration was attained from 1749 to 1754, when more than one hundred ships disgorged upward of 28,000 people.

Writing in 1744, a Palatinate resident explained the cause of the exodus from Germany: "For five years the French troops have overrun our land, confiscated our property, and oppressed us with heavy burdens." The French promised to repay the damages, the writer claimed, but they never did. Then the English army marched through and subjected them to the same treatment. After the English it was the Austrians who "encamped among us. So you can see what unbearable suffering we were forced to endure this past summer." If this was not enough,

> a contagious and deadly disease has spread among our cattle, so that thousands of them have died, and many of the brethren have not a single head left. Our poverty is so great that many of us do not know how to help ourselves any longer. With all these calamities and the high

44 Quoted in Ralph B. Strassburger and William J. Hinke, *Pennsylvania German Pioneers: A Publication of the Original Lists of Arrivals in the Port of Philadelphia from 1727 to 1808,* Pennsylvania German Society Proceedings (Norristown, Pa., 1934), 1:xix and xvii–xviii.

45 This period of German immigration is distinctive primarily because of the sources. From 1727 to the Revolution, ship lists are available for passengers arriving from German and Dutch ports. These lists were taken because Pennsylvania officials became alarmed at the large "foreign" population entering the colony. In 1717 Governor William Keith insisted that masters of vessels "render an Account of the Number and Character of the Passengers," and the new arrivals were to swear allegiance to the province. Except for the registering of the 363 Germans who arrived in that year, nothing official came of that order. However, when Patrick Gordon assumed office in 1726, he shared his predecessor's fear and urged that masters be required to record the name, occupation, and place of origin of all German passengers and that new immigrants be required to declare their allegiance to the king of England and Province of Pennsylvania. This decree resulted in more than 300 ship lists being kept by officials at the port of Philadelphia from 1727 to the Revolution. Strassburger and Hinke, *Pennsylvania German Pioneers,* 1:xvii–xviii. The lists are published in ibid., vols. 1–3.
For the best discussion of the nature of the passenger lists see Marianne Wokeck, "The Flow and Composition of German Immigration to Philadelphia, 1727–1775" *PMHB* 105 (1981), 249–78, esp. Table 1. See also Henry A. Gemery, "European Emigration to North America, 1700–1820: Numbers and Quasi-Numbers," *Perspectives in American History* 1 (1984), 283–342.

taxes and rents, as well as the special bounty for military exemption for our young men, and no relief in sight, we do not know whither to turn in our distress.[46]

The final burst of colonial immigration occurred between 1771 and 1773. In the wake of a crippling famine, almost 2,500 Germans disembarked in Philadelphia.

The growth of unfree labor in Pennsylvania mirrored the economic conditions in the colony: ups and downs of the economy, presence or absence of peace, general trading patterns, and supply of immigrant laborers. After the initial burst of immigration in the 1680s, unfree labor grew by fits and starts. Servant and slave importations into the Quaker colony were insignificant until the late 1720s, largely because of the War of Spanish Succession from 1701 to 1713. This was only the first war to affect the colony's servant and slave populations. Wars not only disrupted the transatlantic flow of indentured laborers, but servants were lured away from their masters to enlist in the British army, thereby voiding their indentures. In 1711 the Assembly received a petition that complained about the injuries and inequities suffered by the inhabitants of the colony when indentured servants were encouraged and "enticed away to inlist themselves with the Officers of the neighboring Government of East New Jersey."[47] In order to compensate the masters for their suffering caused by absconding servants, the Assembly allocated payment to them out of the funds collected for the Queen's war coffer.[48] Merchants refused to import indentured laborers during the colonial wars since no one would buy a servant who was going to run away and enlist. Instead, the traders increased slave importations.

The unfree labor population grew impressively after 1728. The proportion of unfree laborers in Philadelphia remained constant through the early 1730s. However, the relative contribution of servants and slaves to the total number varied because wars affected the supply of particular kinds of unfree labor. In 1729 there were 582 servants and more than 700 slaves in the Philadelphia work force, together constituting about 37 percent of the city's laborers.[49] By 1732 slightly more than 1,500 laborers in Philadelphia were

46 Quoted in C. Henry Smith, "The Mennonite Immigration to Pennsylvania in the Eighteenth Century," *Publications of the Pennsylvania-German Society* 35 (1924), 206.
47 *Votes and Proceedings*, 2:996; James T. Mitchell and Henry Flanders, comps., *The Statutes at Large of Pennsylvania from 1682 to 1801* (Harrisburg, 1896–1911), 16 vols.; 2:398–9.
48 *Votes and Proceedings*, 2:999.
49 From March 1727 to May 1729 approximately 414 slaves were imported into the colony. This figure is based on the amount of import duty collected. *Votes and Proceedings*, 3:1818, 1843, 1863, 1899, 1967, 1994. Also see Darold D. Wax, "The Negro Slave Trade in Colonial Pennsylvania" (Ph.D. diss., University of Washington, 1962), 48. The

unfree, representing about 38 percent of the city's labor force.[50] Throughout the 1730s, the number of servants grew steadily, and although the number of slaves declined, unfree laborers continued to constitute more than a third of the work force.

In spite of an economic boom, the size of the indentured servant population declined from more than 900 in 1739 to 690 in 1741. This was the now typical result of war. The call for enlistees for the booty-rich expedition to Cartagena was too tempting to resist, and about 300 Pennsylvania servants fled from servitude to the fighting forces. The colony's masters complained bitterly about servant enlistment and attempted to cover their labor losses by importing more slaves. In a letter to John Penn, James Logan wrote:

> [They] have indeed in my judgement acted weakly and too inconsistently but the Govr on his part is never to be justified by a Zeal that can be alleged for it in raising 8 Companies . . . no less than between 2 and 300 servants (t'is affirmed full 300) to the very great loss of many of their masters divers of whom being poor country men run in debt to purchase them, and now are ruined by that debt Standing good against them while they are deprived of their servants.[51]

Masters were "unable to carry on their respective trades without the Labour of those Servants"; others had "mortgaged their Estates in the Loan-Office to raise Money to Purchase them."[52]

Economic prosperity heightened the labor demand, but the servant market was too risky. Franklin headed the effort to organize a voluntary militia while the British scoured the colonies for soldiers. Angry servant

New York City slave population, taken from the 1712 census, was 970 in a free population of 4,846. Walter A. Knitte, "The Early Eighteenth-Century Palatine Emigration" (Ph.D. diss., University of Pennsylvania, 1936), 148.

50 Over the next few years the servant population declined while the number of slaves increased. From December 1729 to the end of 1733, duty was collected for 498 slaves imported into the colony. These figures are low because they are based on the assumption that slaves came into the colony only through the port of Philadelphia. *Votes and Proceedings*, 3:2025, 2111, 2181, 2224, 2286.

51 James Logan Letter Book, Logan Papers, vol. 4, HSP. Ironically, the peace-loving Quakers partially encouraged servants to run away and enlist. Not only was the Quaker-dominated Assembly principled "against the bearing of arms or applying Money to any such purposes," but free Pennsylvanians did not want to fight in the army. They were content to let the British do their fighting for them. As a result, in order to gather a fighting force, the British had no other option than to encourage the enlistment of servants. Also, the governor seemed convinced that there were an insufficient number of freemen available for military duty. Thus "servants were encouraged to List, and . . . the names of those who Inlisted were directed to be concealed . . . [giving] Servants an Opportunity of escaping from their Masters." *Minutes of the Provincial Council*, in *Colonial Records* (Philadelphia and Harrisburg, 185–3), 4:435, 436.

52 *Votes and Proceedings*, 3:2564, 2570, 2506–7, 2600–6, 2631.

owners complained about the recruitment of indentured laborers, while potential owners refused to buy and merchants ceased to import servants who would abscond to join the military effort. Without a supply of indentured servants to ease the scarcity of labor, the Quaker capital turned once again to slaves.[53]

Servant enlistments reduced Philadelphia's indentured servant population by more than half during the War of Jenkin's Ear, from a high of 929 in 1739 to fewer than 400 in 1748. During the same period, the slave population grew. Almost 1,000 slaves resided in the city in 1739; by 1748 the number had increased to about 1,235 and in that year unfree laborers accounted for approximately one-quarter of the city's work force.

After the conclusion of King George's War in 1748, the demand for unfree labor resumed. Merchants continuously complained about the "sluggish" dry goods trade, but servants were an item in which they seemed to have faith. In typical fashion, at the end of 1748, the London merchant firm of Hunt and Greenleafe lamented in a letter to John Pemberton that, given the perennial glut of European goods, they wanted to "engage in something that affords a better Prospect of Advantage." Send a ship to Rotterdam, they advised Pemberton, and trade in Palatine servants.[54] Similarly, in the following spring, John Pemberton wrote that "servants would sell regularly at a pretty good price."[55] Even with the downturn in the business cycle merchants reported a strong demand for laborers.[56] In 1750 Pemberton wrote that "several ships arrived with Palatines," but he noted, "they go off pretty fast but not so much cash sterling as last year."[57] In the following year he added, "It seems admirable to me how they get off such numbers of servants as are imported."[58] A notice in the Germantown paper in 1750 announced that the arrival of Captain Hasselwood from Holland with Germans made the fourteenth ship that year. "Besides these," the notice read, "1,000 servants and passengers arrived from Ireland and England."[59] Two years later the demand for servants remained high and Pemberton wrote, "There have been a great number of Palatines ordered this fall, the demand for young people is yet very great."[60] The proportion

53 This assumption about the rise of the slave population is based on the increase in the percentage of black burials in the city.
54 Hunt and Greenleafe Letter Book, December 27, 1748, HSP.
55 John Pemberton to James Pemberton, May 15, 1749, Pemberton Papers, HSP.
56 John Kidd to Neate and Neave, April 5, 1749, John Kidd Letter Book, in Egnal, "Pennsylvania Economy," 100.
57 James Pemberton to John Pemberton, August 17, 1750, Pemberton Papers, HSP.
58 James Pemberton to John Pemberton, September 20, 1751, Pemberton Papers, HSP.
59 *Pennsylvanische Berichte,* December 16, 1750, quoted in Frank R. Diffenderfer, *The German Immigration into Pennsylvania Through the Port of Philadelphia 1700–1775,* part II, The Redemptioners (Lancaster, Pa., 1900), 209.
60 James Pemberton to John Pemberton, December 18, 1752, Pemberton Papers, HSP.

of servants and slaves in Philadelphia's work force reached its highest point in the early 1750s. More than 2,500 labored in the port city, representing more than 38 percent of the city's work force.

The Seven Years' War, like previous wars, greatly reduced the number of indentured servants while heightening the demand for slaves to take their places. The number of servants declined from approximately 1,600 in 1754 to fewer than 700 by 1756. During the same period, the slave population grew steadily. From 1755 to 1765, slave importations into Philadelphia were the highest in the colony's history. Importations peaked in 1763, when more than 500 slaves arrived at the port.[61] Clearly, the diminishing servant population did not indicate a decline in labor demand. Rather, the servant market evaporated as bound laborers flocked to enlist in the British army.[62]

Merchants were so discouraged by the enlistment of white servants that they did not even attempt to bring more into the colony during the Seven Years' War. In a letter to his agent John Perks, merchant Thomas Willing wrote, "I know of nothing to induce me to send a vessel just now to Bristol. No serv[ant]s can be bro[ugh]t here the Sale being Ruined by Enlisting them."[63] In the same year Willing acknowledged that "the same inconvenience to our Farmers and Tradesmen still Subsists, and a grevious and Unequall tax is on them to have their Servants taken from them."[64] In a 1757 letter to Perks, Willing explained, "For by the Enlisting of soldiers all our Labouring men are taken off."[65] The assembly warned the governor that

> if the Possession of a bought Servant . . . is . . . rendered precarious . . . the Purchase, and Of Course the Importation, of Servants will be discouraged, and the People driven to the Necessity of providing themselves with Negro slaves, as the Property in them and their Services seems at present more secure.[66]

This was precisely what occurred. The servant population grew smaller and the slave importations increased. The colonists ignored their supposed preference for white unfree laborers and shifted to slaves.

Following the Peace of Paris in 1763, the unfree labor force in Philadelphia never reattained its prewar level.[67] In 1767 about 331 indentured

---

61 Wax, "Negro Slave Trade," 49.
62 Gary B. Nash, "Slaves and Slaveowners in Colonial Philadelphia," *WMQ*, 3d ser., 30 (1973), 279.
63 July 26, 1756, Willing and Morris Letter Book, HSP.
64 April 22, 1756, Willing and Morris Letter Book, HSP.
65 October 15, 1757, Willing and Morris Letter Book, HSP.
66 Quoted in Nash, "Slaves and Slaveowners," 229.
67 The Tax Assessors' Report of 1767 lists 269 indentured servants. This figure must be increased to account for those servants who were of nontaxable age and thus not included by the assessors. The 1775 Constables' Returns to the Assessor provide the ages for 88

servants lived in Philadelphia, representing not quite 3 percent of the total city population and almost 6 percent of the urban work force. By 1775 the number of indentured servants in the city had increased to 827, or about 4 percent of the urban population and 11 percent of the labor force. Thus in an eight-year interval, Philadelphia's total labor force increased about 30 percent (from approximately 5,334 to 6,989) while the servant population increased by 140 percent from 332 servants in 1767 to 827 in 1775. During the same period, tax assessors' reports reveal that the number of slaves dropped from 814 to 405 in Philadelphia. The proportion of unfree laborers in the city appears to have been on a downward course as well – the number of indentured servants was insufficient to maintain the bound labor force. By 1775 only about 13 percent of the labor force was unfree.

The ethnic makeup of the servant population during the early eighteenth century is difficult to determine precisely, but there is little doubt that it shifted sharply from the predominantly English character of the seventeenth century. Estimates are admittedly rough, since they are based on the advertisements of ship arrivals in the port of Philadelphia. By midcentury most servants came to Philadelphia from the Palatinate. Those who emigrated from the British Isles came predominantly from northern Ireland.

One measurement of servant ethnicity can be made for 1745, the first year for which complete indenture lists exist. Almost nine of ten servants bound in Philadelphia were Irish (86.5 percent), with a few from Scotland (2.6 percent), England (3.2 percent), and Germany (7.5 percent).[68] A second list for 1772 reveals that by the eve of the Revolution the majority of the servants indentured in Philadelphia had emigrated from the Palatinate through the port of Rotterdam (71.7 percent), with an additional 20 percent from Ireland and 9 percent from England.[69] Since the shift in the national origins of servants followed the general emigration patterns, the nationality of servants was determined less by the preferences of potential servant owners than by the internal crises within each country that sent immigrants into Pennsylvania.

percent of the 827 servants in Philadelphia. Of these, 190 (22.9 percent) were below the age of fifteen, and two servants were above the age of fifty. On the basis of this age distribution, I increased the total number of servants listed on the Tax Assessors' Reports by 23 percent—the proportion of servants who would not appear on the tax lists because they were not of taxable age.

68 The obvious difficulty here is that no German ships entered Philadelphia in 1745; thus the picture sketched from these data is distorted. "List of Servants and Apprentices Bound and Assigned before James Hamilton, Mayor of Philadelphia," manuscript, AM 3091, HSP. Abbot E. Smith, *Colonists in Bondage: White Servitude and Convict Labor in America, 1607–1776* (Chapel Hill, N.C., 1947), 321.

69 "List of Servants and Apprentices Bound and Assigned before John Gibson, Mayor of Philadelphia, May 1771–May 1773," manuscript, AM 3795, HSP.

By the middle of the eighteenth century, unfree laborers had become more important for urban than for rural masters. Merchants acknowledged that the demand was for servants with urban skills, and they stressed this need in their correspondence with overseas contacts. Willing and Morris remarked that "men and youths . . . Good husbandmen, house carpenters, weavers, joyners, smiths, hatters, masons . . . and laborers are the best trades."[70] In 1769 Thomas Clifford wrote that all types of tradesmen and manufacturers were prized.[71] Across the Atlantic, advertisements announced:

> Wanted by a gentleman settled near Philadelphia in North America, some tradesmen, such as hair dressers, carpenters, joiners, sawyers, bricklayers, stonemasons, tilers, slaters, plaisterers, surgeons, schoolmasters, bookkeepers, wheel and millwrights, coopers, shoemakers white- and copper-smiths, linen weavers, shoemakers, taylors, gardeners, breeches makers . . . likewise a number of farmers who understand country business.[72]

Advertisements offering servants for sale in Philadelphia appealed to prospective owners in the colony's expanding trades and iron industry: "Just imported a choice parcel of Men and Women among whom are sundry Tradesmen," read one advertisement in 1737.[73] A 1738 shipment of servants included "five forgemen, nine [re]finers, and a hammerman."[74]

Representatives of every imaginable occupation owned unfree labor in Philadelphia. Joseph Vandigrift was one of many innkeepers who depended on bound workers. In 1775 the city's constables recorded that he owned two male servants, William Longwood and George Warren. Longwood was a groom and no doubt assisted Vandigrift by taking care of the stable where guests' horses were boarded. Warren was listed as a laborer and probably performed a large range of tasks from carpentry to odd jobs. Vandigrift's small labor force also included three children who were old enough to assist at the inn. In 1775 Archibald Burns, a Philadelphia hairdresser, had children who ranged in age from a few months to eight years. Because he had four young children, it would not be surprising to find that the three bound laborers Burns owned were domestic servants. However, Burns's servants were all men, from twenty-two to twenty-four years of age, and were skilled. From their occupations it is clear that Burns had aspirations for his

---

70 Thomas Willing to John Perks, October 1754, Willing and Morris Letter Book, HSP.
71 Thomas Clifford to Captain John Livingston, January 10, 1769, cited in Grace Larsen, "The Profile of a Colonial Merchant: Thomas Clifford of Pre-Revolutionary Philadelphia" (Ph.D. diss., Columbia University, 1955), 111.
72 *Gazetteer and Daily Advertiser,* Philadelphia, March 2, 1774.
73 *Pennsylvania Gazette,* October 6, 1737, May 12, 1737, October 14, 1736.
74 *Pennsylvania Gazette,* October 14, 1736, May 12, 1737, April 17, 1738.

Table 3.1 *Distribution of merchant and artisan servant owners and all Philadelphia taxpayers, 1774*

	Servant owners		Philadelphia	
	N	%	N	%
Merchants and retailers	133	37.6	653	13.9
Artisans	144	40.7	2,192	46.6

Source: Philadelphia County Provincial Tax, 1774, City Archives, Philadelphia. For an explanation of the occupation scheme, see note 77.

shop beyond dressing wigs: Richard Saxon was a perukemaker; Moses Haines and Moses Jacobs were both jewellers.[75]

The large number of unfree laborers in the city were bound to individuals in a huge variety of occupations whose businesses and homes required additional labor. Butchers and bakers, graziers and limners, snuffmakers and schoolmasters all owned unfree laborers. However, servant owners were concentrated in the two dominant occupational sectors of the urban economy, which were the key to the demand for unfree labor in Philadelphia. Tom Paine labeled the first sector, merchants and shopkeepers, "convenient but not important." Paine argued that they were a nonproductive class since they filled their time by "exchanging one thing for another and living by the profits."[76] Although unproductive by Paine's standards, merchant capitalists dominated the Philadelphia economy and constituted its elite. As Table 3.1 demonstrates, in 1774 almost 38 percent of the servant owners were from this occupational category, although merchants accounted for barely 14 percent of the city's population.[77]

75 Constables' Returns to the Assessor, 1775, City Archives, Philadelphia: Vandigrift, 143; Archibald Burns, 217. The returns are a census-like document that provide the number of children, servants, slaves, hired servants, tenants, and occasionally age and sex.
76 Thomas Paine to Henry Laurens [Spring 1778], *The Complete Writings of Thomas Paine,* ed. Philip S. Foner (New York, 1945), 2:1142–3.
77 The occupation breakdown is derived from Allan Kulikoff, "The Progress of Inequality in Revolutionary Boston," *WMQ,* 3d ser., 28 (July 1971), 375–412. Kulikoff divides the city into seven occupational sectors. Government workers comprise Group 1. Group 2 includes professional workers such as doctors, lawyers, apothecaries, ministers, and schoolmasters. Group 3 includes all people involved in buying and selling—traders, chandlers, merchants, and shopkeepers. Kulikoff identifies the members of this group as tradesmen. However, an eighteenth-century tradesman was an artisan, not a seller. I have changed the heading to wholesalers and retailers. Group 4 consists of clerical workers, including clerks, scribes, and notaries. The artisan class includes seven subheadings: building crafts, cloth trades, food trades, marine crafts, metal crafts, woodworkers, and miscellaneous crafts. Category 6, composed of those employed in the service trades, includes fishermen, mates, pilots, and

Merchants owned a large number of servants and slaves who served as domestic workers. Wealthy Quaker merchant Henry Drinker, for example, was taxed for two indentured servants a little more than a decade after his marriage to Elizabeth. At various times throughout his career, he also owned two or more slaves. The ownership of unfree labor may have provided Drinker with a status symbol. However, in 1775, with five children that ranged in age from one to thirteen years, a steady round of visitors and guests, and the endless chores associated with eighteenth-century domestic work, Elizabeth Drinker left no doubt that these unfree laborers were indispensable.[78] It is no wonder that with five children, all under the age of six years, merchant John Ross owned domestic labor. His twenty-two-year-old indentured servant and his sixteen-year-old slave must have assisted in the home. Similarly, in 1775 Samuel Pleasants had eight children, from seven years to two months, and the family occupied a substantial house. His household labor force included three indentured servants, three slaves, and two hired servants. It is not difficult to imagine that all of them were kept busy with the care of children and the demands of a large home.[79]

Merchants also utilized unfree laborers in a variety of jobs related to their businesses from clerks and sailors to stevedores and cartmen.[80] Antonio

sailors, and I added ferrymen, shallopmen, and captains. The final category includes unskilled workers such as gardeners, chimney sweeps, and laborers. The data for Philadelphia in 1774 were taken from the occupational breakdown in Jacob M. Price, "Economic Function and the Growth of the American Port Towns in the Eighteenth Century," *Perspectives in American History* 7 (1974), 128–37. I adapted Price's figures to the amended Kulikoff scheme.

In 1767 a total of 23 percent of the servant owners were merchants; by 1775 merchants accounted for more than 26 percent of the servant owners in Philadelphia. It is not likely that these indentured servants were the inventories of their merchant owners. Although Thomas Clifford complained that when servant cargoes sold slowly the servants had to be maintained, he noted that this happened only infrequently. Most servant owners, including merchants, held only one or two servants, hardly a sufficient number to be classified as inventory. See Larsen, "Profile of a Merchant," 16–18.

Wealth and status are the salient factors in the ownership of unfree labor for professionals. In 1745 almost 3 percent of the city's servant purchasers were professionals. By 1775 their numbers had grown to almost 5 percent. Many of society's elite, including such servant-owning notables as Dr. William Logan and lawyer Edward Shippen, Jr., belonged to the professional group.

78 "Philadelphia County Provincial Tax, 1769," manuscript, 174; "Philadelphia County Provincial Tax, 1772," manuscript, 117, Philadelphia City Archives, Philadelphia. I worked from a microfilm copy. Elizabeth Drinker Diary, July 29; August 9, 1779; October 19, 1794; Drinker Papers, HSP.

79 Constables' Returns to the Assessor, 1775: Ross, 199; Pleasants, 28.

80 Carl Bridenbaugh suggests that the "great merchants" had many apprentices to assist them with their large volume of paper work. *Cities in Revolt: Urban Life in America, 1743–1776* (New York, 1955), 286.

Askado was indentured to a merchant "to be taught navigation."[81] Merchants Ross and Vaughan purchased the indentures of William Reddel and Jonas Ackerman. Redell was to serve as a sailor,[82] and Ackerman was to labor on board their ship *Patsy Rutledge* or "any other ships in their employ."[83] In 1775 merchant Benjamin Ross owned indentured servant William Hayes, a skilled hairdresser. Perhaps Ross retailed wigs, in which case Hayes's skills served him in his business. Or it is possible, since Ross had no children and less need for general domestic labor, that Hayes was a personal servant, especially handy for keeping his wig properly styled. Israel Pemberton, one of the wealthiest merchants in prerevolutionary Philadelphia, owned five indentured servants in 1775. Although he no longer had any children living at home, his mercantile enterprise was still thriving, and some of his bound workers no doubt assisted him in business.[84]

Mechanics and manufactors, who according to Tom Paine made the only positive contribution to the urban economy, composed the second occupational category.[85] They depended more on unfree labor than any other group. In 1745, when unfree labor was at its height in Philadelphia, 63 percent of the servant purchasers were artisans, yet they constituted between one-half and one-third of the total work force.

Like merchants, the unfree laborers of wealthy artisans could be found working as domestic servants. John Hanna had six children under the age of seven years. Most likely, his eighteen-year-old female indentured servant tended to children and other household chores rather than the brushmaking business. Similarly, tailor Andrew Hodge's sixteen-year-old bound servant worked with his wife in the home to help care for their eight children and to assist in the countless other duties associated with the household. However, both Hanna and Hodge owned more than these female servants. Hanna had a twenty-one-year-old male slave who most likely did work as a brushmaker. In addition, the other indentured servant and slave owned by Hodge labored with him in his tailor shop.[86]

Most artisans owned unfree laborers to assist them in their trades. In some cases the relationship is obvious. William Ross, a city cordwainer, purchased the indenture of William Chase, also a cordwainer. William Edwards, painter, was bound to Samuel Ridly, painter. And tailor Thomas Martin owed four years of service to his master, tailor George Dillhorn.

81 Registry of Redemptioners, November 23, 1786, HSP.
82 Ibid., October 1785.
83 Ibid., July 21, 1787.
84 Constables' Returns to the Assessor, 1775: Pemberton, 28.
85 Thomas Paine to Henry Laurens [Spring 1778], *Complete Writings of Thomas Paine*, 2:1142–1143.
86 Constables' Returns to the Assessor, 1775: Hanna, 33; and Hodge, 11.

In other cases the relationship between the artisans' careers and their unfree labor was more subtle.[87]

Some artisans, like tailor John Stille, carpenter Richard Roberts, stone-cutter David Chambers, perukemaker James Biddle, and many others, increased their labor forces as their personal wealth grew. Stille is first visible on the tax list of 1767, when he owned one servant and one slave. His assessed wealth more than doubled over the next eight years, and by 1775 he had acquired an additional servant and one slave. In 1767 Chambers had one slave; in 1769 he replaced the slave with a servant. His assessed wealth grew steadily, and by 1775 he had two indentured laborers. Similarly, Biddle had one servant in 1769. Eight years later, his assessment had doubled and his unfree labor force had increased to three – two servants and one slave.[88]

At times, the number of unfree laborers in the household dropped, owing it would appear to a decline in the artisan's fortunes. In 1769 the tax assessor recorded that biscuit baker William Hodge had 75 pounds of personal property, including four slaves. Six years later, Hodge's assessed value had dropped to only twenty pounds and his unfree labor force had declined to two slaves and one five-year-old indentured servant.[89] Tailor John McCalla was rated at sixteen pounds in 1767, but only ten pounds in 1775. In 1767 he owned a servant and a slave; eight years later he had only one servant.[90]

More revealing are artisan households in which the indicators of economic well-being rose yet the number of unfree laborers fell. In some cases the decline in the unfree labor force portends the future of the institution – its ultimate disappearance. However, in other cases the drop in the number of unfree laborers often coincided with the presence of children who were old enough to contribute to the labor of the household. Tailor John Beck's unfree labor force decreased from two indentured servants to only one, from 1767 to 1775, the year his oldest child turned eighteen. Similarly,

87 Constables' Returns to the Assessor, 1775: Ross, 166; Ridley, 205; Dillhorn, 149.
88 Constables' Returns to the Assessor, 1775: Stille, 15; Roberts, 125; Chambers, 138; Biddle, 177. I collected these data by identifying all of the servant owners listed on the 1775 constables' returns. I then traced each servant owner back through the extant prerevolutionary Philadelphia tax lists, 1774, 1772, 1769, 1767, to determine each household's labor history. Since the constables' returns in many cases provide the ages of unfree workers, it was possible to ascertain whether the failure to list unfree labor on the tax list indicated an absence of bound laborers in the household, or whether it was the result of unfree workers whose ages fell above or below the taxable age.
89 Constables' Returns to the Assessor, 1775: Hodge, 5. In addition, Hodge was located on the 1769 and 1774 tax lists. A small part of the drop in assessment is due to the value of the slaves.
90 Constables' Returns to the Assessor, 1775: McCalla, 166. In addition, McCalla was located on the 1767, 1769, and 1774 tax lists.

brewer Reuben Haines's business grew steadily from 1767 to 1775. Yet his demand for unfree laborers declined from a high of five in the first year to three in the latter year, when his oldest child had reached the age of fifteen. Finally, coppersmith Benjamin Harbeson's unfree labor force was at its largest in 1767 – two servants and two slaves. In 1775 he owned two servants and only one slave. Additional labor most likely came from one or more of his six children.[91]

All of these artisan owners purchased labor to help keep up with the demands of the expanding market in the city. A few artisans owned unfree laborers for domestic service. However, the majority of servants in Philadelphia were males owned by Philadelphia's artisan classes – construction workers trying to meet the demands of the immigrant stream; shipbuilders who needed ship carpenters, sawyers, caulkers, riggers, coopers, joiners, and carters to fill the needs of the prospering trading sector; and shoemakers and hatters, butchers and bakers, who found ready work because of the growing local demand.[92]

Even though artisans depended heavily on unfree labor, production in Philadelphia until well into the nineteenth century was conducted on a small scale, and most of the servant and slave owners were of middling wealth.[93] Petty commodity production dominated productive relations in Philadelphia. The producers controlled the means of production, which was organized around the household; they directed production largely to local markets, often "bespoke" or custom work; and they entered the marketplace themselves. Only a few trades like baking, tanning, brickmaking,

91 Constables' Returns to the Assessor, 1775: Beck, 19; and Harbeson, 140. Both were located on the 1767, 1769, 1772, and 1774 tax lists.

92 Of 87 servants who arrived on the ship *King of Prussia* in 1764, 68 (78 percent) were males. "Sales of Palatines Arrived in the ship *King of Prussia,* James Robinson commander, 1764," manuscript, HSP. Of the 118 servants bound in Philadelphia in 1772, 82 (69.4 percent) were men. "List of Servants Bound and Assigned Before John Gibson, Mayor of Philadelphia, 1772," manuscript, HSP. Mildred Campbell reported that only 12.5 percent of a group arriving from Bristol from 1654 to 1685 were women. "Social Origins of Some Early Americans," in *Seventeenth-Century America: Essays in Colonial History,* ed. James M. Smith (Chapel Hill, N.C., 1959), 71.

93 The social and occupational composition of servant owners indicates – not surprisingly – that taxpayers in the lower economic brackets owned proportionately fewer servants. However, the correlation between servant ownership and wealth is not constant. To a large extent this is because taxable wealth is not the best gauge of economic welfare since the tax lists are primarily a measure of property ownership rather than of income. See Sharon V. Salinger and Charles Wetherell, "Wealth and Renting in Prerevolutionary Philadelphia," *JAH* 71 (1985), 826–40. With assessed wealth as the indicator, in 1767 only 15 percent of the servant owners came from the bottom 60 percent of the economic ladder. Eight years later, servant onwers from this bottom position decreased to only 5 percent. More important, between 1767 and 1775, the middle 30 percent of the population acquired servants far out of proportion to their number. By 1775 this group accounted for 75 percent of the servant owners in Philadelphia.

shipbuilding, and ropemaking were regularly carried out with more than a few employees.[94] Thus close to 75 percent of the servant owners possessed only one servant.[95]

The population of female domestic servants being kept by city families did not inflate the number of unfree laborers, nor does the city's proximity to the unfree labor market and its easier access to capital explain its urban character. Women were always in the minority and never constituted more than 20 to 40 percent of the servant population.[96] Almost all female servants with skills were in domestic service – "seamstress, governess, dairy maid, lady maids and the like" – and they were in demand in these jobs. Typical advertisements offering women servants for sale read, "A likely servant girl has a year and a half to serve, can card, wash, knit and iron and is very fit for country work"; or "four years of a likely servant maid's time to be disposed of she works well with her needles." Clearly, women servants did work as domestic servants, but there were never enough of them to affect the character of Philadelphia's unfree labor.[97] And the continual requests for "stout laboring men and boys" indicate that male servants labored in areas thought to have been inappropriate for women.

Philadelphia did not drain off unfree laborers destined for masters in the rural sector, because agricultural production in Pennsylvania did not demand a large number of unfree laborers, as it did in the plantation colonies. Although Pennsylvania farmers throughout the eighteenth century grew a surplus for the market, most of them relied primarily on family labor. During the first half of the century, farmers in southeastern Pennsylvania typically sold about two-fifths of their grain production and often had beef, pork, hemp, flax, cider and whiskey for sale. The market, however, was limited. Most products were "marketed locally to laborers, craftsmen, and townsfolk."[98]

---

94 Steven Rosswurm, *Arms, Country, and Class: The Philadelphia Militia and the "Lower Sort" in the American Revolution* (New Brunswick, N.J., forthcoming 1987); and Eric Foner, *Tom Paine and Revolutionary America* (New York, 1976), 28.

95 Sharon V. Salinger, "Colonial Labor in Transition: The Decline of Indentured Servitude in Late Eighteenth-Century Philadelphia," *Labor History* 22 (1981), 178, n. 21; 188, Table 7.

96 Ibid., 169.

97 Mildred Campbell, "English Emigration on the Eve of the American Revolution," *American Historical Review* 61 (1955), 7; *Pennsylvania Gazette*, January 31, 1748–9, February 15, 1731–2.

98 Historians do not agree on the degree of self-sufficiency in the seventeenth and eighteenth centuries. More than sixty years ago Percy Bidwell and John Falconer argued that farms were self-sufficient. *History of Agriculture in the Northern United States, 1620–1860* (Washington, D.C., 1925), 115–6, 131, 129. James Henretta echoed this view and suggested that the limited market prevented farmers from producing for it. Henretta focused on the communal rural mentality that supported security and balance over market

By the middle of the eighteenth century, Pennsylvania farmers were engaging in a substantial interregional and international trade based largely on the exchange of agricultural products, especially wheat and flour. However, the growth in the market did not have a significant effect on labor. Pennsylvania farmers continued to utilize non-family members only sparingly. Even though farm work was a year round process, most of the tasks – "maize harvesting, second cuttings of hay, two or three plowings, manure spreading and wood cutting" – could be accomplished on a schedule that did not require additional labor. Labor demand was at its peak only during the harvest and farmers found it more efficient to employ casual labor.[99]

Unfree labor in the Quaker colony was overwhelmingly urban by the middle of the eighteenth century. The port city contained no more than 12 percent of the colony's population, yet almost 60 percent of the servants bound in 1745 were purchased by Philadelphia residents.[100] In 1767 nearly

production. "Families and Farms: Mentalité in Pre-Industrial America," *WMQ*, 3d ser., 35 (1978), 3–32.

Carole Shammas presents a most convincing case for the other side of the debate. To her, the vision of the self-sufficient farmer is more nostalgia than reality. Farms could not provide all the necessities, and farmers were obliged to purchase imported items. "How Self-Sufficient Was Early America?" *JIH* 13 (1982), 247–72.

In a study of New England farmers, Winifred Rothenberg seeks to understand the "timing and extent of market imbeddedness among farmers." She concludes that "self-sufficiency" does not describe the New England farm, in part because these farmers had carried from England to America the tradition of the market. But evidence of the market and its accompanying fairs died out within a decade or so from the establishment of towns. However, the fact that specific market days ended does not necessarily mean that farmers became self-sufficient. Although ultimately noncommittal, Rothenberg argues that town governments had to regulate prices, an activity that suggests a regular market. "A Price Index for Rural Massachusetts, 1750-1855," *JEH*, 39 (1979), 975–101.

Most recently, Bette Hobbs Pruitt contends that both views assume self-sufficiency in food. In her study of Massachusetts, Pruitt demonstrates that farms were far from able to supply all food and the local market was a necessary supplement. The communal spirit was actually enhanced by this process since farms tended to complement one another. "Self-Sufficiency and the Agricultural Economy of Eighteenth-Century Massachusetts," *WMQ* 41 (1984), 333-64.

Although this debate is far from being resolved, none of the views claims that family farms required a large amount of additional labor. Henretta goes so far as to suggest that farmers "invariably chose the security of diversified production rather than hire labor to produce more." "Families and Farms," 19. The issue of labor would still be related to the relationship to the market.

99 James T. Lemon, "Household Consumption in Eighteenth-Century America and Its Relationship to Production and Trade: The Situation Among Farmers in Southeastern Pennsylvania," *Agricultural History*, 41 (1961), 69; Lemon, *Best Poor Man's Country*, 108, 177–8.

100 "List of Servants and Apprentices Bound and Assigned Before James Hamilton, Mayor of Philadelphia," in 1745 yields the names of 430 servants. Of these, 253 (58.8 percent) were

9 percent of Philadelphia's households owned at least one servant. By 1775 slightly more than one-fifth of the approximately 2,900 households (597) included at least one servant.[101] A more complete picture of the extent of unfree labor in the city includes the number of Philadelphia families who had direct contact with the institution of servitude, if only for a brief time.[102] By 1775, more than 750 families, or greater than one-quarter of the city's households, had recently owned white unfree labor. If the number of households owning slaves is included, more than 760 Philadelphia families, or almost 30 percent of the households, were directly involved in the ownership of bound labor.[103]

bound to Philadelphia residents, whereas the remaining 177 (41.2 percent) served owners living in the outlying rural Philadelphia, Bucks, Chester, and Lancaster counties. The manuscript is at HSP.

101 The 1767 Tax Assessors' Reports indicate that 298 taxpayers owned servants of taxable age. Again the exclusion of servants under the age of fifteen and over the age of fifty from the tax lists requires an adjustment of the figure. Using the same age distribution for the 1775 Constables' Returns to the Assessor, if we increase the number of taxpayers owning servants by 23 percent, approximately 240, or more than 8 percent, of the taxpayers in Philadelphia in 1767 owned at least one servant. This calculation seems warranted since 75 percent of the servant owners had only one servant. It is true that not all servants of nontaxable age were owned by masters with no other servants, but the number of these appears too small to alter the figures significantly.

By 1775 more than 16 percent of the families owned at least one servant. However, a closer examination of these figures is required. Gary B. Nash reports that "of the 3,319 taxpayers in 1767, 337 were assessed a poll tax, indicating that they were single freemen, usually living at the home of their parents or renting lodging in the house of another." Perhaps another 10 percent of those taxed were tenants. Nash estimates that the number of households could not be more than 80 percent of the total number of taxpayers. "Slaves and Slaveowners," 242–3. For a different calculation of the number of households, see John K. Alexander, "The Philadelphia Numbers Game: An Analysis of Philadelphia's Eighteenth-Century Population," *PMHB* 98 (1974), 314–24. Thus the figures on the number of households involved in the institution of indentured servitude are based on the adjusted number of households—approximately 2,655 (80 percent of the taxpayers).

102 In order to protect both servants and owners, original sales and transfers of ownership were made before the mayor of Philadelphia or, in case of his absence, before the city recorder. Cheesman A. Herrick, *White Servitude in Pennsylvania:* Indentured and Redemption Labor in Colony and Commonwealth (Freeport, N.Y., 1926; reprint, Freeport, N.Y., 1970), 197. "List of Servants and Apprentices Bound and Assigned Before the Mayor of Philadelphia" includes the names and terms of indenture for 220 servants purchased by Philadelphia residents. Of these transactions, only 21 (9.5 percent) were transfers of indenture. Clearly, servant owners were not merely transferring the same population of servants back and forth. Rather, the turnover rate in servant ownership reflects new servants and new owners. For a similar analysis of the slave population see Nash, "Slave and Slaveowners," 243.

103 Nash found more than 700 families with slaves in 1767. These slave-owning families were combined with the 328 servant-owning families during the same period. However, the figure was reduced by 26 percent to avoid counting twice families with both servants and slaves. "Slaves and Slaveowners," 243.

Indentured servants were far more important to the city's labor force than to the neighboring county. In 1767 not quite 3 percent of the work force in rural Philadelphia County were indentured laborers, whereas almost 6 percent of the city's work force were servants. By 1775 more than 10 percent of the labor force in the city were white bound laborers, compared with only 3 percent outside the city. Although the servant population grew in both the rural county and urban Philadelphia, the incidence of servant owning in the city increased to more than three times that in the country-side.

In Philadelphia County, a majority of the residents were engaged in rural occupations, except in the townships of Southwark and the eastern half of the Northern Liberties. These townships contained elements of both urban and rural life. Southwark, lying immediately to the south of Philadelphia and bordering the Delaware River, included many shipyards, ropewalks, tanneries, and the offices and shops involved in the city's growing commerce.¹⁰⁴ The township of the Northen Liberties lay directly to the north of the city. It, too, bordered on the Delaware River and contained many businesses involved in the growing shipping industry. In 1769 sixty-two households owned all of the seventy-nine servants in these townships. Almost three-quarters (70 percent) of the servant-owning households were occupied in nonagricultural labor.¹⁰⁵ Of the 148 households with servants in 1774, only two clearly earned their living in farming. Thus white bound labor was utilized far more extensively in households involved in urban occupations within Philadelphia's peripheral communities as well as in the city itself.¹⁰⁶

The demand for unfree labor was so high in Philadelphia that, even though servants were preferred, white and black unfree laborers filled interchangeable work roles. The Quaker conscience wrestled with the morality of slavery and professed a preference for white indentured

104 For a brief history of the township of Southwark, see Margaret B. Tinkcom, "Southwark, a River Community: Its Shape and Substance," *American Philosophical Society Proceedings* 114 (1970), 327–42.

105 Listed on the 1769 Tax Assessors' Reports as servant owners in Southwark were a smith, vendue master, doctor, butcher, tanner, three ropemakers, two tavern keepers, and three without occupations. Servant owners from the East Northern Liberties in the same year included three innholders, two bakers, three shopkeepers, one distiller, one widow, three butchers, two brewers, two milkmen, two brickmakers, three tanners, and a carter, smith, and miller.

106 The servant population in the rural townships of Philadelphia County were typical of the colony. Bedford and Northhampton counties had a far smaller percentage of servants than did Philadelphia County. Lancaster and Chester counties had almost the same percentage of servants as Philadelphia County, but none of the counties approached the incidence of servitude characteristic of the city of Philadelphia.

servants. However, each time indentured servants were unavailable, Quakers suppressed their consciences and stepped up slave importations to fill the labor shortage caused by the diminishing servant supply.

At times, the interchangeable nature of the two systems is obvious. Help-wanted advertisements in the *Pennsylvania Gazette* enunciated the laborers' duties and general requirements for the jobs, but a "servant man white or black" would fill the need.[107] In addition, the labor histories of individual owners disclose that servants and slaves were substituted for one another. Ropemaker James Craig vacillated between slaves and servants. In 1774 his two slaves were replaced by two servants. Whether Craig's slaves died, were manumitted, or sold is unclear, but his household labor force was maintained at the same level first with slaves, then servants. John Palmer's bricklaying business required two unfree laborers. In 1769 both unfree laborers were slaves; six years later, Palmer owned one servant and one slave. Edmund Milne gradually increased the number of unfree laborers he owned. He had one slave in 1769, purchased the indenture of a servant in 1774, and raised his total to four in 1775 with an additional servant and slave.[108] Although interchangeable, Pennsylvania owners voiced a preference for indentured servants, but if servants were unavailable, demand eclipsed preferences.

Quakers felt no pangs of conscience over the institution of indentured servitude. However, the Friends wrestled often with the morality of slavery. This concern was expressed as early as 1688, when the first antislavery tract was published in Pennsylvania.[109] In that same year the Germantown Friends' Meeting voiced their protest against the institution of slavery, arguing that Negroes had the right to freedom. The meeting concluded that such a weighty matter could not be resolved by the Monthly Meeting and so it was referred to the Quarterly Meeting. They, too, refused to take action, and so the debate passed to the Yearly Meeting, where once again nothing was done. The Yearly Meeting considered the issue again in 1696 and cautioned that "it is the advice of this meeting that the Friends be careful not to encourage the buying of any more Negroes and that such as have Negroes, be careful to bring them to meetings."[110] In a presentation to the meeting in 1700, Penn stated "that Friends ought to be very careful in

---

107 See, for example, *Pennsylvania Gazette*, supplement 2090, 1769, and May 17, 1775.
108 Constables' Returns to the Assessor, 1775: Craig, 180; Palmer, 204; Milne, 140. In addition, all were traced to the other tax lists.
109 This first antislavery tract was thought to be authored by Daniel Pastorius. Samuel W. Pennypacker, "Daniel Francis Pastorius," *PGSP* 9 (1898), 114.
110 Edward R. Turner, *The Negro In Pennsylvania: Slavery – Servitude – Freedom, 1639–1831* (New York, 1911; reprint, New York, 1969), 14; Thomas E. Drake, *Quakers and Slavery in America* (New Haven, Conn., 1950), 11–12.

discharging good conscience toward them in all respects, but much more especially for the good of their souls."[111]

The morality of the slave trade presented Quaker merchants with an additional dilemma. Isaac Norris pleaded with Jonathan Dickinson to "send me no more nor Recommend me no more Negroes for sale I don't like that Sort of Business." In another letter Norris explained that "I have recd. a Lame Negro and Sickly I know not what to do with I have no Inclination to be Concerned in Selling Negro's at all and desire to avoid it as much as possible."[112] Dickinson also voiced a desire to avoid participation in the slave trade. Although Dickinson and Norris imported and sold slaves in Philadelphia, by the 1730s most Quaker merchants had withdrawn from the trade.[113] This had little effect on the importation of slaves, however, since other merchants willingly took up the slack.[114]

While the Quakers articulated their opposition to slavery, other Pennsylvania writers acknowledged the benefit of slave labor in a society where the supply of free workers was so unpredictable. Benjamin Franklin explained in 1751 that Americans purchased slaves because "slaves may be kept as long as a Man pleases, or has Occasion for their Labour while hired men are continually leaving their Master (often in the midst of his Business) and setting up for themselves."[115]

Economic considerations encouraged the investment in indentured servants rather than slaves. The average eighteenth-century price for a servant was fourteen pounds, but slave prices were more than three times that amount. Clearly, the higher initial cost of slaves was returned over a longer period. However, the price differential suggests that different people were able to purchase servants and slaves. In addition, some masters could not take advantage of the long-term investment and needed a return more quickly. Compounding the problems of the high cost of slaves was the uncertainty of the slave investment. Masters owned slaves for life; thus they had to absorb the financial risk in case their slaves became ill, grew too old to be productive, or died. In contrast, servant masters realized their investment in three to four years. Support for elderly slaves must have been a problem, because in 1726 the Pennsylvania Assembly was compelled to pass a law coercing masters to provide for their elderly or infirm slaves.[116]

111 Quoted in Richard Wright, *The Negro in Pennsylvania: A Study in Economic History* (New York, 1912), 15.
112 Quoted in Darold D. Wax, "Quaker Merchants and the Slave Trade in Colonial Pennsylvania," *PMHB* 86 (1962), 150.
113 Dickinson was involved in the slave trade until his death in 1722; Norris participated until 1732. Ibid., 151.
114 Nash, "Slaves and Slaveowners," 266; Turner, *The Negro in Pennsylvania*, 4–6.
115 *The Papers of Benjamin Franklin*, 4:230.
116 Alan Tully, "Patterns of Slaveholding in Colonial Pennsylvania: Chester and Lancaster Counties, 1729–1758," *JSH* 6 (1973), 286–7; James T. Mitchell and Henry Flanders,

Slave ownership included additional costs. In Philadelphia, servants and slaves were taxable property but were not of equal value. During the mid-eighteenth century, servants over the age of fifteen years were valued at thiry shillings, and owners paid the collector two shillings and three pence. Slaves above the age of twelve were assessed at four pounds and slave owners were obligated to pay six shillings of tax per slave.[117]

In the contemporary view, the choice between a servant and a slave was an economic decision. In the 1740s a petition to the Assembly complained that the working classes struggled to pay the purchase price of a servant only to have their investment vanish when the servant enlisted. The more wealthy, "having no other Servants but Negroes, contribute nothing."[118] The Assembly proposed that, because of the servant shortage, "an advantage may be gained by the introduction of slaves, which could likewise be a means of reducing the exorbitant price."[119]

Wealth was not the critical factor in determining which type of unfree laborer a prospective master would buy. For some, owning slaves may have been an example of conspicuous consumption since the costs were so high and the less expensive servants were usually available.[120] However, the correlation between wealth and servant or slave ownership is weak. Only within the artisan category and among mariners did servant and slave ownership diverge. Artisans represented a large wealth spectrum. Those on the bottom of the economic ladder, especially cloth and food workers, tended to invest in the less expensive servant. Mariners, however, an occupational category that included the more wealthy captains, seemed to prefer slaves. Although the Quakers became vigorous opponents of slavery after 1760, even they manumitted only rarely before 1775.[121] When the demand for labor was high and servant supplies small, most Philadelphia residents ignored their preferences, suppressed their consciences, and bought slaves.

In addition to high labor demand and a large supply of uprooted people, another reason for the continuing flow of immigrant laborers into the British colonies was that trade in human cargo, white or black, was lucrative, and many people shared the spoils. Servants who came to

comps., Statutes at Large, 4:61.

117 Herrick, *White Servitude in Pennsylvania*, 204. In Lancaster and Chester counties, slaves were assessed at a value equal to one hundred acres of good land, the equivalent of two to four times the value of an indentured servant. Tully, "Patterns of Slaveholding," 299, n. 24.

118 *Votes and Proceedings*, 3:2564.

119 Ibid.

120 Tully, "Patterns of Slaveholding," 284–305; see also Wax, "Negro Slave Trade," 52.

121 Nash, "Slaves and Slaveowners," 236; Jean Soderlund, "Conscience, Interest and Power: The Development of Quaker Opposition to Slavery in the Delaware Valley, 1688–1780"

Pennsylvania were treated like any other imported goods. "A person could purchase, according to his inclination," writes R. J. Dickson, "a pound of garden seeds or passage to America from McKedy and Elder at the sign of the Orange Tree in High Street, Belfast."[122] Advertisements for the sale of servants suggest how humans became indistinguishable from other commodities. For example:

> Lately imported from Bristol, several likely Servants, Men and Women bred to most sorts of Business: also most sorts of European Goods, as, Fine Salt, Glass Bottles . . ."[123]

One trip to the store would yield "Rum, Sugar, and Mellases [*sic*] with some likely Men and Women Negro Slaves."[124]

It was possible to transport just a few servants at a time, thereby enabling other individuals to emigrate as free persons. In a letter to an acquaintance in Ireland, merchant Robert Parke explained how to bring some old friends to Pennsylvania. "I would have you Procure three or four lusty Servants and agree to pay their passage on this Side. [Then] he might sell two and pay the others passage with the money." It was also feasible, as Philadelphia merchant Daniel Clark recommended in 1761, to use a single servant cargo to help with current financial problems. Clark wrote to his English correspondent with advice for a Mr. Casey, who was apparently experiencing financial reversals. If Clark could procure about twenty or thirty servants, "he could return with the produce of his jaunt the Next fall and thus, if favour'd by Fortune would be enabled to bring Mrs. Casey with him the next year again in a more desireable Condition than he could this year."[125]

Slave traders in early Pennsylvania reaped profits as well, although before 1727 the trade into the Quaker colony was small. Slaves were transported from the West Indies and South Carolina on consignment to Philadelphia merchants.[126] Most of the slaves were described as of poor quality and were referred to as "refuse" or "waste" slaves.[127] After 1730, although the slaves arriving in Pennsylvania continued to come almost exclusively from the West Indies, merchants no longer purchased them solely on consignment. With the demand for slaves increasing, merchants imported larger cargoes

(Ph.D. diss., Temple University, 1982), 1–160; Thomas E. Drake, *Quakers and Slavery in America* (New Haven, Conn., 1950), 71.

122 Dickson, *Ulster Emigration*, 110.
123 *Pennsylvania Gazette*, February 15, 1731.
124 Ibid., June 15, 1738.
125 Quoted in Meyers, *Quaker Immigration*, 99; "Letters, Invoices, Etc of Daniel Clark Merchant of Philadelphia from May 1760 to June 1762," manuscript, AM 911, HSP.
126 Darold D. Wax, "Negro Imports into Pennsylvania, 1720–1766," *Pennsylvania History* 32 (1965), 255; Wax, "Quaker Merchants," 144–5.
127 Wax, "Quaker Merchants," 151.

and arranged for the sale after arrival.[128] By the late 1750s, the demand for slaves was so high that Pennsylvania merchants traded directly with the African coast.

Transporters' profits from the servant voyages depended on the ship's capacity, the length of the voyage, the quality of the provisions, and the value of the other goods on board. The price of passage to Pennsylvania from the Old World was approximately five to six pounds through the seventeenth century and three to four pounds through the eighteenth.[129] Using four pounds as the average cost for transporting an individual across the Atlantic, servant traders earned significant profits from the sale of a servant parcel. The average price of a servant ranged from fourteen to sixteen pounds for a three- to four-year indenture. Approximately forty servants comprised a parcel. Thus importers netted about ten pounds from each servant sold and close to four hundred pounds for the shipment – a sum often more than sufficient to cover the operating costs of a voyage.[130] Traders lavished praise on the servant trade because, as merchant Thomas Clifford wrote, it was a cash business.[131]

The trade in indentured labor only occasionally engendered doubts about its morality. James Pemberton, a partner in a prosperous family-run business and a leading member of the Philadelphia Quaker community, felt a nagging concern in 1749 about entering the servant trade. In a letter to his brother John in London, James lamented that "now a commission of this sort, I mean of Palatines, is attended with some trouble and it is not the most agreeable business which has all along been my objection to meddle with this adventure."[132] In contrast, Thomas Clifford identified servants as the

128 Robert Ellis Letter Book, 1736–1748, HSP. This letter book contains the most lengthy correspondence concerning the Pennsylvania slave trade and for this reason is unusual. Although many merchants engaged in the slave and servant trade, they corresponded very little about their enterprises.

129 Dickson, *Ulster Emigration*, 86; Richard B. Morris, *Government and Labor in Early America* (New York, 1946), 319.

130 On the basis of merchants' letter books and newspaper advertisements, I estimated that servant parcels from areas other than Germany averaged forty persons. See Willing and Sons to John Perks, October 1754, Willing and Sons Letter Book, HSP.

131 Larsen, "Profile of a Colonial Merchant," 111, 115. The indentured servant trade to Pennsylvania contrasts markedly with the trade in slaves to the Chesapeake and southern colonies. For example, traders from the Quaker colony did not deal exclusively in servants or slaves, nor were their ships built solely to accommodate the trade in human cargo. In addition, only the largest merchant houses, those that owned their own vessels, were consistent participants. Many merchants were involved, but most participated in only one venture. Only the following mentioned it regularly in their correspondence: Willing and Morris, Willing and Sons, Drinker and Sons, the Pembertons, Thomas Ellis, and Thomas Clifford. All are at HSP. One volume of Thomas Clifford's letters is at Columbia University.

132 James Pemberton to John Pemberton, May 30, 1749, Pemberton Papers, HSP.

ideal commodity. Clifford felt that indentured laborers not only provided him with an almost sure profit, but also enabled him to make a positive contribution to the welfare of the colony by providing those in need of labor with extra hands.[133]

Besides acting as a subsidiary source of profit for a number of Philadelphia merchants, the servant trade offered two other important advantages to traders. First, servants protected merchants' businesses when English dry goods glutted the colonial market. Pemberton agreed to deal in servants since "I . . . think it better than to bring goods to so dull a market as I imagine ours will be."[134] Hounded by the prospect of a glut of English manufactures, merchants repeatedly set their sights on the servant trade. London correspondents informed John Pemberton that since the American market could handle no more goods, "we think to engage in something that affords a better prospect of Advantage, in which thy Brother Jimmy seems to incline to be concerned with us. And that is, to Charter a ship here for Rotterdam to freight with Palatines."[135] Willing and Sons similarly depended on the servant trade. "Our trade is in such an unhappy state," they wrote, "that we have not been able to sell the rest of your potts since our last." However, they enclosed the proceeds from a sucessful servant sale.[136] A few months later, Willing and Sons reported that "our trade is still in a melancholy situation. . . . We have a great quantity of goods by us." They requested thirty or forty servants to help revive business.[137]

The second advantage afforded to merchants by the servant trade occurred during periods of the nonimportation agreements. Merchants had difficulty securing enough goods to fill their vessels for the homeward passage since so many colonial shippers competed for the few imports permitted. Thomas Clifford claimed that especially during periods of restricted trade, servants were prized. Importing indentured laborers would not only help to fill cargo space but would eventually offset the shortage of manufactured goods in the colonies by bringing servants who were skilled tradesmen and "manufactures." In 1769 Clifford hoped that nailmakers might be encouraged to emigrate to Pennsylvania since the nonimportation restrictions had created shortages of nails.[138]

Convict servants provided another source of profit in the servant trade. Most convict servants went to the tobacco colonies, but a sufficient number landed in Pennsylvania to arouse concern. For protection in 1683 the colony

133 Larsen, "Profile of a Merchant," 110.

134 James Pemberton to John Pemberton, May 30, 1749, Pemberton Papers, HSP.

135 Hunt and Greenleaf, London, to John Pemberton, Philadelphia, February 27, 1748, Pemberton Papers, HSP.

136 Willing and Sons to Thomas Day and James Stevens, August 6, 1754, Willing and Sons Letter Book, HSP.

137 Willing and Sons to John Perks, October 1754, Willing and Sons Letter Book, HSP.

138 Larsen, "Profile of a Merchant," 110.

"proposed that no felons be brought into this country."[139] Benjamin Franklin feared that Pennsylvania would not be protected from the convict trade. In 1751 he wrote that in some of the more remote areas of Pennsylvania "there are a Number of these venomous Reptiles we call Rattle-Snakes Felons-convict from the beginning of the World." Franklin proposed that the snakes be spared and, instead, a bounty "allowed per Head, some Thousand might be collected annually, and transported to Britain," to be distributed in "places of Pleasure about London. . . . Rattle Snakes seem the most suitable Return for the Human Serpents sent us by the Mother Country."[140]

A long chain of people profited from the convict trade. In order to transport a felon, a merchant or captain petitioned for the cargo by paying a contractor three pounds for each convict.[141] These servants were sold in the colonies for amounts ranging from nine pounds for unskilled laborers to as much as twenty-five pounds for skilled workers. Allowing for the minimal transportation costs, both the shippers and the contractors turned a profit.

The Pennsylvania Assembly acted to limit the importation of convict servants by passing a series of laws. In 1722 a five-pound duty was placed on all convicts imported into Pennsylvania, and a fifty-pound bond was to be posted by the importer to ensure the good behavior of each servant. This act was repeated seven years later, primarily because merchants and transporters were evading the order by bringing convict laborers into adjacent colonies and smuggling them into Pennsylvania. Acts to prevent convict servants from entering the Quaker colony were passed until 1742 without ever being sent to the home government for approval. When the laws were presented, they were disallowed. The strongest opponents of these laws were the European contractors of convict servants, who hoped to keep the convict trade open and the profits rolling in.[142]

Although the majority of indentured servants participated in the institution voluntarily or were transported to the colonies to escape punishment at the hands of the English courts, an involuntary form of recruitment accounted for a large number of seventeenth-century English servants as well as eighteenth-century German redemptioners. These transporters added one more to the list of individuals who profited from the servant trade. "Spirits" were of little importance in the peopling of Pennsylvania because the English government successfully eliminated this aspect of the servant trade before Penn carried his charter to the New World. However,

139 Quoted in Morris, *Government and Labor,* 334.
140 "A Letter to the Printers of the Gazette, May 9, 1751," *Papers of Benjamin Franklin,* 4:131–2.
141 Morris, *Government and Labor,* 336.
142 Ibid., 334–5.

an occasional petition makes it clear that some vestiges of the seventeenth-century recruitment tactics remained. In 1725 and again in 1727, Edward Busby wrote to the deputy governor of Pennsylvania begging him to have his son released from indenture. According to Busby, Captain Sparkes of Bristol had taken his fourteen-year-old son and sold him to David Evans in Philadelphia for sixteen pounds of paper money.[143]

Shady recruitment techniques continued to operate on the Continent. The "newlanders," counterparts of the English spirits, traveled through the countryside of Germany and Holland singing the virtues of life in the New World. Fancily dressed and displaying the accoutrements of wealth, they claimed to represent the possibilities afforded by emigration.[144] Acting as a recruiting agent for servants to go to America must have been a fairly profitable venture. An advertisement in the Philadelphia newspaper alerted inhabitants that a "servant-procurer" in Cork, Ireland, was offering his services.[145] Many of the eighteenth-century servants and redemptioners were lured by the promises of recruiters or shipmasters. Potential servants paid them for assistance, and merchants or captains compensated the agents for each individual in the cargo.

In addition to the development of regularized trade in servants and slaves, the growth and urban character of indentured labor affected the institution in other ways. Servants in the eighteenth century served significantly longer terms than the colony's first servants. More than one-quarter of the first group of servants were obligated for three years or less, whereas fewer than 10 percent of servants indentured in the mid- eighteenth century signed on for such short terms. Table 3.2 compares the length of indenture among three groups of servants. The first were indentured during the early years of the colony. The second group signed their indentures primarily during the third decade of the eighteenth century, whereas the final group were bound in 1745–6. Only 15 percent of the colony's first servants served five years or more, whereas more than one-quarter of the eighteenth-century group served for extended periods of time. In addition, early Pennsylvania servitude had vestiges of the English institution and was guided in part by custom. However, the institution became increasingly rigid and formal – oral contracts were replaced by formal written indentures.

The dramatic alterations in indentured servitude – longer terms, altered ethnic composition, an impersonal transportation system, and an urban labor force – greatly affected the experiences of servants in the eighteenth century. Not only did the transatlantic system exploit them miserably, but the level of social conflict escalated as well. Strong incentives existed for

143 Colonial Office Papers, CO 324, 35, 297, [no date]; 297, January 13, 1727, PRO.
144 Herrick, *White Servitude in Pennsylvania*, 184–5; Smith, *Colonists in Bondage*, 59–62.
145 *Pennsylvania Gazette*, February 3, 1742.

Table 3.2 *Length of indenture among servants indentured in selected periods,*
1681–1746

	Date of indenture					
Number of	1681–7(1)		1718–31(2)		1745–6(3)	
years	N	%	N	%	N	%
1	8	4.1	—	—	6	1.5
2	12	6.2	—	—	13	3.2
3	31	15.9	—	—	23	5.6
4	113	57.9	79	56.4	257	62.5
5	8	4.1	28	20.0	50	12.2
6	2	1.0	13	9.3	23	5.6
7	9	4.6	16	11.4	28	6.8
8 +	13	6.1	4	2.9	11	2.6
Total	195		140		411	

Sources: (1) Marion Balderston, "Pennsylvania's 1683 Ships and Some of Their
Passengers," *Pennsylvania Genealogical Magazine* 24 (1965), 69–114; Balderston,
"William Penn's Twenty-Three Ships," *Pennsylvania Genealogical Magazine* 23
(1963), 27–67. (2) Jack Kaminkow and Marion Kaminkow, *A List of Emigrants
from England to American, 1718–1759* (Baltimore, Md., 1964). (3) "List of
Servants and Apprentices Bound and Assigned Before James Hamilton, Mayor of
Philadelphia, 1745 and 1746," Manuscript, AM 3091, Historical Society of
Pennsylvania, Philadelphia.

servants to run away – to shorten the long terms of service and to escape the
conflict. As a result, the Pennsylvania legislature developed a legal code to
define the limits of behavior for both servants and masters. The code left
nothing to the imagination, with statutes covering virtually every aspect of
servants' lives. Servants were not only prevented from fornicating, marrying
without consent, and purchasing liquor; they were to serve additional time
for absconding, to work a full day, and to abide by their masters' wishes.[146]
  Portions of the law did include provisions for the protection of servants.
If masters were "tyrannical" and abusive, they would be admonished not to
"provoke" the servant.[147] Masters could not sell their servants out of the

146 *Duke of York's Book of Laws, 1676–1682* (Harrisburg, Pa., 1897), September 22, 1676,
    28, 37, 38; Staughton Geroge, Benjamin M. Nead, and Thomas McCamant, comps.,
    *Charter to William Penn, and the Laws of the Province of Pennsylvania, Passed between
    the Years 1682–1700, Preceded by Duke of York's Laws in Force from the Years 1676 to
    1682, with an Appendix* (Harrisburg, Pa., 1879), for 1683 see p. 153; for 1693 see p. 237;
    Mitchell and Flanders, comps., *Statutes at Large*, 2:35, 54–55, 285, 389; 4:1701–171;
    6:358, 440; 8:8, 30
147 *Duke of York's Book of Laws*, 38

province without the servant's consent and authorization from two justices of the peace.[148] In 1729, as the tide of immigration increased, all sales and assignments of servants were to be made before the mayor or city recorder.[149] When indentures were completed, servants were entitled to freedom dues. A 1765 law not only concerned healthier voyages, but included a provision making it illegal to separate married couples.[150]

The character of indentured servitude had changed dramatically in eighteenth-century Pennsylvania. The demand for unfree labor in Philadelphia, especially among artisans, soared and servants and slaves poured into the colony. Adverse economic conditions in Europe and Ireland propelled thousands of Germans and Scots-Irish to Pennsylvania. Slave traders took advantage of a regularized trade in Africans. Enormous alterations occurred in transportation as well. Servants no longer accompanied family and friends to Pennsylvania; rather, they became human cargo in a big business that brought substantial profits to individuals on both sides of the Atlantic. Potential masters preferred to buy the time of white servants rather than black slaves, but as the demand for bound workers escalated, masters appeared unconcerned about the type of unfree labor, and servants and slaves became the workers in interchangeable labor forces. No longer governed by custom, indentured servitude had taken on a peculiarly American form. We turn now to the way servants experienced the eighteenth-century institution.

---

148 Mitchell and Flanders, comps., *Statutes at Large,* 2:54; and Minutes of the Provincial Council, 1:61
149 Mitchell and Flanders, comps., *Statutes at Large,* 4:170
150 Ibid., 440.

4 Servants in the eighteenth century

IN 1773 JOHN HARROWER chronicled his personal trail from freedom to servitude. Harrower had been a businessman in Scotland but was forced to leave his home and family on December 6, 1773, to find relief from his economic woes. With only eight and a half pennies and stockings to sell, Harrower hoped to find work in eastern England. He certainly would go no farther from home than Holland. But at each stop along the way, no work was available and no ships had space to take him to Holland. He survived by selling his small inventory of stockings, borrowing a bit of money, and living very frugally.[1]

Harrower's travels took him first from Scotland to Newcastle. There he contemplated "engaging the M[aste]r of the *Elizabeth* Brigatine bound for North Carolina" but, he wrote, "the thoughts of being so far from my family prevented me."[2] After a futile search for work in Newcastle and no better luck at the next stop, Portsmouth, Harrower trudged eighty miles to London. Six weeks after leaving home, Harrower lamented that he "was like a blind man without a guide, not knowing where to go, being friendless and having no more money but fifteen shillings and eight pence farthing a small sum to enter London with."[3]

Harrower survived in London on almost no money. One day, while waiting for a possible business contact, he drank three pennies worth of punch and "was obliged to make it serve me Dinner." The only advertisement for employment Harrower felt qualified to answer was one for "bookkeepers and Clerks to go to a Gentlemen [in] Philadelphia." He arrived at the stated address but was too late; the position had been filled. With each further effort Harrower faced the same dilemma: "more than a dozen Letters before me, so that I hade little expectation."[4]

1 Edward M. Riley, ed., *The Journal of John Harrower: An Indentured Servant in the Colony of Virginia, 1773–1776* (Williamburg, Va., 1963).
2 Ibid., 7.
3 Ibid., 14.
4 Ibid., 15–16.

On January 24, Harrower wrote "a petition in generall to any Merch[an]t or Tradesman setting forth my present situation . . . offering to serve any for the bare support of life fore some time." But, he recorded, it was "all to no effect, for all places here at present are entirely carried by friends and Interest." Harrower discovered that the city of London was full of "many Hundreds . . . starving for want of employment, and many good people are begging." By this time, he was reduced to his last shilling and was "obliged to engage to go to Virginia [as an indentured servant], for four years as a schoolmaster for Bedd, Board, washing and five pounds during the whole time."[5]

Although indentured servants rarely kept journals, we know that Harrower's tale was not unique. Hundreds of others shared similar economic circumstances. Their quest for work forced them to leave their families and homes and trek to the nearest seaports. After a futile search for employment and with resources depleted, these individuals often solved their most immediate problem, their economic condition, by signing on as indentured servants. Perhaps by the end of their servitude, the future would look more promising. It is unlikely that prospective servants had any realistic notion of what awaited them in the New World. But thousands came. And most signed their contracts voluntarily, spurred by economic difficulties, concerns of conscience, and "the ever present factor of encouragement from America."[6]

Emigrating servants did leave a record of what pushed them to leave their homelands and drew them to Pennsylvania. Servants embarking from London, Stomaway, and Leith longed to "procur[e] better livelihoods"; for "want of employ," to better "pursue ones calling"; or to "better [their] fortune."[7] Servants on board the ship *Clementine* bound for Philadelphia echoed the hope of "procuring a better livelihood."[8] Passengers and servants on board the *Friendship* thought that Philadelphia would provide

---

5 Ibid., 17.

6 R. J. Dickson, *Ulster Emigration to Colonial America, 1718–1775* (London, 1966). Dickson included a quotation from a 1729 newspaper account that described farmers "condemned to the fringe of sufficiency by high rents" and thrown into a "scene of misery and desolation . . . crowded along the roads, scarce able to walk and infinite numbers starved in every ditch in the midst of rags, dirt and nakedness" (pp. 44, 80).

7 "An Account of Passengers and Servants on board the *Friendship,* Thomas Gann, Master, Port Leith to Philadelphia, May 9, 1774; *Two Friends,* London, Peter Bruster, Master, October 10–17, 1774; *Dolphin,* John Randall, Master, April 19–26, 1774; *Minerva* Arthur Hill, Master, January 24–30, 1774," Treasury Office T47/12, PRO. Port authorities were required "to make weekly returns to the Treasury on the number of emigrants and the causes of emigration." Dickson, *Ulster Emigration,* 16.

8 "An Account of the Number of Persons Who Have Emigrated to America in the Ship *Clementine* of Philadelphia, Patrick Binn, Master, July 13, 1774, Treasury Office, T47/12, PRO.

a better opportunity to "better their fortunes and pursue their callings than remaining in England."[9] Emigrants from Scotland expressed similar sentiments:

> The chief cause which gave rise to and propagated the prevailing spirit of Emigration among the Highlanders is that for some years the Land holders and Chieftans of the North have rais'd their rents so high and screwed their Tenants to such a degree that they have been greatly oppressed and reduced to Indigent and necessitous Circumstances . . . It is easily conceived that a people oppressed in this manner would grasp at any opportunity to be relieved from a condition but one degree removed from slavery.[10]

Customs officers in Wigtown summarized the cases of David Ireland, a smith, and George McCandlish, a farmer. Ireland and McCandlish opted to go to Pennsylvania because "they were informed and understood they could live much better and with more ease in the country to which they are going than they could in their country."[11]

German servants held similar hope for life in the New World. Jacob and Hannah Duncan agreed to indenture themselves because in exchange for four years of labor they would receive a "stake in the future."[12] For these individuals, emigration meant removing the shackles that burdened them in the Old World and replacing them with opportunity in the New.

Tantalizing reports in letters from Pennsylvania drew them to the Quaker colony. Very little of this correspondence has survived, but "letters from north Irish emigrants influenced the direction and volume of succeeding emigrations."[13] In 1728 an emigrant sent an account of the New World to northern Ireland,

> inviting and encouraging them to transport themselves thither, and promising the liberty and ease as the reward for their honest industry with a prospect of transmitting their acquisitions and privileges safe to their posterity, without the imposition of growing rent and other heavy burdens.[14]

In 1729 the northwestern Irish justices reported "that the highly colored accounts of life in America" were a more important cause of emigration than conditions at home. In 1737 James Murray, an Ulster emigrant to New York, wrote to express "from the viewpoint of laborers and tradesmen" the

9 Port Leith, May 9, 1774, T47/12, PRO.
10 Treasury Papers, T1/500, PRO.
11 Customshouse, Wigtown, Scotland, January 5, 1774, Treasury Papers, T1/500, PRO.
12 Chester County Petitions, Court of Quarter Sessions, 1720–1750, May 1748, Chester County Historical Society, West Chester, Pa.
13 Dickson, *Ulster Emigration,* 53.
14 Quoted in ibid., 44.

superiority of life in the American colonies to life in Ireland.[15] Emigrants from Scotland also received letters from relatives and friends "advising of their beneficial Settlements there, and of their having purchased for a trifling sum the property of a considerable extent." Customs officials at Wigtown, Scotland, admitted that the letters from North America "fell accidentally into our hands."[16]

Potential German servants also received encouragement from the colonies. A gentlemen of Wittgenstein described the effect of a letter received from Christopher Sauer, a well-known Germantown printer. Sauer praised Pennsylvania as an earthly paradise and, the German resident alleged, two women resolved immediately to leave for the Quaker colony. Other families decided to emigrate as well. Sauer explained that he "wrote largely to my friends and acquaintances, of the civil and religious liberties. . . . My letters were printed and reprinted whereby thousands were provoked to come to the province."[17] In the final count one hundred persons from the area responded to Sauer's letter by making their way to the New World.[18]

Because letters from the New to the Old World were not always favorable, a group of forgers and shady ship captains emerged to censor the correspondence. Some shipmasters involved in the Irish trade felt little aversion "to censoring the letters they carried and making sure that unfavorable reports of America never reached their destinations."[19] German immigration agents also altered unfavorable accounts. These letters were either discarded or "falsely copied." A few individuals in Germany earned their living forging these letters.[20] Advertisers wanted the view of America to be synonymous with the "promised land."

Less commonly, potential servants were encouraged to emigrate by colonial recruiting agents. Merchant Thomas Clifford sent a former servant back to his native Bristol to "acquaint poor laboring people with the genuine State of this Country, and the Opportunities industrious honest poor men have of supporting themselves by their labor here."[21] Visitors in Europe or departing emigrants occasionally advertised for servants. John Harrower may have answered an advertisement like the one Charles Taylor placed in a London newspaper in 1773 – Wanted "blacksmiths, taylors,

15 Quoted in ibid., 45, 17–18.
16 Customshouse, Wigtown, Scotland, January 5, 1774, Treasury Papers, T1/500, PRO.
17 Quoted in Karl F. Geiser, *Redemptioners and Indentured Servants in the Colony and Commonwealth of Pennsylvania* (New Haven, Conn., 1901), 14.
18 Donald F. Durnbaugh, "Christopher Sauer, Pennsylvania-German Printer," *PMHB* 82 (1958), 324.
19 Dickson, *Ulster Emigration*, 17.
20 Cheesman Herrick, *White Servitude in Pennsylvania: Indentured Labor in the Colony and Commonwealth* (Freeport, N.Y., 1926; reprint, Freeport, N.Y., 1970), 185.
21 Grace H. Larsen, "Profile of a Colonial Merchant: Thomas Clifford of Pre-Revolutionary Philadelphia" (Ph.D. diss., Columbia University, 1955), 118.

coopers, shoemakers and a genteel lad that understands waiting on a single person" to accompany him to Pennsylvania.²²

Shipping advertisements bolstered the image of the colonies as a source of relief for those in the throes of economic misery. Potential servants from Ireland were tempted by the pictures of a pleasant passage and the promise of a successful future. A 1766 advertisement for the departure of the *Hopewell* declared,

> It would swell the advertisement to too great a length to enumerate all the blessings those people enjoy who have already removed from this country . . . suffice to say, that from tenants they . . . become landlords, from working for others they now work for themselves, and enjoy the fruits of their own industry.²³

How could anyone have resisted a 1767 advertisement in the *Belfast News Letter* that equated the departure of the *Britannia* to a religious experience? "The ship, by the blessing of God, will then proceed on her intended voyage for the Land of Promise."²⁴ Writing from the colonies in the 1770s, emigrant William Eddis claimed that the streets of London were filled with advertisements

> offering the most seducing encouragements to adventurers under every possible description; to those who are disgusted with frowns of fortune in their native land and to those of an enterprising disposition, who are tempted to court her smiles in a distant region.²⁵

From Scotland, people were tempted by many "enticing accounts of America published everywhere by the shipmasters and agents, [which] have a great affect."²⁶

Women who traveled the distance alone confronted special difficulties, and we can only imagine how they must have felt as they contemplated the journey to America. They too left their homes and families to escape a desperate poverty, to seek some alternative to the increasingly difficult lives of their mothers and sisters before them. Perhaps, like many of their contemporaries, they had already moved from the countryside to seek work in the cities, to labor as domestic servants in the homes of wealthy families. Most likely, they cherished dreams of a better life than they had known, a modest prosperity, stalwart husbands, homes, and perhaps servants of their own. They could not have known that merchants were warning their agents abroad to "send no more women."

22 Dickson, *Ulster Emigration*, 118–19.
23 Ibid., 17.
24 Ibid.
25 William Eddis, *Letters from America*, ed. Aubrey Land (Cambridge, Mass., 1969), 37.
26 Abbot E. Smith, *Colonists in Bondage: White Servitude and Convict Labor in America, 1607–1776*, (Chapel Hill, N.C., 1947; reprint, New York, 1971), 54.

Once they had made the decision to go to America, prospective servants arranged for the indenture, boarded ships advertised as "well suited for passengers," and soon found themselves in the midst of a nightmare. The journey to the "promised land" became a "middle passage" with horrors that sometimes rivaled those of the slave trade. Illness and death from overcrowding, crude sanitary conditions, and meager diets plagued the passengers, who found themselves thrust into the role of human cargo in an eighteenth-century profit business. The on-board provisions were generally calculated to last for twelve weeks, fourteen if the captain was "liberally inclined."[27] The daily diet at sea consisted of bread, ship's biscuits, meat, peas, cheese, and, if the passengers were fortunate, fish. But when the ship's progress was delayed, usually owing to inclement weather or unfavorable winds, provisions dipped dangerously low, especially since quantities were calculated to accommodate "freights" rather than the number of people. A "freight" was a passenger over the age of fourteen. Children between the ages of four and fourteen counted as half-freights. On voyages where there were a high proportion of children, as on the redemptioner ships, provisions were less adequate and delays at sea often disastrous.[28]

The most vivid account of the transatlantic journey comes from the journal of Gottlieb Mittelberger. His graphic descriptions make the sounds and smells almost palpable. Mittelberger was witness to a tragic journey even though he had paid for his ticket. He made the trip from Germany to the New World with a commission to deliver an organ to a Lutheran congregation in Pennsylvania. In May 1750 he left his birthplace in the district of Vailhinger for Heilbronn, picked up the organ, and then followed the typical route down the Neckar and the Rhine rivers to Rotterdam. The Rhine boats had to stop at thirty-six customshouses between Heilbronn and Holland, where officials examined the ship and required passengers to pay a toll. After four to six weeks, the ships finally arrived in Holland, where once again they were detained. "In Rotterdam and to some extent also in Amsterdam, the people are packed into the big boats as closely as herring." The sleeping area for each person measured only two by six feet. Between four hundred and six hundred passengers were crammed into these ships, forced to share quarters with "the immense amount of equipment, tools, provisions, barrels of fresh water, and other things."[29]

With favorable winds, the passage from Holland to Cowes, off the southern coast of England, might take eight days or less; with contrary winds, it could take as long as four weeks. In Cowes, everything was

27 Ibid., 213.
28 Ibid., 213–14.
29 Gottlieb Mittelberger, *Journey to Pennsylvania in the Year 1750 and Return to Germany in the Year 1754*, translated by Oscar Handlin and John Clive (Cambridge, Mass., 1960), 11.

reexamined and additional customs charges were levied. Mittelberger writes, "It can happen that ships have to ride at anchor there from eight to fourteen days, or until they have taken on full cargoes."[30] By the time the ship sailed, most of the passengers had spent their last remaining money, had consumed their meager stock of provisions, and had nothing left. Families that had planned to arrive in Pennsylvania free were now forced to travel as redemptioners.

When the ship weighed anchor for the last time, "both the long sea voyage and misery begin in earnest."[31] Almost five hundred passengers crowded onto the *Osgood* for this journey to Pennsylvania. Signs of distress filled the ship:

> smells, fumes, horrors, vomiting, various kinds of sea sickness, fever dysentery, headaches, heat, constipation, boils, scurvy, cancer, mouth-rot, and similar afflictions, all of them caused by the age and the highly-salted state of the food . . . as well as by the very bad and filthy water.[32]

Mittelberger also witnessed food shortages, frost, heat, thirst, and "so many lice, especially on the sick people, that they have to be scraped off the bodies." The climax of the journey was reached, Mittelberger claimed, when a storm hit, and for two or three days, "everyone was convinced that the ship with all on board" would sink.[33] Six months of steady traveling finally brought Mittelberger to Pennsylvania; the journey from Rotterdam to Philadelphia had taken fifteen weeks.

If the shipboard accommodations were miserable for paying passengers like Mittelberger, the conditions below deck were even worse for indentured servants. The tragic nature of the trade in servants was not merely a function of the enormous number of immigrants who poured into the Quaker colony after the second decade of the eighteenth century. Thousands of immigrants had arrived in Pennsylvania during the seventeenth century as well. The difference resides in the nature of the transportation system. In the early period, servants were not segregated from paying passengers, nor was the transportation of servants a special business. Indeed, servants often accompanied their masters. In the eighteenth century, however, the transportation of servants became a profitable enterprise. Traders delivered thousands of bound laborers to Pennsylvania and exhibited a callous disregard for their servant cargoes. As a result, passengers on these voyages suffered from a high rate of disease.

30 Ibid., 12.
31 Ibid.
32 Ibid., xiv.
33 Ibid., 12–13.

The number of diseased passengers was so alarming that Pennsylvania officials became concerned about the spread of sickness within the colony. In 1720 the Provincial Council recommended a law entitled "An Act to Prevent Sickly Vessels coming into this Government."[34] This law stipulated that surgeon Patrick Baird be authorized to board all incoming passenger vessels,

> to examine the State of Health of the Mariners & Passengers aboard, and upon reasonable Cause of Suspicion of any pestilential or Contagious Distemper being aboard to warn and require the master or Commander of such Sickly Ship or Vessel not to presume to land.[35]

The master would either have to anchor the ship a mile from the city or be obliged to land any sick passengers a safe distance from the city and to accommodate them at his own expense in "Country" houses. Thus servants were often stopped just short of the New World, with land in sight, and forced to remain quarantined on board ships in which they had just spent a horrifying ten to twelve weeks.

As the flow of servants into Pennsylvania swelled, the problem of disease became acute.[36] In 1738 Doctor Thomas Graeme reported to the Council that, if the ships *Nancy* and *Friendship* were allowed to land, "it might prove Dangerous to the health of the Inhabitants of this Province and City."[37] The masters of these vessels were ordered to remove a distance of one mile from the city, were fined, and had to give five hundred pounds' security. In the same year, alarmed at the risk of disease from immigrant vessels, Governor Thomas recommended the building of a "pesthouse" to quarantine new arrivals.[38] Conceding that Pennsylvania had flourished in large part because of the great number of immigrants from the Palatinate and other areas of Germany, he warned that the unhealthy condition of these arrivals threatened the resident population and burdened passengers

---

34 *Minutes of the Provincial Council of Pennsylvania*, in *Colonial Records* (Philadelphia and Harrisburg, 1852–3), 3:112.

35 Ibid.

36 For the lengthy debate see Minutes of the Provincial Council, 3:293–4; 4:498, 568, 569, 587, 674; and 5:410. Billy G. Smith estimates that the annual crude death rate in Philadelphia jumped markedly from 31.5 burials per 1,000 population in 1737 to 53.2 per 1,000 in 1738. In that year, sixteen ships landed passengers from Germany, whereas only seven ships landed passengers the year before. "Death and Life in a Colonial Immigrant City: A Demographic Analysis of Philadelphia," *JEH* 37 (1977), 871; see also Ralph B. Strassberger and William J. Hinke, *Pennsylvania German Pioneers: A Publication of the Original Lists of Arrivals in the Port of Philadelphia from 1727 to 1808*, Pennsylvania-German Society Proceedings (Norristown, Pa., 1934), 1:xxix.

37 Minutes of the Provincial Council, 4:306.

38 Ibid., 512.

confined while ill on board the ships.[39] The Council responded by reiterating the positive contribution the German population had made to Pennsylvania society but refused to appropriate the necessary funds for a facility.[40] This statement provided small consolation to the sick passengers. As Mittelberger observed, "The miserable people who are ill must often still remain at sea and in sight of the city for another two or three weeks – which in many cases means death."[41]

Ships filled with diseased passengers continued to land. In 1741 Governor Thomas once again petitioned for a pesthouse to make a "charitable provision" for the immigrants rather than confine them to the ships.[42] This time the Assembly was more responsive. After a lengthy debate with the governor, they appropriated funds to purchase Fisher Island, at the mouth of the Schuylkill River, to be used as the site of a pesthouse and hospital. Although the hospital was not erected until 1750, sick immigrants were taken off the ships and quarantined in the existing buildings on the island.[43]

The creation of the pesthouse was an official acknowledgment that the city was under great risk from the continued arrival of unhealthy immigrants. But the establishment of a quarantine area did nothing to protect the health of future arrivals, and the island was reminiscent of an institution of punishment rather than a haven for the sick. A visitor to the island in 1764, perhaps Pastor Helmuth, described "a land of the living dead, a vault full of living corpses." He had intended to preach to the inhabitants but "the stench and the revulsion of body as well as mind, yes the feelings of humanity, forbade me to carry out my intention of speaking or praying with them."[44]

Female servants were particularly susceptible to shipboard illnesses, and merchants warned their captains and European correspondents about their vulnerability. Merchants James and Drinker, announcing the arrival of the ship *Anna* in May 1769, reported that all was in good order except "several of the women servants if not all, [are] bad with the itch."[45] They wrote again the following month that "but one of the woman sold, the other three [are] at the hospital to be cured of convulsion Fits and the Itch and [we]

39 Ibid., 315.
40 Ibid., 317.
41 Mittelberger, *Journey,* 16.
42 Minutes of the Provincial Council, 4:507–8, 509–24.
43 Smith, *Colonists in Bondage,* 216. In 1749, there were 2,000 German passengers who died at sea; approximately 6,800 persons arrived in Philadelphia. Strassberger and Hinke, *Pennsylvania German Pioneers,* 1:xxx- xxxi.
44 Edgar C. Hastings, "Labor in Pennsylvania to 1790" (M.A. thesis, Pennsylvania State College, 1926), 32.
45 James and Drinker to Lancelot Cowper, May 19, 1769, James and Drinker Letter Book, HSP. The itch was an infestation of scabies. It is not clear why the women were so severely afflicted by the disease whereas there was no mention of the difficulty among men.

shall be glad to get clear of them at any rate. Pray keep clear of the Sex in all further supplies of servants."[46]

Death was also common on the transatlantic voyages. Encouraged to seek their fortunes in the flourishing Quaker society and promised suitable provisions for the voyage, prospective servants suffered a staggering loss of life on board eighteenth-century vessels. Although it is difficult to derive precise mortality figures, a crude rate approximation at various points throughout the eighteenth century can be calculated using scattered data. In 1710 fully 25 percent of the German immigrants to Pennsylvania perished.[47] Of the sixteen ships that arrived in Philadelphia in 1738, only two could land passengers without a quarantine period. On one of the ships, 70 percent of the passengers died. Overall, a total of 1,600 individuals perished, a crude mortality estimate of more than 50 percent.[48] In 1749, the year of heaviest German immigration into the colony, approximately one of five passengers died on route.[49] Although only spotty data exist for the mortality on vessels carrying servants from Ireland, Irish servants may have fared even worse.[50] In 1729 statistics from two vessels indicate a mortality of more than 50 percent. A 43 percent mortality occurred on the *Seaflower* voyage in 1741 and a 26 percent death rate on the voyage of the *General Wolfe* in 1772.[51]

Scattered data reveal that the mortality for servants at certain times equaled that for slaves in the "middle passage," and during other periods actually exceeded the death rate for slaves. Analyses of mortality in the eighteenth-century French slave trade from Nantes yield a mean rate of 16.2 percent for the period from 1715 to 1775. These data also show a general decline in mortality between 1748 and 1792.[52] A recent study of the middle

---

46 James and Drinker to Lancelot Cowper, June 7, 1769, James and Drinker Letter Book, HSP.

47 Herbert S. Klein, *The Middle Passage: Comparative Studies in the Atlantic Slave Trade* (Princeton, N.J., 1978), 70. Ten ships carried these German emigrants to Philadelphia. Klein also reports other, more random mortality data for eighteenth-century European immigration, which average 15–20 percent. Karl Geiser notes that in 1732 a vessel lost 100 of 150 passengers (67 percent). *Redemptioners*, 50. See also Frank R. Diffenderfer, *The German Immigration into Pennsylvania Through the Port of Philadelphia, 1700–1775*, part 2, *The Redemptioners* (Lancaster, Pa., 1900), 262. On a 1745 vessel, 350 of 400 (87.5 percent) perished.

48 Smith, *Colonists in Bondage*, 216. Mortality was calculated by comparing the number of dead reported in Smith with the number of arrivals (approximately 2,750) for that year. Strassberger and Hinke, *Pennsylvania German Pioneers*, 1:197–251.

49 See note 44.

50 Dickson, *Ulster Emigration*, 95.

51 Ibid., 208–9. Approximately 175 persons died on two vessels. Each ship carried about 150 passengers.

52 Philip D. Curtin, *The Atlantic Slave Trade: A Census* (Madison, Wis., 1969), 276–80, Table 78.

passage reports a death rate of 9.3 percent over the entire eighteenth century as well as a decline in the rate as the century progressed.[53] Thus slave mortality throughout the eighteenth century fell within the 10 to 20 percent range, compared with almost 25 percent for servants traveling to Pennsylvania.

A number of factors contributed to excessive servant death. Although profit motivated both trades, slaves were more valuable than servants. Each slave represented a substantial investment well before reaching the slave market. In contrast, transporters of servants paid at most a small sum to an agent to procure the servant and were out of pocket only for the provisions on the transatlantic voyage. In addition, slave traders operated ships designed and used exclusively for the transportion of their human cargo and the business of slaving was the sole venture. Servant traders did not make quite the same commitment nor reap comparable profits. They were content to make operating costs or have additional cash, but servant cargoes usually accounted for only a portion of a venture.

The high mortality in the servant trade was avoidable. As horrible as the middle passage was, death rates actually improved through the eighteenth century. Servant transporters were aware of the requirements for a healthy voyage. Merchants Abel James and Henry Drinker cautioned their Captain Enoch Story to pick out healthy servants and warned him that the journey's success depended upon the "Provisions laid in and furnished for the Voyage."[54] Merchant Thomas Clifford prescribed that his vessels have frequent washings with vinegar "every ten days if weather permits, fore and aft between decks." When the ships were not crowded, Clifford ordered them scrubbed with water.[55] Servant traders were also aware of the advantages of citrus and proper ventilation. It had been known for some time that citrus prevented scurvy. In addition, proper air circulation had been identified with healthy voyages and well before the midcentury a ventilation system for ships had been developed. When the English Board of Trade planned to send a group of settlers to Halifax in 1749, they commissioned the inventor of the "Sutton Air Pipes" to estimate the costs of installation of the system for the transport vessels. Sutton agreed to outfit

---

53 Klein, *Middle Passage,* 68. Although the mortality figures for the eighteenth-century servant and slave trades were comparable, Klein reports that the death rate dropped far more in the nineteenth-century European trade than in the slave trade. Klein suggests that the drop is related to the length of time at sea (p. 92). The data from the European trade are too scant to reveal any trends for the eighteenth century. However, the drop in mortality to 2 percent in the nineteenth century might also reflect the decrease in the servant trade. Nineteenth-century emigrants were predominantly paying passengers.

54 James and Drinker to Captain Enoch Story, May 6, 1769, James and Drinker Letter Book, HSP.

55 Larsen, "Colonial Merchant," 122; Smith, *Colonists in Bondage,* 216.

the ships at a cost of thirty pounds per ship, "or thirty-five if with furnace." The board ordered the work and was pleased to discover that the English arrived in Halifax in excellent health, "while John Dick's Germans, who came on a ship without ventilation, were all sickly."[56] Whether ventilation systems did in fact provide a more healthy atmosphere on ship is not our concern, since contemporary wisdom thought that proper ventilation would protect the health of passengers. By not incorporating ventilation technology, shippers revealed that the health of their servant passengers was not a priority.

Transporters took great pains to reassure paying passengers that their transportation was separate from that of servants. In an advertisement announcing the departure of the *Elizabeth and Mary* for Philadelphia in 1769, paying passengers were urged to travel on this ship because they would experience a superior voyage. The advertisement promised that "as she will take no servants, will have good accommodations for passengers."[57] Thus if servant traders had wanted to, they could have protected the health of their servants. Clearly, few incentives motivated them to do so, and as long as they did not jeopardize the health of paying passengers and separated free from bound travelers, both businesses could operate.

In order to make the maximum pecuniary gain in the servant trade, shippers crammed as many souls as possible into their vessels, confident that even with the most callous disregard for human life, the monetary return would still make it worth the effort. A number of immigrants testified that the treatment during the voyage caused much of the suffering. On the vessel carrying John Harrower to Virginia, the servants came close to mutiny on two different occasions. They were incensed because the captain had put them on strict rations.[58] Harrower also reported that two servants were placed in irons "for wanting other than what was served."[59] Testimony from a 1729 trip suggests that the danger to the passengers came from a combination of too many passengers and too much time spent in travel. A hard trip was made nightmarish when "meanly provided, many starve for want and may die of Sickness being crowded in such numbers on board one Vessel."[60] The ship *Love and Unity* left Rotterdam bound for Philadelphia in 1731. Hardly living up to its name, the passengers endured a dreadful voyage, many lives were lost, and the vessel was unable to reach Philadelphia. It landed instead off the coast of Massachusetts. In testimony written

56 Smith, *Colonists in Bondage*, 216–17.
57 From the *Dublin Mercury*, February 18–21, 1769, cited in George R. Mellor, "Emigration from the British Isles to the New World," *History* 40 (1955), 74.
58 Riley, ed., *Journal of John Harrower*, 19–20.
59 Ibid., 25.
60 *Pennsylvania Gazette*, November 20, 1729.

by five survivors, the captain was accused of being "a wicked murderer of souls, thought to starve us, not have provided provisions enough, according to agreement."[61] An English emigrant who traveled to Baltimore in 1774 reported that as soon as the vessel left Land's End the master "used the passengers in a most cruel manner." He reduced the food to "one and one half biscuits, three small potatoes, and two ounces of salt beef, six spoonfuls of pea soup being substituted for potatoes and beef on Tuesdays and Fridays." The traveler alleged that complainers met severe punishment.[62] Captains involved in the redemptioner trade also gained an infamous reputation. Transportation rules specified that if the passenger survived the voyage beyond the halfway point in the journey, the family would be responsible for the cost of passage, whether or not the individual survived. Many masters were notorious for providing adequate provisions for only the first half of the trip and then virtually starving their captives to the journey's end.[63]

The staggering risk to servant life did not escape the notice of the Pennsylvania government, and colonial officials blamed overcrowded vessels for the high rate of disease and mortality.[64] In 1750 the Pennsylvania Assembly passed the first act to limit the number of passengers per ship. The

---

61 Quoted in Diffenderfer, *German Immigration,* 64.

62 Dickson, *Ulster Emigration,* 209.

63 Diffenderfer, *German Immigration,* 211.

64 Tight packing is a possible explanation for the high mortality in the eighteenth-century German trade. The tight-packing theory for the slave trade was developed by Daniel P. Mannix in collaboration with Malcolm Cowley in *Black Cargoes: A History of the Atlantic Slave Trade* (New York, 1962), 105–6. However, the tonnage record for ships transporting German passengers to Pennsylvania are unavailable. The estimated average number of persons per vessel in the European trade was three hundred on ships averaging just less than two hundred tons. The resulting one and a half person per ton is considerably lower than the corresponding rate for the slave trade. Klein, *Middle Passage,* 70; Strassberger and Hinke, Pennsylvania *German Pioneers,* 1:xxxi.

Klein refutes the tight-packing theory as an explanation for increasing slave mortality through the eighteenth century. He demonstrates that the most important cause of death was the length of the voyage rather than the number of passengers per ship. *Middle Passage,* 65–8.

Scattered tonnage data exist for the more humane Irish servant trade. These reveal that, during periods of high emigration, the number of passengers exceeded the tonnage of the vessels and mortality rose. Also, the advertisements for passage doubled the actual tonnage of the ships in order to attract the maximum number of persons. Dickson, *Ulster Emigration,* 210. No restrictions were ever imposed by the Irish or English Parliaments during the eighteenth century to limit the number of passengers per ship. In 1828 the British Passenger Acts determined the number of passengers per vessel at "three to every four tons burthen" (p. 211).

Some merchants, like James and Drinker and Thomas Clifford, equated good voyages with healthy cargoes. For many others, however, the goal was to "procure all the servants you can." Orr, Dunlop, and Glenholme Letter Book, 1767–1769, July 25, 1767, HSP.

Assembly conceded that quarantining was merely a stopgap measure and proclaimed that masters and owners imported too many Germans and other passengers in one vessel, which resulted in rampant disease and death. In order to improve conditions the Assembly ordered that each freight be allowed a space of six feet in length and one foot six inches in breadth. If a passenger was under the age of fourteen, the same space would accommodate two persons.[65]

This law had little effect; servants continued to arrive ill. In 1754 Doctors Graeme and Thomas Bond submitted a health report after investigating a large number of cases of ship's fever among recently arrived Palatines. The doctors concluded that "from the great number that have dyed, we are certain . . . the people have been sick since we visited them, or that the sick have been wickedly conceal'd from us."[66] They described how masters unloaded the sick from their vessels before the doctors' visit. This particular ship "lay below [Philadelphia] on Pretense of being aground, but . . . she was kept back only to have time to take out the sick."[67] In 1754 Jacob Shoemaker, who was in charge of the "stranger's burial ground," reported that more than 250 recently arrived Palatines had been buried during the previous three months, and he noted that this was not the final total.[68]

In 1765, after intense pressure from the Pennsylvania German Society, the Assembly once again legislated to halt the overcrowding on ships because "it is found by experience to require some further provision and regulation."[69] This supplement to the 1750 law itemized all of the abuses German passengers were subjected to during the transatlantic voyage. It reiterated the previous horizontal space to be allowed each passenger and included a provision to ensure a vertical space. Each passenger was to have not less than three feet nine inches in the forepart of the ship, and in the cabin and steerage area at least two feet nine inches of vertical space was required between the decks. In addition, vessels were to be fumigated and

65 James T. Mitchell and Henry Flanders, comps., *Statutes at Large of Pennsylvania from 1682 to 1801* (Pennsylvania, 1902), 5:95. The need to pass laws in order to prevent disease and death is striking evidence of the magnitude of the problem.

66 "A Colonial Health Report of Philadelphia, 1754," *PMHB* 36 (1912), 477–78.

67 Ibid., 478.

68 Minutes of the Provincial Council, 6:175–6; Diffenderfer, *German Immigration*, 263; Herrick, *White Servitude in Pennsylvania*, 189. Herrick reported the year as 1757.

69 Mitchell and Flanders, comps., *Statutes at Large*, 6:432. In 1764 the Pennsylvania German Society was formed to aid German immigrants. Led by prominent merchant Henry Kepple, the prosperous German community had sufficient clout to push passage of this law. One fascinating stipulation granted redemptioners thirty days to find a labor contract. During this time the ship's captain was required to house and feed them. My guess is that the timing of this law reflects both the emergence of powerful lobbyists on behalf of the German community and the resumption of the trade after the Seven Years' War.

washed with vinegar twice per week, and each ship carrying German passengers was to provide a surgeon equipped with medicines for the journey.[70] The Assembly approved a law that was designed to improve the travel conditions of transatlantic passengers, and yet the new statute allocated the most meager amount of space for each person. Without the interference of colonial officials, merchants' behavior went unchecked and the route to the promised land was lined with the horrors of disease and death.

If prospective servants survived the passage, the next ordeal began as the ship neared the port. Servants did their best to wash, groom, and gather their belongings. Often, chests were missing or possessions had been pilfered. At other times, passengers discovered that their trunks had never made it on board.[71] In 1749 the *Pennsylvanische Berichte* reported the arrival of a ship that carried the personal belongings of Germans who had arrived some weeks before. The article lamented that many found their chests had been broken open "but the Germans pay and must pay when their chests are robbed or when famished with hunger even though their contracts are expressly to the contrary."[72]

Servants and their belongings were so mistreated at the hands of the Pennsylvania traders that the 1765 law not only clarified matters of health, but addressed a whole range of abuses. To prevent ships' crews from gouging the passengers, the maximum profit from the sale of items to passengers could not exceed 50 percent. To ensure that German passengers were not ignorant of the law, an interpreter was to board the ship before landing and explain their rights. To increase the chances that servants' baggage made the journey, shippers were required to issue bills of lading and were liable for losses and damage. This law also forbade masters from charging family members for the cost of passage of any who died in transit.[73]

After the ship docked, announcements appeared in the local papers noting the ship's arrival and advertised all of the goods on board, including the indentured servants. In the seventeenth century, most servants had arranged their indentures on the eastern shores of the Atlantic. For eighteenth-century servants, the docking signaled the opening of the servant market in which they were the commodities. A typical advertisement read that newly arrived servants were available for all "sorts of business, inquire at Willing and Shippen."[74] Philadelphia residents could purchase a general

---

70 Ibid., 432–40. See also Minutes of the Provincial Council, May 17, 1765, 9:248.
71 Herrick, *White Servitude in Pennsylvania,* 185.
72 *Pennsylvania Gazette,* November 16, 1749, quoted in Diffenderfer, *German Immigration,* 208.
73 Mitchell and Flanders, comps., *Statutes at Large,* 1764–5, 4:432–40.
74 *Pennsylvania Gazette,* February 7, 1731.

assortment of imported spring goods, as well as a few barrels of Irish beef and Scotch herring, and, in addition, examine the 250 servants included in the ship's cargo.[75]

Those interested in purchasing a servant boarded the ships to inspect them. Reminiscent of the slave market, servants were displayed like cattle. Prospective buyers felt their muscles, checked their teeth and health, verified occupations, inquired about their behavior, and then, if satisfied, paid the master the costs and took the servant home. As the ship neared its return departure date, the remaining servants were removed from the vessel and housed in the merchant's buildings. Newspaper advertisements directed buyers to the places of business.[76]

Female servants were particularly "troublesome" and difficult to place. To a great extent, the problems were caused by the limited demand for domestic laborers. In 1754 Thomas Willing wrote to his agents requesting a cargo "with 20 to 30 man and boy servants. . . . The servants should not be above 30 or less than 16 years old and no women."[77] In their instructions to a ship's captain, Abel James and Henry Drinker requested that "if servants are dealt in avoid women altogether or as much as possible."[78] In 1764 Benjamin Marshall warned Thomas Murphy that "the less Women the better as they are very troublesome."[79] In the same year, Marshall wrote to Barnaby Eagen that "Stout able Labouring men and Tradesmen out of the Country with Young Boys and Lads answer best, Women are so troublesome it would be best to send few or none as there is often so many Drawbacks on them."[80] Because domestic servants were in such close contact with their masters' families, prospective owners were particularly selective and required more detailed information than most servants could provide. In 1769 Thomas Clifford warned his captain to "avoid so much as possible bringing women servants, [for] 'tis not easy to get good places for them . . . without Character reference."[81]

For redemptioners, the landing was followed by a frantic search to procure the funds to repay the captain or to contract for the most favorable indenture. The process often proved frustrating. Announcements appeared

---

75 Ibid., May 5, 1773.

76 See ibid., October 23, 1729, December 14, 1731; *Pennsylvania Packet and General Advertiser*, March 8, 1773, August 9, 1773; *American Weekly Mercury*, August 4, 1724.

77 Willing and Sons to John Perks, October 24, 1754, Willing and Sons Letter Book, HSP.

78 James and Drinker to Captain Enoch Story, May 6, 1769, James and Drinker Letter Book, HSP.

79 Benjamin Marshall to Thomas Murphy, November 9, 1765, "Extracts from the Letter Book of Benjamin Marshall, 1763–1766," ed. Thomas Stevenson, *PMHB* 20 (1896), 209–10.

80 Benjamin Marshall to Barnaby Egan, November 9, 1765, "Extracts From the Letter Book of Benjamin Marshall," 209.

81 Quoted in Larsen, "Colonial Merchant," 115.

in newspapers warning redemptioners to pay or "they will be proceeded against according to Law."[82] If the servant market was poor, redemptioners were thrust into society. "For none would take a man with the encumbrances of a Wife or small Children . . . and by that means many of them . . . are hardly able to maintain themselves."[83]

For eighteenth-century German servants, the jarring experience of being a piece of cargo in the labor market was complicated by language problems. For every servant like Johannes Fierly or Hans Surnan who was purchased by a German family, there was a Christopher Stoffel or Johannes Fretzel acquired by an English-speaking master.[84] Comments like "broken English" or "little or no English" testify to the difficulties.[85]

Henry Muhlenberg, a minister of the Lutheran Church, arrived in Pennsylvania in 1742 and experienced the language problems firsthand. On his way home from missionary business, Muhlenberg stopped in Providence and was asked to preach a sermon in German. "An English justice of the peace," Muhlenberg writes, "said there was [*sic*] a great many poor German servants, men and women, indentured to the English people in this neighborhood." Muhlenberg commented that these German servants spoke no English and longed for a sermon they could understand. Apparently redemptioners received the service eagerly, for Muhlenberg wrote, "There was weeping among the Germans, as is usually the case when they have been deprived of the Word of God for a long time."[86]

Once servants had been purchased, their lives were filled primarily by rigorous work and inflexible schedules. Male servants labored at a great variety of jobs. Those who toiled in the homes of the city's elite included among their responsibilities driving carriages, running errands, and caring for the horses.[87] The bound laborers in the city's inns and taverns were expected to perform household chores, wait on tables, do the marketing, and tend horses.[88] In a city board yard, the servant was counted on to take care of the accounts and to be familiar with the varieties of lumber.[89] In

82 *American Weekly Mercury,* November 7, 1728.
83 Joseph Turner to Jacob Bosanquat, September 1756, Allen and Turner Letter Book, Library Company Collection, HSP.
84 *Pennsylvania Gazette,* October 7, 1749; January 4, 1745.
85 Comments are from the runaway advertisement in the *Pennsylvania Gazette,* and from *American Weekly Mercury.*
86 Harold D. Eberlein and Cortrandt Hubbard, *The Church of Saint Peter in the Great Valley, 1700–1740: The Story of a Colony County Parish in Pennsylvania* (Richmond, Va., 1959), 67.
87 *Pennsylvania Gazette,* suppl. 2090, January 12, 1769; suppl. 2095, February 16, 1769.
88 Ibid., May 10, 1770.
89 Ibid., August 17, 1769.

merchants' businesses, servants performed as clerks and were expected to "write a tolerable hand and understand figures."[90]

The majority of Philadelphia's eighteenth-century servants worked for artisans in a tremendous array of craft establishments. Petty commodity production was organized around the household, and servants and masters lived and worked togeher. Servants were part of a household labor force, supplementing rather than replacing family members. James Gardener, a tanner, skinner and leather dresser, was indentured in 1745 to tanner John Howell.[91] They probably worked side by side, performed many of the same tasks, and shared the stench of the tan yard. Paul Mahoney arrived in Philadelphia one year later and was indentured for four years to shipwrights John Lawton and Simon Sherlock. For Mahoney, each day seemed like another because he spent his time sawing, an indispensable skill in the shipyard.[92] John McCan was indentured to Philadelphia cabinetmaker Matthew Hand. McCan was "most accustomed to chair making."[93] Servant John Hopkins, who was owned by a shoemaker, made children's shoes and pumps, "of which he was uncommonly ready."[94]

Work was hard in early America and not without its dangers, especially for servants. An article in the *Pennsylvania Gazette* reported that "a man ordered his servant to take some Fowls in from Roost every night for fear of the Fox." Thinking he was a fox, the master shot the servant in the arm.[95] John Martin was a brewer's servant. While loading beer casks on board Captain Annis's ship, he "missed his footing and fell into the River"; the cask tumbled after him, striking him in the head, and he drowned.[96]

Much of urban production in the eighteenth-century port city was controlled by the weather. More hours of daylight meant longer periods at the workbench. When it rained or snowed, housewrights, shipwrights, and others who labored out-of-doors were forced to call a halt to their labors. When the weather turned severe, the river froze and supplies were stuck on board ships until the thaw. Winter sleet prevented the cooper from molding the barrel staves outside or the ropemaker from walking the rope. No doubt, during these downtimes, servants and masters performed other necessary jobs. While huddled around the fire, they could sharpen or fix tools. Perhaps they sought new jobs or discussed new styles. At times

90 Ibid., September 7, 1769.
91 "List of Servants and Apprentices Bound and Assigned Before James Hamilton, Mayor of Philadelphia, 1745–6," manuscript, AM 3091, HSP; *Pennsylvania Gazette*, November 28, 1745.
92 "List of Servants and Apprentices, 1745–6;" *Pennsylvania Gazette*, September 3, 1747.
93 *Pennsylvania Gazette*, October 17, 1775.
94 Ibid., June 18, 1767.
95 Ibid., November 3, 1729.
96 Ibid., October 2, 1729.

masters may have given up getting anything accomplished and trudged off to the neighborhood tavern to hear the latest news and to drink to the health of the king and the end of winter. If all else failed and winter stayed around too long, masters might be forced to sell their servants. In January 1775 a cooper fell vicitm to the vagaries of the weather and placed this advertisement: "To Be Sold, a servant man with three years and ten months to serve, a cooper by trade, and is a good hand at making flaxseed casks and pork barrels. Sold for no faults but their master's declining business."97

The work pace for female laborers was similarly difficult and varied. Domestic servants were accountable for a wide range of chores, from cooking and housework to carding and spinning, washing and "doing up the linen."98 Domestic tasks were endless, often disagreeable, and occasionally dangerous. Servants were required to be available twenty-four hours per day. Child care took up much of the time, and servants acted as wet nurses, as well as baby nurses, and tended the children.99 Household chores often fit into a set pattern, so that a day of clothes washing was invariably followed by a day at the ironing table. It was not unusual in the Drinker household for servants to be required to prepare a meal for twelve to fifteen people – the family, visitors, and borders.

Domestic servants were called upon by their masters for the slightest excuses – a barking dog or a scary noise. They were also to be on hand for more serious matters in case of illness or when the fire alarm sounded. The chambermaid slept at the foot of Elizabeth Drinker's bed.100 She was expected to rise before the family and stoke the fires to spare the Drinkers the inconvenience of dressing in a cold house or to make sure that family members did not wait for their hot morning beverage.101 One particularly rainy winter, Elizabeth Drinker reported that the privy filled and flowed into the house. The cleanup was a most objectionable job and fell to the servants.

Most household work was not dependent on the seasons, especially in the city. However, work schedules in the summer were slightly different. The Drinkers, like many upper-class Philadelphia families, vacated the city during the summer months. Servants usually spent three to four days preparing the summer home for occupancy. Drinker reported that "my Nancy and Jacob went to Frankford to clean the home," and of course they helped with the move.102 In the city, Sally Brant worked as a maid. While on their summer plantation, Sally helped turn the hay.103

97 Ibid., January 4, 1775.
98 Ibid., June 7, 1770.
99 Elizabeth Drinker Diary, June 2, 1771, HSP.
100 Ibid., August 11, 1794.
101 Ibid., January 17, 1796.
102 Ibid., July 28, 1772.
103 Ibid., July 31, 1794.

Philadelphia's elite undertook the exodus to the country not merely for a change in scenery. In addition, they vacated the city to escape the virulent summer epidemics. The epidemic season impinged on servants' lives in terrifying ways. Molly Rhoades, the Drinkers' youngest daughter, had a maid who died presumably of yellow fever. When Elizabeth Drinker insisted that her own maid, Judea, go to assist her daughter, Judea refused. She apparently feared for her own safety and did not want to work in a home where yellow fever had recently taken a life. Drinker finally convinced Judea to go, although the method of persuasion is unclear.[104] In addition, servants were often required to remain in the fever-ridden city to protect their masters' vacant homes. Patience was left behind to tend the house while the family and all of the other servants escaped from the city.[105] No one wanted to leave a house unattended, and the onerous task fell to the servants.

Domestic servants shouldered a special group of burdens. As servants in a household, they found themselves thrust into an ambiguous position. They were simultaneously workers to be controlled and extended members of the family to be disciplined. Conflict is inevitable in all economic relationships defined by inequality, no matter how well intentioned the employer. In such an exploitative relationship as that between domestic servant and master, when the servant resided and labored within the household, where living and working spaces were close, and when the relationship was to last for four years or even longer, latent conflict could easily become overt.

Urban life affected the tone and character of the servants' experience. Servants belonged to a distinct subculture that embraced both the free and unfree laboring classes. Not only did these social relations separate the working classes from those above them, but their "betters" were aware of the association and felt threatened by it. Throughout the eighteenth century, petitions to colonial officials from the inhabitants of Philadelphia complained about the social gatherings of the unfree classes. In 1741 the Philadelphia Grand Jury reported "the great disorders" committed on Sundays by "servants, apprentice boys and numbers of Negroes."[106] During the weekday evenings, "many disorderly persons" gathered at the court-house, the Grand Jury claimed, "and great numbers of Negroes and others sit [until late] and many disorders were committed."[107] The semiannual

104 Ibid., June 25, 1799.

105 Ibid., July 21, 1799.

106 Quoted in Eric Foner, *Tom Paine and Revolutionary America* (New York, 1976), 50. The first complaint about these disorders was made in 1693. Edward R. Turner, *The Negro in Pennsylvania: Slavery – Servitude – Freedom, 1639–1831* (Washington, D.C., 1911; reprint, New York, 1969).

107 Quoted in Foner, *Tom Paine*, 50. This also occurred in 1741. Turner, *Negro in Pennsylvania*, 33. The problems persisted until as late as 1761, when the mayor had the

fairs in Philadelphia, held in May and November, were important occasions of lower-class life. In 1731 city residents complained that "diverse inhabitants . . . by custom think they have a right to liberty of going out." Not only did these individuals partake of spiritous drink, but they "conspired to run away more than at any other time." Even worse was the corruption of the city's youth, "who are at times induced to drinking and gaming in mix'd companies of vicious servants and negroes."[108] By 1775, at the urging of the mayor and Common Council, the Assembly abolished the fairs. Fairs, according to the Assembly, were "useless" and tended to "debauch the morals of the people." The people "debauched" were not just the servants but the journeymen and slaves who participated in the gaming and drinking.[109]

All classes frequented the many taverns and dram shops in the city, even though the law prohibited tavern keepers from serving spirits to servants or slaves. Lawrence Herne, who was indentured to a tavern keeper, managed nicely. And Thomas Minor, a servant owner, petitioned the court for "considerable damage and trouble by his servants getting liquor and giving a pledge for it as the house of Robert McKee tavernkeeper and by . . . running away from his master's service when intoxicated with liquor."[110]

Urban life not only provided servants with access to strong drink, the drinking establishments frequented by the "lower sort" were virtually segregated from the middling and upper classes. In 1744 the Philadelphia Grand Jury referred to Hell Town, a neighborhood where the proportion of houses that served strong drink was extremely high. The great number of tippling houses presumably caused a great "temptation to entertain Apprentices, Servants and even Negroes." The activities in these places, "nurseries of Vice and Debauchery," changed little through the course of the century.[111] "Spiritous liquors" were an important part of the lives of the laboring classes and stealing away from one's master to share a pint must have eased the pain of servitude.

Paternalism still governed the associations between servants and masters because productive relations in prerevolutionary Philadelphia remained unchanged. Masters and servants continued to live under the same roof, paused together over the midday pint, perhaps shared the supper table, and worked toward the same productive goals. Unlike the paternalism characteristic of a slave society, the class structure did not prevent the servant

Pennsylvania Gazette publish an account of the previous legislation, November 12, 1741.

108 Quoted in Foner, *Tom Paine*, 50.

109 Steven Rosswurm, *Arms, Country, and Class: The Philadelphia Militia and the "Lower Sort" in the American Revolution, 1765–1783* (New Brunswick, N.J., forthcoming), chap. 1.

110 Petitions, Chester County Court, May 27, 1750, Chester County Historical Society.

111 Rosswurm, *Arms, Country and Class*, chap. 1.

classes from developing a social network. Although the same productive relations dominated labor, the institution of indentured servitude had changed, mainly because of the ordeal servants suffered in reaching America, the shifting ethnic balance of the population, and the erosion of skill. The behavior of servants leaves little question that a heightened level of social conflict induced servants to seek ways of escape. This is evident from the steady rise in the number of runaways in the eighteenth century.[112] Only three seventeenth-century servants are known to have escaped from service.[113] In contrast, at least 10 percent of the servants indentured in 1745 were advertised as runaways over the next five years. Throughout the late colonial period approximately 6 percent of the city's servants protested by running away.[114]

Runaways pursued two strategies. The first, open to both men and women, was simply to escape from one's master. These servants dodged and hid from colonial officials and jail keepers eager to earn the reward offered for a captured runaway. Outbound ships were also a target for runaways, and masters of vessels were warned not to take them on board. The second strategy, available only to men, was to enlist in the British forces during periods of war. The British army eagerly recruited soldiers, and if a servant joined the king's forces, usually for the duration of a campaign, his indenture was voided.

Servants ran away for a variety of reasons. Many servants were sold and resold, and they reacted to the insecurity by fleeing. Pennsylvania laws

112 Servants rarely resorted to suicide; only three cases were found. In 1732 a servant girl hanged herself near Christina Bridge. *Pennsylvania Gazette,* May, 7, 1732. A few years later a servant man was found "where he hang'd himself." No reasons for the suicide were given, except that the man "thru' shame and Remorse" for a theft "put an end to his life." *Pennsylvania Gazette,* September 5, 1734. Servant John hanged himself "having been disordered in his senses." *Pennsylvania Gazette,* November 26, 1741.

113 Although Richard Morris provides the number of runaways advertised in the *Pennsylvania Gazette* during the eighteenth century, he had no way of determining the relation between the number of advertisements, the number of runaways, and the number of servants. The best estimates for calculating a runaway rate are for years in which we have data for the servant population and the number of runaway advertisements. This calculation would tend to be on the low side since it would be based on advertisements and not all runaways were advertised.

The supposition that the newspapers did not contain records for all of the colony's runaways is supported by the fact that runaways who appeared in court often did not have a corresponding newspaper advertisement. Some servants may have been recovered quickly and advertisements were unnecessary. Also, masters may not have had the funds to buy an ad. Presumably, city owners would have been more likely to advertise since they had greater access to the newspapers.

114 I calculated a runaway rate by using the lists of servants bound for 1745 and 1772 and comparing the servants' names with the runaway advertisements in all of the Philadelphia newspapers.

attempted to prevent arbitrary transfers of ownership, but they were not always successful. Martha McLoud was an eighteen-year-old Scottish servant runaway who had "lately lived with a certain Alexander Chisholm, innkeeper in Burlington." Chisholm sold her to George Bartram, Philadelphia merchant, and was assigned by him to John Zell.[115] Few servants were juggled as many times as runaway Edward Houton. Houton came from London in 1743 to serve a seven-year term. He was sold to Norton Grimes of Philadelphia, from whom he ran away. After he was recovered, Grimes sold him to Richard Deaver at the Susquehanna Ferry. Deaver died and Houton was part of the estate that went to the widow, from whom he ran away. He was captured again and sold to Michael Webster. Houton ran away again and was sold to James Giles, who was advertising for him in 1750.[116]

Servants ran away mainly because of conflicts with their masters. The day-to-day reminder of the power relationships and the servant's lack of freedom in combination with an unpleasant master, work, or living situation would have frustrated even the most patient servant. The names of some owners became familiar to newspaper readers because so many different servants ran away from them. In 1721 Benjamin Hillyard absconded from William Hunt of Bucks County. In 1722 and 1723 Daniel Rives also escaped from Hunt.[117] In 1721 John Wheldon, a Philadelphia shoemaker, advertised for runaway servant James Swain; one year later he advertised for Swain again. Six years later Wheldon was searching for Ed White.[118] Lawrence Reynolds lost George Rogers in 1725 and John Wilson in 1726.[119] The same was true for Philadelphia shopkeeper Evan Morgan. John Forst escaped from him in 1730, and in 1731 his servant Mary Davis left.[120]

For so many different servants to have run away from the same owners strongly suggests that these masters were at the very least difficult to work for. Charles Ridgely seems to have been responsible for his servants' escape. Charles Campbell and an unnamed Irish lad had been in the country about six months. When they fled, "they had iron collars on."[121] Apparently these shackles were not unusual. Eighteen-year-old John Coffee, taken into custody on the suspicion of being an escaped servant, was also wearing an iron collar around his neck.[122]

115 *Pennsylvania Gazette,* August 10, 1774.
116 Ibid., February 8, 1750.
117 *American Weekly Mercury,* June 1722, September 1722, June 1723.
118 Ibid., March 1721, July 1722, September 1728.
119 Ibid., September 18, 1725, May 8, 1726.
120 *Pennsylvania Gazette,* April 30, 1730, June 24, 1731.
121 Ibid., May 14, 1767.
122 Ibid., May 31, 1775; suppl. 2387, September 21, 1774.

Runaway patterns reveal that the servants from rural areas of the colony ran away at a far greater rate than city servants. More than two- thirds of the servants absconding in the period from 1735 to 1744 resided in the countryside. In the later colonial period, 1767–69, almost 75 percent of the advertised runaway servants escaped from rural servitude,[123] even though less than half of all Pennsylvania servants lived outside the city.[124]

The isolation of rural labor and the lack of a support network clearly took a toll. The social organization of the city enabled urban servants to lead far less isolated lives than rural servants. During the period from 1744 to 1751, more than one-quarter of all urban runaways traveled with other servants or slaves of different masters.[125] Rural servants, however, fled with another servant or slave only 17 percent of the time. Throughout most of the eighteenth century, less than one-fifth of rural bound laborers who ran away absconded with another unfree person from a different household. More than 25 percent and occasionally as many as 30 percent of urban runaway servants joined with another servant or slave to escape from servitude. These runaway patterns are clear testimony to the social relationship of the unfree classes in Philadelphia.

The relatively high incidence of rural runaways suggests that, for all the problems of urban servitude, rural servitude was more onerous. In part, city bondpeople had a social network that was not possible in the rural countryside because of the lack of a concentrated population. Also, skilled urban servants were often able to work at their crafts. If the master-servant relationship was tolerable, servants survived the period of unfreedom and could fantasize about someday being their own masters, possibly with servants of their own. For many rural servants, labor was just endless drudgery. George Owens, a Chester County servant, despaired because his work consisted entirely of chopping wood.[126]

The British army offered servants the other alternative for escape. Each time the recruiters beat their drums in the Philadelphia area servants flocked to enlist. Data on the number of servant enlistees are available for only two periods. During the campaign of the 1740s more than 188 servants from

---

123 It is possible that escape from the rural areas was easier, but that cannot have been the motivating force.

124 In 1745, 58.6 percent of the servants were bound to Philadelphia residents. The remaining served owners living in the outlying rural counties. "List of Servants and Apprentices, 1745–6."

125 Petitions, Chester County Court of Quarter Sessions, August 1748.

126 From 1744 to 1751, the *Pennsylvania Gazette* ran advertisements for 365 rural servants and 87 urban servants. Of these, 23 urban servants absconded with other unfree laborers and 63 rural servants fled with other people. Cases of hired laborers absconding with servants and slaves were reported as well. For servants and slaves running away together, see *Pennsylvania Gazette*, July 1745; August 30, 1739; July 3, 1740; September 17, 1741.

Philadelphia City and County enlisted in the British forces.[127] This represented at least 10 percent of the area's servant population. When the recruiters appeared during the Seven Years' War, almost 12 percent (190) of the city's servants enlisted to gain their freedom.[128] Even this rate undercounts the actual number of servants who absconded, because it does not take account of individuals like those on Joseph Turner's 1756 shipment from Rotterdam. Turner reported that many redemptioners were forced to enlist because they were unable to find masters.[129] These individuals were not included in the lists of masters compensated for their enlisting servants.

The inducements that lured servants into the Anglo-Spanish War of 1739 were primarily financial. Promises of bounty enticed servants to join the assault on Porto Bello and Cartagena. Numerous advertisements appeared in the newspapers, and handbills describing the war actions and captured riches and encouraging enlistment were liberally posted throughout the colony. In November 1740 the *Pennsylvania Gazette* published a letter describing in excited detail the meeting of the *Townshend* packet and the Spanish ship *S. del Carmes*. According to the account, the Spanish did not have a chance against the superior British forces. A June 1740 article recounted the heavy Spanish losses from a skirmish that left the Americans virtually unscathed and listed the prizes captured.[130] In the spring of 1740 a broadside was printed and repeated over the next several weeks asking for men "willing to inlist [*sic*] in the important Expedition now on Foot for Attacking and Plundering the most valuable Part of the Spanish West Indies."[131] The *Gazette* also advertised for "Gentlemen" sailors and others interested in a privateering voyage against the Spanish. The notice promised that one-half of the prize booty would be divided among the officers and men and the other half would go to the owners of the vessel. Also, the soldiers would receive monthly wages and compensation for any loss of limbs.[132] Another letter in May 1740 announced that the plunder from this expedition would abound "in Gold, Silver and every sort of Riches. There such of our North Americans, as please, may become possessors of large and fruitful Plantations! . . . from private Soldiers, and Men of no Fortunes,

---

127 *Votes and Proceedings of the House of Representatives of the Province of Pennsylvania,* Pa. Arch. (Harrisburg, Pa., 1931–5) 3:2677.

128 "A List of Servants Belonging to the Inhabitants of Pennsylvania and Taken into His Majesty's Service, 1757." The original is at the Huntington Library, San Marino, Calif. I worked from a photocopy of the original at HSP. Philadelphia had about 1,430 indentured servants in 1756.

129 Joseph Turner to Jacob Bosanquat, September 1756, Allen and Turner Letter Book, Library Company Collection, HSP.

130 *Pennsylvania Gazette,* June 5, 1740, from London dated February 17, 1739–40.

131 *American Weekly Mercury,* May 1, 1740, repeated May 8 and May 15.

132 *Pennsylvania Gazette,* July 16, 1741.

to great and opulent Planters."[133] The extravagant promises must have been seductive. Considering the hope of potential booty, the decision to enlist is understandable. Servants thought that they were exchanging a three- to four-year term of servitude for a six-month expedition that would transform them into wealthy planters. They had no way of knowing that the death rate from this particular expedition, to Cartagena, would be so staggering. The Philadelphia newspapers did not begin to print the death statistics until June 1741. The advertisements and notices luring servants into the forces said nothing about death, only freedom, excitement, riches, and the remote possibility of injuries, which were to be compensated.

Something other than the promises of plunder and riches lured servants into the War of the Austrian Succession (1744–8) and the Seven Years' War. Some apparently joined to escape from their indentures. More than 80 percent of the servants who enlisted escaped from rural servitude and 60 percent of the enlistees had served less than half of their terms.[134] Somewhat surprising were those servants who absconded to the army with less than 10 percent of their indentures left to complete. John Oswald and Adam Rifle must have thought that their indentures would never end. Oswald enlisted with the British after having served thirteen years and five months of a sixteen-year indenture. Rifle owed three years and three months of an eleven-year and nine-month indenture when he enlisted. Others joined the army out of economic need. The group of redemptioners imported by Joseph Turner in 1756 were unable to secure indentures and were forced to leave their families in Philadelphia and sign up for a tour of duty with the British army.[135]

Overall, one-tenth of all servants and perhaps one-eighth of male servants found a way to escape their full terms. This level of social conflict, absent in the seventeenth century, suggests that the institution had become sufficiently oppressive to warrant servants' taking large risks including harsh sentences, the wrath of one's master, and the dangers of war. The law dealt severely with servants who absconded. William Pallet was ordered by the court to serve his owner, Jeremiah Collett, sixty additional days for the twelve days he was absent. He was also to pay four pounds five and one-half shillings for the costs incurred during his capture or serve nine extra months.[136] Since most servants had no money, Pallet most likely served the additional time. Alexander Frazier was awarded eleven months plus an additional seven years of labor from his servant Lawrence Finny for the time he lost and the

---

133 *American Weekly Mercury*, May 8, 1740.
134 "Servants Belonging to the Inhabitants of Pennsylvania." Of these 61 percent had served half or less of their indentures.
135 Robert Turner to Messrs. Wolffinder and Birchinsha, September 1756, Allen and Turner Letter Book, Library Company Collection, HSP.
136 Petitions, Chester County Court of Quarter Sessions, 1729.

expense of his capture.[137] William Fisher had to work an extra six years and 250 days to settle with his master for running away.[138] Servants, if caught, not only faced strict penalties; they returned to an irate master. If a difficult situation had caused them to abscond in the first place, their attempted escape most likely exacerbated an already strained relationship. Those who opted for the more dangerous and circuitous way out of servitude and joined the British army discovered that this route to freedom afforded little glamor. The desertion rates were high, and during wars advertisements for deserting servants were common.[139]

The pressures female servants faced were different, and so were their reasons for running away. Only occasionally did men run away to join wives or lovers. Women, however, most often fled to be reunited with the men in their lives. In 1767 Rose O'Bryan, a sixteen-year-old Irish servant, ran away from her owner Jacob Kaiser. He speculated that she had not left the city since "she says she is married to a taylor that lived in the same house she formerly belonged to . . . who sold her about twelve months ago."[140] Christiana Weeks, an English servant, had been in the colony only three months when her owner advertised that she was missing. Since Christiana had a certificate of marriage to Nathanial Weeks, her master assumed that she was headed toward New York to be reunited with him.[141] Mary Cotney, an Irish servant, was thought to have left her service to seek out her husband in Boston.[142] Mary Musgrove apparently ran away because she was "remarkable fond of a sweetheart."[143]

The condescending attitude of masters toward their female servants was expressed in demeaning descriptions, and if this language was conveyed to the servants it must have inspired many to run away. Some sense of the relationship is gleaned from the advertisements masters composed describing their female runaways. Jane Jacobson escaped repeatedly and her owner's attitude was summed up by the phrase, a "stout fat woman."[144] Runaway Catherine Caisey's master could muster no kinder description than that she was a "chunky fat lump."[145] Elizabeth Drinker was convinced that her servant Patience Clifford faked illness and lied. Drinker characterized Clifford as "intolerable," "sick," "thoughtless," and "careless" and

137 Ibid., August 1731.
138 Ibid., June 1732; see also September 1726 and August 1732.
139 For example, "Deserted from his Majesty's service the following persons, viz. Patrick Burk . . . Lately servant to Willaim Moore, esq., Chester County." *Pennsylvania Gazette,* May 28, 1748.
140 Ibid., June 25, 1767.
141 Ibid., October 19 1774.
142 Ibid., November 15, 1775.
143 Ibid., December 27, 1786.
144 Ibid., April 5, 1775.
145 Ibid., July 17, 1776.

seemed to be particularly irked by her servants' tendency to "eat green fruit." Drinker attributed the problems she had with Betty Burge to the "ill nature of the old woman."[146] Perhaps the use of derogatory language allowed masters to underscore their servants' inferiority while legitimizing their own positions of authority. Some masters clearly had little respect for their servants and did not spare them ridicule. These attitudes were easily communicated to the servants, and some responded by running away.

Masters claimed that pregnancy was the most common reason women servants ran away and often assumed that if their female servants fled they must be pregnant. Sarah Clarke's master claimed that she looked "very suspicious of being with child."[147] Master William White said that his runaway servant Elizabeth Young "appears as if with child."[148] Of the women who were pregnant, many were married or had a loving partner. Ann Carson escaped from her Philadelphia master in search of John Herson. Carson was "supposed with [his] child." They traveled to Pennsylvania on the same ship, but she was indentured to a Philadelphia master and he to a Lancaster County resident.[149] Masters provided these descriptions of their potentially pregnant servants in order to identify the runaways as well as to offer a plausible explanation for their escape.

Servants who became pregnant while under indenture paid a stiff price. In January 1777 Margaret Sexton delivered two female mulatto children. Her owner, Hugh McCullough, petitioned the court to compensate him for the loss of her service while she recuperated from the birth and for the charges paid for nursing and attendance while she was lying in. Sexton's term of service, which was to expire in 1779, was extended by the court for two more years. In addition, the overseers of the poor bound her children to serve McCullough.[150]

In the Elizabeth Drinker household, pregnancy created intense strain in the relationship between mistress and servant. Drinker was a wealthy Quaker who wrote in her diary almost daily for more than half a century. She first suspected that her servant Sally Brant was pregnant on August 8, 1794. This possibility so distressed Drinker that "for a week past [she] labored under great anxiety of mind on account of our poor little and I fear miserable S[ally] B[rant]. 'Tis possible I am mistaken though I greatly fear for the worst." Moreover, the suspected pregnancy angered Drinker. "I could not have thought," Drinker lamented, "that a girl brought up from her 10th year with the care and kindness that S[ally] B[rant] has experienced

---

146 Drinker Diary, July 10, 1796; August 7, 1796; November 30, 1796, HSP.
147 *Pennsylvania Gazette*, March 29, 1775.
148 Ibid., June 14, 1775.
149 Ibid., September 7, 1774; also March 29, 1775, and June 14, 1775.
150 Philadelphia County Court of Quarter Sessions Docket, vol 4, September 1779, 150, City Archives, Philadelphia.

with our Family, could be so thoughtless." The situation was not alleviated by the fact that Sally Brant showed little remorse and "appears to be full of Glee as if nothing ailed her."[151] Elizabeth Drinker was so embarrassed by her servant's pregnancy that Sally stayed at Clearfield, the Drinker's summer home, when the family returned to the city. "What could I do with S[ally] B[rant] in her present appearance with a crowd of company?" Drinker pleaded.[152]

A few weeks after the baby was born, Sally Brant returned to work in Philadelphia, but without her baby, who was left with a hired nurse. Not only did Elizabeth Drinker prevent Sally from caring for her baby, she did not even allow Sally to name the child as she wished. Sally planned to give the baby its father's surname, but this so horrified the Drinkers they named the child Catherine Clearfield, after their summer home. Joe, the father, tried unsuccessfully on several occasions to visit Sally and see the child, but Henry Drinker warned him that if he ever "found him sculking about our neighborhood he would lay him by the heels."[153] Neither Joe nor Sally ever saw the baby again, for the infant died.[154]

Sally Brant was required to serve additional time to make up for the expenses incurred as a result of her pregnancy, the time she lost while she recovered from the birth, as well as the nurse's salary. The irony of this punishment is particularly striking since Sally had had no say in the hiring of the nurse, and she may have blamed the nurse for her baby's death. Elizabeth Drinker expressed sadness at the news of Catherine's death, musing that perhaps they should have had the baby with them in Philadelphia. Yet Drinker philosophically surmised that all had most likely worked out for the best, although she clearly had less affection and respect for Sally afterwards.

Sally Brant's frustration not only reveals how problematic and inconvenient a servant's pregnancy could be for the mistress or master, but also highlights the intensity of feeling between servant and mistress and the ambiguities inherent in this labor relationship. Drinker expected Sally Brant to behave both as family and as worker, and when Brant became pregnant, Drinker reacted with hurt and anger, the same feelings she expressed over infractions by her children. Yet Drinker also reacted like an employer, for even though Brant had worked faithfully for the Drinker household for years prior to her pregnancy, Drinker meted out a swift and stern punishment and never regained her feelings of affection for the young woman.

151 Elizabeth Drinker Diary, August 20, 1794; September 30, 1794, HSP.
152 Ibid., September 27, 1794.
153 Ibid., February 14 and 26, 1795.
154 Ibid., July 2 and 6, 1795.

Merchants no doubt had the troublesome nature of pregnancy in mind when they inveighed their agents to send no more women. Even if servants did not abscond, pregnancy was inconvenient for masters because their servants were unable to work, at least while they were lying in and recovering from the birth. However, the legal code enabled masters to transfer the "troublesome nature" of women servants to a net gain. The law dealing with runaways remained in effect throughout the colonial period and required a runaway servant to work five additional days for every day of absence incurred and to reimburse the master for all costs sustained in her or his capture.[155] Additional laws dealt with bastardy and fornication among servants, and it is clear that Pennsylvania lawmakers and masters equated servant pregnancy with "trouble."

The earliest laws punished the crimes of fornication and bastardy by requiring the convicted individuals to marry, serve time in jail, pay a fine, or undergo corporal punishment. Nicholas More, the president of the Free Society of Traders, requested in 1683 that this "Law against Fornication" be amended because masters received little compensation when their servants were convicted. More "prayed some severe punishment may be Enacted" that would better serve the interests of the master.[156] In 1700 the law was changed. A woman servant convicted of bearing a bastard child was required to "serve one whole year after her time by indenture or covenant expired."[157] Six years later, the law was made more severe. A woman found guilty of having a bastard child while under indenture was required to "serve such further time beyond the term of her indenture or covenant mentioned as the justices of the peace in their quarter-session shall think fit . . . provided it be not more than two years nor less than one."[158]

It is impossible to assess the relation between servant pregnancies and abuse by masters. The likelihood of such assault is high since female servants were usually considerably younger than their masters, lived under the same roof, were the property of their owners, and the losers in the power relationship. If the assault resulted in a child, the master was rewarded with extra time from the servant. In 1720 John Worral took his servant Eleanor Taylor to court on the charge of fornication. Worral was awarded ten pounds thirteen shillings as compensation for the crime. This amount included eleven shillings eleven pence for the midwife and six shillings for the man who fetched her. Worral argued that he was also due five pounds for the time lost due to the delivery. Since servants rarely if ever had money,

---

155 Minutes of the Provincial Council, 1:80; the law was repeated in 1700. Mitchell and Flanders, comps., *Statutes at Large*, 2:54.
156 Minutes of the Provincial Council, 1:61.
157 Mitchell and Flanders, comps., *Statutes at Large*, 2:6.
158 Ibid., 181–2.

Taylor probably worked off the debt.[159] In 1750, when Lettice McConway was accused of bastardy, Thomas Holden received two more years of her service. Margaret Brook was ordered to serve two additional years after she was "delivered of a bastard child."[160]

No cases were found in which servants prosecuted masters for sexual abuse; however, female servants did take masters to court for assault. The court awarded Elizabeth Matthews freedom and dues because her master, Robert Guty, was convicted of beating her.[161] Anne Pynard petitioned the court to be released from servitude, for she was "much abused and severely whipped."[162]

The alteration in the ethnic composition of the servant population contributed to the intensity of social conflict among servants and masters. Although servants from all ethnic groups ran away, including a few French and Spanish servants, the majority of Pennsylvania's runaways were from Ireland. Only a small number were from Germany, with a few more from England. The reasons for this are not clear. Part of the explanation may be that many German redemptioners emigrated as family units, and running away may have been logistically more difficult or less desirable. Occasionally, when German servants did abscond, husbands and wives traveled together.[163] Another explanation for the low incidence of German runaways is that they may have been inhibited by language difficulties. Most likely, the Irish ran away at a high rate in response to the profound anti-Irish sentiment in Pennsylvania. The English had a long history of anti-Irish feeling, and the large proportion of Irish servants must have inspired the colonists' hatred. The Irish were more abused than any other ethnic group in Pennsylvania, and much of the abuse was overt. German servants were described as industrious;[164] the Irish "have such an ill-name, they won't sell for any tolerable price."[165] Irish runaways were portrayed like Dennis Hurly, who was "remarkably subject to swearing and drinking," or Patrick Tumony, who although he writes a good hand "pretends to be a miller."[166]

159 Petitions, Chester County Court Quarter Sessions, May 1720.

160 Ibid., February 1749–50.

161 Ibid., August 1732.

162 Philadelphia County Court of Quarter Sessions Docket, vol. 2, September 1764, City Archives.

163 *Pennsylvania Gazette*, October 30, 1746.

164 Herrick notes that the German servants ran away far less frequently than the Irish and attributes the difference to three main factors: The Germans were less impulsive and adventuresome, better able to accept the exacting toil, and more unfamiliar with the country and its laws than the newly arrived Irish. *White Servitude in Pennsylvania*, 230.

165 Pemberton Papers, HSP, quoted in Robert O. Heavner, "Indentured Servitude: The Philadelphia Market, 1771–1773," *JEH* 38 (1978), 709.

166 The wealth of the master had little to do with whether the quality of servant life was sufficient to convince servants to abscond or remain. Servants ran away from wealthy and

The variation in runaway patterns among the servile classes exposes the basic distinction between the two forms of bondage for the individuals involved. Servitude and slavery did have much in common. Both were highly exploitative labor systems. White and black unfree laborers performed the same tasks, had little to say about their lives, were at the whim of their masters, and were subject to a very similar legal code. And during the eighteenth century, the nature of the servant market dispelled any doubts that this was a humane and benign institution. Although the distinctions between the systems of servitude and slavery were blurred, the psychological realities for the bound workers were vastly different. For all of the horrors in both systems, the one fundamental difference was that the servant's bondage was for a finite period of time. The slave's burden of perpetual bondage was hardly comparable to a three- to four-year indenture. The level of frustration for skilled slaves might very well push them beyond the threshold. The master reaped the benefit not only of his own labor but of his slaves' as well.

The experiences of eighteenth-century Pennsylvania servants had changed dramatically from those of the colony's first unfree workers. Hundreds of

middling owners. Merchants like Reese Meredith, George Emlin, Samuel Howell, and Isaac Norris had to resort to the newspapers to advertise for lost servants. *Pennsylvania Gazette*, July 31, 1741 from Reese Meredith; July 8, 1744, and June 29, 1746, from George Emlen; July 5, 1747, from Samuel Howell; and October 1731 from Isaac Norris. Both skilled and unskilled servants ran away, although the proportion of each cannot be accurately determined. Of those who were listed in the newspaper advertisements, approsimately one-fifth listed a skill, as shown in the following tabulation (data from *Pennsylvania Gazette*):

Year	Runaways listing a skill	Total runaways	Percent skilled
1728–32	32	105	30.4
1735–44	40	258	15.3
1745–51	71	452	15.7
1767	11	79	13.9
Total	154	694	22.1

These data indicate that the minority of servants were skilled or, more likely, reflect a process opposite to the one Gerald Mullin identifies in the skilled slave population. Mullin finds that skilled slaves ran away at a higher rate than unskilled slaves. He suggests that skilled slaves had greater resources for escape. In contrast, skilled servants, appear to have run away less often than unskilled servants, since the former were concentrated in the city and urban servants ran away at a lesser rate than rural servants. Gerald R. Mullin, *Flight and Rebellion: Slave Resistance in Eighteenth-Century Virginia* (New York, 1972), 36–8. Mullin reports that 32 percent of the runaway slaves (359 of the 1,138) were listed as skilled (p. 94).

Scots-Irish and Germans, having failed to secure employment and convinced they had no options remaining, signed indentures to provide themselves and their families with temporary economic relief. Many experienced unrelieved horror from the time they boarded the vessel through the completion of their terms of indenture. They were articles for sale, shipped to Pennsylvania in a business in which the transporters were concerned more with the number of servants they could ship than with the servants' health and welfare. The increasing complexity of the legal structure of indentured servitude, the escalation in the number of runaways, as well as the complaints about female servants all reveal heightened social tensions over the course of the eighteenth century. The change in the ethnic composition of the servant population contributed to the strained relations. Masters, it seems, became increasingly abusive, and even some servants who had only a limited time left to serve found absconding preferable to serving out their time. Servants chose to emigrate because they equated a three- to four-year indenture with more prosperous futures; but they were caught by a labor system in a period when the Philadelphia economy was also undergoing enormous change.

5 Eighteenth-century servants in freedom

THE MOST SALIENT FEATURE of the postservitude lives of eighteenth-century indentured laborers was their obscurity. Although mortality and geographic mobility may have been high, these two factors cannot account for the large number of former servants never located in the records nor the many servants found just once. Consider, for example, Dennis Bryan, who came to the Quaker colony in 1745 and signed a four-year indenture to serve David Jenkins, a Chester County yeoman.[1] One year after he had gained his freedom, a Dennis Bryan was rated in East Nantmeal Township at the lowest assessment and listed as an inmate, an adult, usually single, who rented a room. Dennis Bryan does not appear again on Chester, Philadelphia, or Bucks County tax lists nor in the probate records. By 1773 Dennis Bryan had made his way to Philadelphia. He was admitted into the Pennsylvania Hospital with dropsy; the overseers of the poor put up his security.[2] It would appear that Bryan survived a hand-to-mouth existence for almost twenty-five years. John Falls served Samuel Flower of Chester County for four years in exchange for the thirteen pounds Flower paid for his servant's passage from Ireland in 1745. In 1750 Falls was rated at the lowest assessment and listed as an inmate in East Nantmeal Township. Falls never appears again in the Chester, Bucks, or Philadelphia records. John Henry Kalbfleich emigrated from Germany in 1745. Since he was unable to pay the cost of his passage, Kalbfleich was indentured for two years to Stephen Goodman, a Philadelphia County yeoman.[3] Twenty years after the terms of his indenture were completed, a John Henry Kalbfleich was assessed at four pounds in Upper Merion Township in Philadelphia County. His minimal property included two horses and two cows. It is possible that Bryan, Falls, and Kalbfleich moved constantly and no consistent records could exist for them. More likely, they, like many of the city's residents,

1 "List of Servants and Apprentices Bound and Assigned Before James Hamilton, Mayor of Philadelphia, 1745–46," manuscript, AM 3091, HSP.
2 Attending Managers' Accounts, 1752–1781, Pennsylvania Hospital Records, American Philosophical Society. I worked from a microfilmed copy.
3 "List of Servants and Apprentices, 1745–46."

were too poor to be of interest to tax assessors. They rented small flats or parts of apartments and were overlooked by the tax collectors, who spent their efforts where the results would be greater.[4] Thus the lives of former servants and other poor folks went unrecorded and are lost to historical sleuthing.

Female servants are even more difficult to find after their indentures were completed. The few who can be located reveal that the women carried a disproportionate share of the burden of poverty. Elizabeth Drinker provides information on a few of her former servants, both indentured and hired, who reappeared many years after they ceased to serve her. Mary Brookhouse knocked on the Drinkers' door twenty-one years after she had worked for the Drinkers and asked for money.[5] The request upset Drinker for it was clear that Mary Brookhouse had been reduced to begging in her later years.[6] Betty Burge worked for the Drinkers at some time before 1796. In October of that year she was rehired. Three years later she called upon Elizabeth Drinker to report that she was indisposed. She had injured herself falling out of a wagon and she wanted Henry Drinker, Elizabeth's husband, to recommend her to the overseers of the poor. "I gave her some victuals and some money," Drinker recorded, "but I don't expect H[enry] D[rinker] will give her a good character, he can't, tho' perhaps she may be recommended as a proper object of charity." Betty Burge drops from sight after this entry, but obviously her work as a domestic servant did not spare her from the need for charity in her later years.[7] The only servant who returned to the Drinkers with a happy tale was Polly Neugent. She had served a four-year indenture, now had four children, all daughters, and an "industrious husband." But soon after she visited, Neugent's fortunes changed. When she called again a year later, it was to solicit business for her blacksmith husband.[8] The Drinker home was probably among the best places to work in all of Philadelphia. They were a devout, wealthy family who respected family members and workers alike. And yet a stream of servants returned to the Drinkers after they had served their time, all requiring some sort of aid.

Historians do not agree about the prospects for mobility in eighteenth-century America. Some writers conclude that Pennsylvania provided a relatively high standard of living and ample opportunity. They report that

4 Sharon V. Salinger and Charles Wetherell, "A Note on the Population of Prerevolutionary Philadelphia," *PMHB* 109 (1985), 376–8.
5 Elizabeth Drinker Diary, August 24, 1799, HSP.
6 Drinker noted that Brookhouse died just three months later at the age of 63. Ibid., November 10, 1799.
7 Ibid., October 17, 1796; November 2, 1799.
8 Ibid., March 4, 1795; June 8, 1796.

diligent labor was rewarded by an ascent up the economic ladder.[9] For more than a decade now, historians of early Pennsylvania have amended these favorable accounts through systematic research and a healthy dose of skepticism. Rather than general affluence and mobility in Philadelphia, they have found shrinking opportunity and increased poverty as the eighteenth century unfolded.[10] A mobility study of freed eighteenth-century servants not only furthers our understanding of the effects of the Pennsylvania economy on individual mobility, but also allows us to compare and contrast the experiences between the seventeenth and eighteenth centuries. Finally, the concern is with more than mobility and the extent to which former servants obtained a decent competency, because their elusiveness belies the notion that opportunity was widespread.

The first group of eighteenth-century servants traced through their postservitude careers were 191 men and women who arrived in Pennsylvania during the second and third decades of the eighteenth century (Group II).[11] Of these, 133 (70 percent) arrived in the colony between 1722 and 1728. As in all other servant groups indentured in Pennsylvania, the majority were males (116, or 61 percent). And like the colony's first group

9 Alexis de Toqueville, *Democracy in America*, ed. J. P. Mayer and Max Lerner, trans. George Lawrence (New York, 1966); Carl Bridenbaugh, *Cities in Revolt: Urban Life in America, 1743–1776* (New York, 1955); Carl Bridenbaugh and Jessica Bridenbaugh, *Rebels and Gentlemen: Philadelphia in the Age of Freedom* (New York, 1942); Sam Bass Warner, Jr., *The Private City in Three Periods of Its Growth* (Philadelphia, 1968); Richard Hofstadter, *America at 1750: A Social Portrait* (New York, 1971); Jackson Turner Main, *The Social Structure of Revolutionary America* (Princeton, N.J., 1965); Charles S. Olton, "Philadelphia Mechanics in the First Decade of Revolution, 1765–1775," *JAH* 59 (1972), 311–26.

10 Gary B. Nash, "Urban Wealth and Poverty in Pre-Revolutionary America," *JIH* 6 (1976), 545–84; Nash, "Poverty and Poor Relief in Pre-Revolutionary Philadelphia," *WMQ*, 3d ser., 33 (1976), 3–30; Nash, "Up From the Bottom in Franklin's Philadelphia," *Past and Present*, no. 77 (1977), 57–83; Nash, *The Urban Crucible: Social Change, Political Consciousness, and the Origins of the American Revolution,* (Cambridge, Mass., 1979); John K. Alexander, "Poverty, Fear and Continuity: An Analysis of the Poor in Late Eighteenth- Century Philadelphia," in *The Peoples of Philadelphia: A History of Ethnic Groups and Lower-Class Life, 1790–1840* (Philadelphia, 1973), pp. 13–36; Billy G. Smith, "Struggles of the Independent Poor: The Living Standards of Philadelphia's 'Lower Sort' During the Last Half of the Eighteenth Century," *WMQ*, 3d ser., 38 (1981), 163–202; Smith, "Up, Down, and Out in Late Eighteenth-Century Philadelphia," (Ph.D. disser., University of California, Los Angeles, 1981).

Except for the path-breaking work by Nash and James T. Lemon, there have been no detailed studies of property accumulation or wealth distribution among the individuals residing in the rich agricultural areas of the colony. James T. Lemon and Gary B. Nash, "The Distribution of Wealth in Eighteenth-Century America: A Century of Change in Chester County, Pennsylvania, 1693–1802," *JSH* 2 (1968), 1–24.

11 The list was drawn from Jack Kaminkow and Marion Kaminkow, *A List of Emigrants from England to America, 1718–1759* (Baltimore, Md., 1964).

Table 5.1. *Ethnic origins of Pennsylvania's indentured servants in selected periods, 1682–1746*

| | 1682–7 (1) | | 1718–31 (2) | | 1741–6 (3) | |
Country	N	%	N	%	N	%
England	218	85.8	138	94.5	14	4.0
Ireland	31	12.2	4	2.7	324	93.6
Other	5	2.0	4	2.8	8	2.3
Total	254		146		346	

Sources: (1) Marion Balderston, "Pennsylvania's 1683 Ships and Some of Their Passengers," *Pennsylvania Genealogical Magazine* 24 (1965), 69–114; Balderston, "William Penn's Twenty-Three Ships," *Pennsylvania Genealogical Magazine* 23 (1963), 27–67; "A Partial List of Families Who Resided at Bucks County, Pennsylvania Prior to 1687 with the Date of Their Arrival," *Pennsylvania Magazine of History and Biography* 9 (1885), 223, 240; "Some Early Arrivals: Settlers in Chester County, Pennsylvania," *Pennsylvania Genealogical-Society Publications* 4 (1911), 281–304. Also see Michael Ghirelli, *A List of Emigrants from England to America, 1682–1692* (Baltimore, Md., 1963). (2) Jack Kaminkow and Marion Kaminkow, *A List of Emigrants from England to America, 1718–1759* (Baltimore, Md., 1964). This specifies servants and includes information on length of indenture, age, port of destination, and occupation. (3) "List of Servants and Apprentices Bound and Assigned Before James Hamilton, Mayor of Philadelphia, 1745 and 1746," manuscript, AM 3091, Historical Society of Pennsylvania, Philadelphia.

of bound laborers, almost all emigrated from England (Table 5.1) and were obligated to serve their masters for at least four years.

The second eighteenth-century group followed through their postservitude careers were 414 individuals indentured in Pennsylvania between 1745 and 1746 (Group III).[12] More than 60 percent owed their masters four years of labor in exchange for the cost of their passage. The masters of this group resided in Philadelphia City (54 percent), Philadelphia County (16 percent), Bucks County (24 percent), and Chester County (5 percent). Unlike previous servant groups in Pennsylvania, these individuals emigrated primarily from Ireland; only a handful came to Pennsylvania from England.

As Table 5.2 reveals, eighteenth-century servants, once freed, were far more elusive than their seventeenth-century counterparts. Of 191 individuals in Group II, slightly more than one-quarter (28 percent) could be located as free persons. Some (26, or 14 percent) had to be dropped from the list because their names, like James Anderson or John Smith, were too common. There was no hope of identifying the correct person from the

12 "List of Servants and Apprentices, 1745–46," HSP.

Table 5.2. *Visibility of servants indentured in selected periods in Pennsylvania records, 1681–1746*

	1681–7		1718–31		1741–6		Total	
	N	%	N	%	N	%	N	%
Common names	22	11.2	26	13.6	54	13.0	102	12.7
Not Found								
Women	28	14.3	27	14.1	72	17.4	127	15.9
Men	47	24.0	84	44.0	152	36.7	283	35.3
Found								
Women	16	8.2	0	0.0	0	0.0	16	2.0
Men	83	42.3	54	28.3	136	32.9	273	34.1
Total	196		191		414		801	

Sources: Philadelphia, Bucks, and Chester County tax assessment records; Philadelphia and Chester County commissioners' minutes; Minutes of the Pennsylvania Hospital for the Sick Poor; poor records; deeds; court records; wills and inventories.

various lists of eighteenth-century residents. Of those who were found, many were located at only one point in their postservitude careers, as they entered the Pennsylvania Hospital for the Sick Poor or bore witness at a trial. The information was often insufficient to reveal very much about their lives. Straightforward measurements of property accumulation were difficult enough; it was almost impossible to ascertain whether former servants established households and married. The task was all the more frustrating because an occasional glimmer of these individuals' lives was sufficient to suggest that they had remained in Philadelphia.[13]

Similarly, 414 persons were indentured before the mayor in 1745–6. After 54 (13 percent) common names were dropped, only 136 (33 percent) could be located after gaining freedom. They too often appeared only fleetingly in the sources.[14] This persistence rate contrasts markedly with the taxables of Philadelphia. More than two-thirds of the assessed population in late eighteenth-century Philadelphia could be found on the tax lists three to five years later.[15]

The extreme difficulty of tracing individuals cannot be attributed to the lack of sources. Through the eighteenth century, the extant records become

13 Women servants (twenty-seven, or 14 percent) could not be found at all; twenty-six names (14 percent) had to be dropped from the search because they were too common; and an additional eighty-four (44 percent) never appeared in the sources.
14 Of the seventy-two women (17 percent), none were found; common names like William Smith or William Anderson accounted for 13 percent; and 152 (37 percent) were never located in the sources.
15 Salinger and Wetherell, "Note on the Population," 377.

richer as the ability to locate former servants contracts. Table 5.2 also reveals that during the late seventeenth and early eighteenth centuries, with scant records, half of the freed servants were found. With richer sources from the middle and third quarter of the eighteenth century, the proportion of former servants that could be traced dropped to approximately 30 percent. Beginning in the mid-eighteenth century, tax lists are intermittently available for Philadelphia City and Philadelphia and Bucks counties.[16] Chester County tax records are consecutive after 1715.[17] In addition, the Philadelphia and Chester County commissioners' minutes list the names of persons from whom no tax could be collected.[18] Also, the minutes of the Pennsylvania Hospital for the Sick Poor, founded in 1751, contain the records of daily admissions including name, place of residence, and medical diagnosis for each patient.[19] Finally, records are available from agencies that were responsible for relieving the poor.[20] Taken together, these records are comprehensive enough to suggest that, if former servants do not appear on them, they were dead, no longer in the area, or impoverished and invisible.

Tax records indicate that former servants experienced very limited mobility. At no time did more than 35 percent of those located appear on tax lists.[21] An analysis of the aggregate tax data from Table 5.3 reveals that

16 Lamp Tax, 1765, City Archives, City Hall Annex, Phliadelphia; Philadelphia County Provincial Tax, 1767, Rare Book Room, Van Pelt Library, University of Pennsylvania, Philadelphia; 1772 and 1774 Philadelphia County Provincial Tax, City Archives, City Hall Annex, Philadelphia; Hannah Benner Roach, comp., "Taxables in Chestnut, Middle and South Wards, Philadelphia, 1754," *PGM* 21 (1959), 159–96; Roach, comp., "Taxables in the City of Philadelphia, 1756," *PGM* 22 (1961), 3–41; Bucks County tax lists, 1742, 1759, 1761, 1762, 1763, 1764, 1775.

17 The Chester County tax lists are at the Chester County Historical Society, West Chester, Pennsylvania. I worked from an alphabetized composite in multivolumes in the reading room at HSP.

18 I worked with Philadelphia County Commissioners' Minutes, vol. 1718 to 1766, City Archives, City Hall Annex, Philadelphia, and vol. 1771 to 1774, HSP. Volume 1774 to 1776 was discovered in the late 1970s and is in the Tax and Exoneration Records, Pennsylvania State Archives, Harrisburg, Pa. For Chester County, Chester County Commissioners' Tax Discounts, Chester County Historical Society.

19 Attending Managers' Accounts, 1752 to 1781, Pennsylvania Hospital Records, American Philosophical Society, Philadelphia.

20 Philadelphia Poor Daybook, 1739, Gratz Collection, Box 4, HSP; Philadelphia Poor Records, 1750–1767, Miscellaneous Collection, Box 7a, HSP; Records of the Contributors to the Relief and Employment of the Poor, Almshouse Managers, Minutes, 1766–1778, City Archives, Philadelphia.

21 This high of 35 percent was reached in the first decade after the attainment of freedom for Group II (Table 5.4). Nineteen of the fifty-four servants found appeared in the tax record. All of the servants from Group II found on early tax records were Chester County residents—the only county with extant tax lists for this period. The proportion found declined through the former servants' careers. The high point for Group III was reached

Table 5.3. *Distribution of taxable wealth after servitude among former servants indentured in selected periods and age mates, 1718–46*

Assessment (pounds)	Servants		Age mates	
	N	%	N	%
Servants indentured 1718–31				
20 or less	32	66.7	22	95.7
21 or more	16	33.3	1	4.3
Total	48		23	
Servants indentured 1745–6				
20 or less	81	79.4	30	81.1
21 or more	21	20.6	7	18.9
Total	102		37	

Note: Because of the changing exchange rate between Pennsylvania currency and the value of sterling, I converted all assessments from Pennsylvania currency to sterling. Billy G. Smith made the conversion table available. See Ann Bezanson, Robert D. Gray, and Marian Hussey, *Prices in Colonial Pennsylvania* (Philadelphia, 1935), 431–2; *Historical Statistics of the United States* (Washington, D.C., 1949), 733; John J. McCusker, *Money and Exchange in Europe and America, 1600–1775* (Williamsburg, Va., 1978), Table 3.7, 183–8.
Sources: Chester County tax lists are available after 1715; Bucks County 1742, 1759, 1761–4, and 1765; Philadelphia County, 1754, 1756, 1765, 1767, 1772, 1774, and 1775.

servants clustered around the lowest tax assessments. More than 65 percent of Group II who were taxed, never accumulated more than twenty pounds of taxable property. Similarly, of the Group III servants who appeared on the tax lists, almost 80 percent were taxed on property valued at twenty pounds or less.

If the former servants are followed through the tax record at ten-year intervals, those from Group II who did acquire property did so quickly. Table 5.4 reveals that the largest group of servants found were the nineteen (35 percent) who had acquired some property within the first decade after attaining freedom. However, almost three-quarters (fourteen of nineteen) were assessed for twenty pounds or less. Two decades after gaining freedom, fewer servants appeared on the tax record, and those who did had made no further gains in property accumulation. All clustered in the categories that represent meager to modest wealth. Of the sixteen former servants found on the tax lists in the second decade after gaining freedom,

during the second decade after the attainment of freedom when 34 percent (46 of 136) were located in the tax records.

Table 5.4. *Distribution of taxable wealth after servitude among former servants in selected periods, 1718–46*

Value (pounds)	First decade		Second decade	
	N	%	N	%
Servants indentured 1718–31				
20 or less	14	73.7	7	43.8
21 or more	5	26.3	9	56.2
Total	19		16	
Servants indentured 1745–6				
20 or less	36	76.6	42	91.3
21 or more	11	23.4	4	8.7
Total	47		46	

Note: Because of the changing exchange rate between Pennsylvania currency and the value of pounds sterling, I converted all assessments from Pennsylvania currency to sterling. Billy G. Smith made the conversion table available. See Ann Bezanson, Robert D. Gray, and Marian Hussey, *Prices in Colonial Pennsylvania* (Philadelphia, 1935), 431–2; *Historical Statistics of the United States* (Washington, D.C., 1949), 733; John J. McCusker, *Money and Exchange in Europe and America, 1600–1775* (Williamsburg, Va., 1978), Table 3.7, 183–8.
Sources: Tax lists are available for Chester County after 1715. Bucks County tax lists cover the years 1742, 1759, and 1761–4. For Philadelphia, I used the lists for 1754, 1756, 1767, 1772.

more than 40 percent had personal property of twenty pounds or less. By the end of their careers, Group II servants continued to remain on the bottom. In the third decade after freedom, the tax records are increasingly meager. Only thirteen servants were assessed; almost 70 percent held less than twenty pounds of taxable property.[22]

The stories of Joseph Hargrave and Peter Nonsette help bring the numerical analysis of Group II to life. Hargrave arrived in Pennsylvania in 1723 to serve a five-year indenture.[23] Almost thirty years after he was granted freedom, a Joseph Hargrave, measurer, was assessed at sixteen pounds in Lower Delaware Ward.[24] No further record of Hargrave was found. When Peter Nonsette was sixteen years old, he traveled to Pennsyl-

22 These proportions are derived from the number of servants found on each list. For Group II, more than 65 percent includes 32 of the 48 servants located in the tax record. Similarly, for Group III, the 80 percent taxed on property valued at less than 20 pounds reflects the experiences of 81 of 102 fromer servants.
23 Kaminkow and Kaminkow, *List of Emigrants*, September 3, 1723.
24 Roach, comp., "Taxables in the City of Philadelphia," PGM 22 (1961), 3–41.

vania to serve a four-year indenture.[25] In 1739, seven years after he had completed the terms of his indenture, Nonsette paid tax in East Bradford Township in Chester County. Nonsette was not seen again until 1751, when a letter of administration was filed for him. His inventory of estate revealed that he had been a yeoman with thirty-two acres of land, owned a servant, and had accumulated personal wealth of more than 300 pounds.[26] Group II members entered society as free persons at a time when the Pennsylvania economy was growing, and this economic expansiveness may have helped them in their intitial stages of mobility. Two and three decades after gaining freedom, however, during continuing colonial prosperity, these former servants made no further advances up the scale of property accumulation.

The process was no easier for nonservants.[27] Since the age mates of Group II were married in Philadelphia in 1730, the tax record from Chester County is the only adequate source for tracing their early career patterns. However, even as the Bucks County tax records become more complete, members of the control cohort remain invisible. Twenty years after marriage, only two were found and both were assesed at below twenty pounds. By the end of their careers, when tax lists are available from all three counties, fifteen members of the control group were located on the tax lists and all were clustered in the modest wealth brackets. More than 85 percent had personal property assessed at ten pounds or less, an amount that reflected a few horses, cows, and minimum acreage but only rarely home ownership or unfree labor. Even living in an era when the economy was strong, these individuals achieved only the most modest mobility.

The people who served their indentures during the mid-eighteenth century also appeared only rarely on the tax records. The few who were located fought an uphill battle to accumulate property. During the first decade after attaining freedom, the members of the servant group experienced rates of property accumulation that were similar to those of their age mates. Forty-seven of the former servants and fourteen of the control cohort appeared on the tax records; only one member of the control group was assessed at the minimum rate. All but one former servant, William Andrew, remained in the lowest bracket. Andrew arrived in Pennsylvania from Scotland in 1745 and signed a five-year eleven-month indenture with John Kerr, a Philadelphia plasterer.[28] Five years after Andrew completed the

25 Kaminkow and Kaminkow, *List of Emigrants*, August 4, 1728.
26 Chester County Court House, West Chester, Pa.
27 The cohorts were taken from Philadelphia marriage records. Group II's control cohort is from the year 1730 and includes 190 men married in Christ's Church, and the First Presbyterian Church, both in Philadelphia. The control cohort for Group III consists of 76 males who married in Christ's Church and in the German Reformed Church, Philadelphia, in 1750.
28 "List of Servants and Apprentices," HSP.

terms of his indenture, the tax assessor located him in West Nantmeal Township, Chester County. Andrew had accumulated a small amount of property. Five years later, however, he was assessed at slightly more than seventy-two pounds, one of the largest assessments in the township. Fifteen to twenty years after gaining freedom for the servants and after marriage for the control cohort, both former servants and cohort members continued to cluster within the one- to ten-pound assessment range. For Christopher Gygor this meant that twenty years after the termination of his two-year indenture to Philadelphia wheelwright Reuben Foster,[29] Gygor appeared on the Philadelphia County tax list as a yeoman with eighty acres of land, his own dwelling, one horse, three cows, and an assessment of eight pounds.[30]

Tax records provide only a relative index of mobility and ultimately of welfare. They measure and allow us to compare wealth only in terms of capital stock. This presents a problem because only a very small number of people owned Philadelphia's capital wealth. Of the individuals assessed on the 1769 Philadelphia tax list, the wealthiest 10 percent possessed nearly 70 percent of the property with the highest value. Similarly, 10 percent received almost 90 percent of the money paid in rents. With such a skewed distribution of the ownership of property, it is no wonder that few former servants made it into the class of property holders.[31]

The tax lists provide a clue to the difficulty in following former servants through the sources. Fully 20 percent of the individuals culled from the 1769 tax list were not listed as heads of household. They appeared on the tax list only because they paid rent to a property owner. It is impossible to measure the assessed wealth of this group because the only information available for these individuals is the amount of rent they paid. The data on rents paid confirm that this group is distinct from the rest of the population not simply because the tax collector missed them. In addition, they paid lower rents than other renters, which suggests that they were poorer, and a greater proportion were females, which also hints at greater economic vulnerability. Although not all of them were former servants, many were. They had remained in the city but were not counted by the collectors because their assets warranted little attention.[32]

John Kelso's story illuminates the experiences of the unassessed group. Kelso paid an annual rent of fifteen pounds to Samuel Emlen, a Philadelphia shopkeeper, most likely for an apartment. However, Kelso was neither listed nor assessed as a head of household, nor did he appear as a head of household on the surviving prerevolutionary tax lists. Kelso may have been

29 Ibid.
30 Philadelphia Provincial Tax, 1767.
31 Sharon V. Salinger and Charles Wetherell, "Wealth and Renting in Prerevolutionary Philadelphia," *JAH* 71 (1985), 831.
32 Ibid., 835.

missed by the tax assessors because he moved often. More likely, the collectors overlooked Kelso because he owned no taxable capital stock.[33]

Ultimately, tax lists do not provide the best measure of mobility. In part, too few survive and those that do exclude a large number of people who should have been listed as heads of household. In addition, tax records underestimate the relative real wealth of the poor, precisely because taxes were levied on capital goods. As a result, they exclude income or book debts or even trading stock.[34] For the small proportion of servants who made it into the tax records, most accumulated only minimal amounts of property. However, these records leave unanswered many questions about mobility.

Additional clues to the mobility of former servants can be gleaned in the land records, although they too measure capital stock. An analysis of the deeds reveals that eighteenth-century servants only rarely acquired land. John Bartlett was the only former servant from Group II located in the deed books. Bartlett arrived in Pennsylvania in 1722 to serve a four-year indenture. Bartlett had been a free man for eighteen years in 1744 when he purchased seventy-nine and a half acres in Olney Township in Philadelphia County.[35] Landownership was slightly more common among members of the age-mate cohort. Of the sixty-nine members, eight owned acreage outside the city and four purchased city lots.

Former servants from Group III also acquired land only rarely, strongly suggesting that, despite the economic expansiveness of the era, they were unable to move upward in society. Only nine former servants owned farm acreage, and three of these held parcels of forty acres or less, an amount that would provide only a marginal existence. Although only four members of the control group owned farmland, nine purchased city lots. Control group member Albertoon Richlost, a Philadelphia boatbuilder, was deeded a city lot in 1749. Six years later he purchased a second lot in Philadelphia County on the Delaware River. Carpenter Matthew Keyser, also a member of the control cohort, resided in Germantown. He owned three city lots by 1763, and when he died, three years later, his estate was valued at more than 200 pounds. Neither servant nor control group members owned land in significant numbers, but a higher proportion of the control cohort held land both in the city and in the rural areas of the neighboring counties. It appears that especially in the port city, where most of the property was owned by a small number of residents, landownership did not provide a viable means of mobility for the colony's servants who served their terms during the eighteenth century.

33 Ibid., 836.
34 For a discussion of the problems of the tax record see Jackson T. Main, *Society and Economy in Colonial Connecticut* (Princeton, N.J., 1985), 37–9.
35 Deeds are located at the City Archives, City Hall Annex, Philadelphia, except for a few scattered volumes held by Harrisburg.

Probate records provide another gauge of servant mobility. It is not surprising that proportionally very few inventories survived for former servants and their age mates. Inventories of estate were located for eleven members (20 percent) members of Group II and twenty-two (16 percent) of Group III.[36] The probate record for the control cohort is even more skimpy; only four (2 percent) probate inventories were uncovered for control Group II and nine (11 percent) for control Group III. The small number of these documents suggests either that few of the individuals left sufficient property to warrant an inventory or that they migrated outside the area. However, whereas the total amount of wealth left in the estates by former servants fell below the mean extant Philadelphia inventories as a whole, the few control group documents followed the pattern of the city. Almost two-thirds of the servants from Group II and one-half of the servants from Group III left estates valued at fifty pounds or less. Within the city as a whole, only 17 percent of the estates recorded property valued at the same modest amount. Similarly, only 18 percent of the former servants left estates of two hundred pounds or more, whereas more than half of the inventories left by members of the control groups and by Philadelphians at large had property valued in the higher wealth brackets.

The following vignettes capture the probate histories of some eighteenth-century servants. A letter of administration was filed for Job Carpenter in 1733.[37] He had arrived in Pennsylvania in 1722 and signed a five-year indenture.[38] Carpenter was listed as a laborer in Falls Township, Bucks County; his assets at death came to slightly less than fifteen pounds. Conrad Abel arrived from London in 1745.[39] He was first indentured to Nicholas Prossius, a Philadelphia tailor, and then to Jacob Newman, a Philadelphia resident whose occupation is unknown.[40] Abel was to serve a total of eight years. In 1767, fourteen years after he had attained his freedom, Abel appeared on the Philadelphia tax list. He resided in Mulberry Ward, owned his own dwelling, and paid on an assessment of nine pounds. By 1772 Abel had a slave and was listed as a dyer. He died twenty-two years later with personal property valued at almost three hundred pounds, one of the highest inventories of any former servant.[41] Not only did servants leave fewer inventories than the Philadelphia population as a whole, their

---

36 The percentages were derived by subtracting the common names and those never located in the sources from the total number of servants in each group. Thus instead of 191 servants in Group II, I used 54. Similarly, rather than calculate 414 servants for Group III, I used 136 (414 minus 54 common names and 224 never found). See Table 5.2.
37 Bucks County Court House, Doylestown, Pennsylvania.
38 Kaminkow and Kaminkow, *List of Emigrants,* July 2, 1772.
39 "List of Servants and Apprentices, 1745–46."
40 Ibid.
41 City Hall Annex, Philadelphia, Pennsylvania.

Table 5.5. *Proportion of former servants located in the poor records*

	Group II	Group III
Poor records	12	84
Taxes deferred	11	26
Total	24	110
Percentage of total found	44.4	80.9

Note: The percentages and numbers undercount the number of poor because I was unable to control for death. Thus in the third decade after gaining freedom, the population of Group II was certainly fewer than 54. Similarly, for Group III fewer than the 136 individuals used to calculate the data were living 30 years after attaining freedom. In addition, the records of the poor are much richer after 1750, when the institutions for the poor were established. Thus the data for Group III are most likely a better gauge of servant poverty.

Sources: Poor records include Attending Managers' Accounts, 1752 to 1781, Pennsylvania Hospital Records, American Philosophical Society, Philadelphia; Minutes of the Overseers of the Poor, 1768–1774, Historical Society of Pennsylvania, Philadelphia; Pennsylvania Poor Records, 1750–1767, Misc. Col., Box 7a, Historical Society of Pennsylvania; Chester Country Court Records, Chester County Historical Society, Wast Chester, Pa; Bucks County Court Records, Doylestown, Pa; Philadelphia Poor Daybook, 1739, Gratz Collection, Box 4, Historical Society of Pennsylvania; Records of the Contributors to the Relief and Employment of the Poor, Almshouse Managers Minutes, 1766–1778, City Archives, City Hall Annex, Philadelphia. Information on tax deferments is from Philadelphia County Commissioners' Minutes, 1718–1766, City Archives, City Hall Annex, Philadelphia; 1771–1774, Historical Society of Pennsylvania; Chester County Commissioners' Tax Discounts, Chester County Historical Society, West Chester, Pa.

accumulated property at the end of their careers was far smaller than that of other inhabitants of the city.

The admittedly skimpy record of former servants, from tax lists, deed books, and probate data, has created an impression of minimal mobility. However, the records of the poor corroborate this conclusion and indicate that former servants struggled for a decent competency. Aggregate data, displayed in Table 5.5, reveal that over 40 percent of the servants from Group II (twenty-three of fifty-four) needed public assistance of some sort. They had their taxes abated or depended on help from one of the institutions for the poor. The extent of postservitude difficulties is even worse than these figures reveal, since institutions for the poor and thus the records are quite thin through the first half of the eighteenth century. By the time the third group of servants gained their freedom, the poor records are rich and the indices of servant poverty more complete. Servants indentured in the mid–eighteenth century struggled – more than three-quarters were forced at some time in their lives to depend on the public dole.

An analysis of the poor records over time accentuates the grim details of former servants' struggle for movement up the economic ladder. During their first decade of freedom, nine (almost 17 percent) required some form of public assistance; they either were too poor to pay their tax or requested direct aid. During their midcareers, members of Group II appeared only rarely on the poor lists. One individual needed a tax deferment, and three others required direct aid. Into the third decade after the attainment of freedom, however, the years from 1755 to 1760, these former servants relied on assistance in more significant numbers. Ten persons (19 percent) either needed their taxes abated or required a charitable dole. During the same period, only about 5 to 6 percent of the city's population as a whole could be identified as poor. The most striking comparison is the record of former servants in contrast with that of the cohort. Only two members of the control group, thirty years after their marriages, were listed in the poor records.

If the servants who served their indentures during the 1740s are also followed over time, their struggle as free persons is clearer. Within only ten years after gaining freedom, one-quarter (thirty-five, or 26 percent) had to call upon public aid, whereas during these years, 1755–60, only 5 to 6 percent of the city's inhabitants appeared on the same lists. Dennis Gorman came from Ireland in 1746. His four-year indenture was purchased by Philadelphia bricklayer Isaac Roberts.[42] Eight years after gaining his freedom, Gorman was listed as a poor patient in the Pennsylvania Hospital. The overseers of the poor were responsible for his security.[43] Gorman was suffering from a "scorbutik" tumor – a vitamin C deficiency common to the poor. Thomas Welsh, a former servant of Joseph Ellis, was admitted to the Pennsylvania Hospital as a poor patient seven years after completing his indenture.[44] Welsh requested an early discharge from the hospital because he was concerned about procuring enough business to support his family. The managers of the hospital agreed to treat him as an outpatient.

Times became increasingly hard for the members of Group III. Fifteen to twenty years after they had gained their freedom, the number of former servants who were receiving some sort of aid was more than four times greater than the figure for the city's population as a whole. Nearly half (46 percent) of Group III members were listed as poor, compared with about 10 percent of the port city's population. In 1767 Bernard Kerr was required to

---

42 "List of Servants and Apprentices, 1745–46."
43 Attending Managers' Account, Pennsylvania Hospital Records.
44 "List of Servants and Apprentices, 1745–46"; Attending Managers' Accounts, Pennsylvania Hospital Records.

request a tax discount from the Chester County commissioners because he was in the hospital.[45] Kerr had arrived from Ireland in 1745 and served a four-year indenture with Philadelphia tailor John Kattoringer.[46] When George Vance came to Pennsylvania from Ireland in 1746, he was obligated to serve John Moore for four years.[47] George Vance of Southwark lived as a free man for almost twenty years before he was sent to the almshouse by the overseers of the poor in 1769.[48] At about the same time, Mary Vance, also of Southwark, presumably his wife, was ordered to the House of Employment.[49] The individuals of Group III were regular dependents at the institution of the poor. Again, a great gulf exists between the members of Group III and the cohort. Only one member of the control group was located on the poor records.

We can only speculate about the causes of the striking differences between former servants and the cohort. It appears likely that the cohort had greater resources. They presumably had lived in Pennsylvania longer, many were perhaps natives, and if they did experience financial difficulties, they had families and friends to lean on. Servants, in contrast, had few if any personal resources. Their friends were most likely in similar economic straits, and their families were three thousand miles away. Their only recourse when the cupboard was bare or the wood supply depleted was to seek public assistance. In addition, it is possible that immigrant servants were stigmatized, especially if they were non-English. Since the vast majority of Group III were Scots-Irish, their inability to succeed economically as free persons might have been due in part to the rampant anti-Irish feeling in Philadelphia.

As dependent as the male servants were on public aid, female servants required assistance in greater proportion. The admission dockets of the Guardians of the Poor reveal that servant women all over Philadelphia shared the likelihood of bleak futures. Indeed, women carried more than their share of the burden of poverty in late-eighteenth-century Philadelphia. They constituted a disproportionate number of the population of the poorhouse. Although more men were admitted and discharged, the population of the poorhouse contained a significant sexual imbalance, for almost two-thirds of the residents were women.[50] The causes of female poverty in

---

45 Chester County Commissioners' Tax Discounts, February 6, 1767, Chester County Historical Society, West Chester, Pa.
46 "List of Servants and Apprentices, 1745–46."
47 Ibid.
48 Minutes of the Overseers of the Poor, January 19, 1769, HSP.
49 Ibid.
50 The mean sex ratio was 73.8 for the years 1787 to 1790. These are the only years for which the total poorhouse population is given. Admission Dockets of the Guardians of the Poor, City Archives, Philadelphia.

Philadelphia were not the same as in Boston, where poor women were primarily war widows. In 1742 a "staggering 30 percent of [Boston's] married women had no spouses to contribute to the support of their households."[51] Since the Quaker capital traditionally took a pacifist role and only rarely recruited men to fight, the origins of female poverty must lie elsewhere.

Women were vulnerable in specific ways, and it is not surprising that the large female population of the poorhouse reflects, in part, the fact that women sought its refuge as a maternity hospital. Mary Bough, pregnant by her master and "destitute of necessaries," was admitted to the poorhouse to lie in in 1787.[52] In the same month, four other women were admitted with the same need.[53] Philadelphia women who bore illegitimate children were frequently forced into the poorhouse because often they had no one with whom to share the financial burden. These women tended to remain for relatively long periods. Some, like Susannah Jones, remained for only a month. Jones lay in almost immediately after being admitted, but she ran away exactly one month later.[54] More typical, however, was Mary Owen. She arrived in the poorhouse on March 10, 1788, gave birth, and remained for more than two months.[55] Women who had illegitimate births were usually the poorest members of the community, the most vulnerable, the least likely to be able to force their partners to share support, and, if they had been indentured servants, the least likely to have families to aid them.[56]

The poorhouse doubled as an immigrant aid home and often provided recent arrivals with their first housing in Philadelphia. Ann Larky traveled to Philadelphia from Londonderry. Since she was pregnant, she gained admission to the poorhouse. Apparently her importers did not think she could be sold; they were liable for her costs.[57] Four women were admitted to the poorhouse directly from their ships in 1794. They had arrived from Belfast on the brig *Susannah* and were all victims of ship's fever.[58]

More important, the disproportionate number of women in the poorhouse is further testimony that, once on the bottom of the economic ladder,

51 Gary B. Nash, "The Failure of Female Factory Labor in Colonial Boston," *Labor History* 20 (Spring 1979), 166.
52 Guardians of the Poor, December 4, 1787.
53 Ibid., December 3, 13, 20, 21, 1787.
54 Ibid., December 20, 1787; January 20, 1788.
55 Ibid., March 10, 1788; May 23, 1788.
56 From the period when the Guardians of the Poor Daily Occurrence Docket begins in November 1787 to December 1800, many women were admitted as "pregnant." Louise A. Tilly and Joan W. Scott found that women "who bore illegitimate children were often those with no ties to their family of origin." *Women, Work, and Family* (New York, 1978), 39.
57 Guardians of the Poor, March 5, 1788.
58 Ibid., July 14, 21, and 23, 1794.

it was virtually impossible to move upward. Poverty continued to be a reality in late-eighteenth-century Philadelphia, and former servants were among the most vulnerable. The following examples reveal how few options were available to the struggling poor. A constable came upon Mary Johnston on a Sunday as she was "about to Drown her Child" and she was carted off to the poorhouse.[59] Eight persons were admitted to the poorhouse on the same day. All were suffering from a fever, "and they are all brought in from the same cellar or Hovel in Plumb Street Southwark." The men, women, and children in this group were "sick, helpless and destitute," shut away in some cellar, and temporarily baled out of their misery by the city's overseers.[60] Ann Wilson and her six-week-old baby had just arrived from Ireland in 1797 when they sought relief. Her husband was forced to seek work in the country, and in a distressed state she and her baby entered the poorhouse.[61]

The large number of women who resided in the poorhouse bears testimony to the difficulties faced by many indentured servants who had served their time but who had no place to go or any means of support when they were freed. Margaret Harrison had served an indenture with Peter Souder in the Northern Liberties and arrived at the poorhouse door destitute and "severly poxed" in 1788.[62] Margaret Fisher had been indentured to Frederick Stall, a Philadelphia rope maker. She requested admission to the poorhouse in 1800 because she was sick and venereal.[63] Nancy Dougan came to Pennsylvania from Ireland and entered the poorhouse sick just after she had finished serving her time.[64] Alice Brady finished serving her time with Widow Sutor and came to the poorhouse "neglected and distressed."[65] After Susannah Kirk completed her indenture to Abner Lukens, she worked "at service for six years past with different families in this city." Because Kirk was sick and incapable of "helping herself," her only recourse was to gain entry to the poorhouse.[66] The names of former servants roll off the pages of the admissions docket. These women arrived in the colony, served their time, and landed in the poorhouse sick, destitute, and totally without resources.

Other indicators enhance our sense of the difficulties faced by former servants in the eighteenth century. Many of those who served indentures in the seventeenth century participated actively in government. This does not

59 Ibid., June 30, 1788.
60 Ibid., July 19 and 26, 1794.
61 Ibid., December 11, 1797.
62 Ibid., November 15, 1797.
63 Ibid., February 18, 1800.
64 Ibid., August 19, 1796.
65 Ibid., November 15, 1797.
66 Ibid., July 16, 1800.

appear to have been the case for the eighteenth-century servants. No members of Group II or III ever served on juries, let alone as constables or Assembly representatives. Admittedly, court records for Philadelphia are fragmentary until midcentury, but records do exist for Chester County. Members of the control cohort held offices but not to the same degree as the seventeenth-century servants. Thomas Morgan served as coroner of Chester County beginning in 1743.[67] In 1754 Edward Hughes was a member of a grand jury.[68] And Thomas Marden served for at least one term as a constable for Byberry Township beginning in 1757.[69] These three individuals were the only members of the Group II cohort who served in an official capacity. The Group III controls also rarely served in governmental office. Only Jasper Scull, who served for many years as the coroner from Northhampton County, held an office.[70] Several reasons account for the tremendous differences in the rates of governmental participation between seventeenth- and eighteenth-century servants and their cohorts. Group I had a slightly higher rate of economic mobility, and it must have increased their opportunity to serve. Also, the openness of colonial government in the early years of the colony may have provided opportunity for a larger number of potential participants. Finally, the changing ethnic and class background of eighteenth-century servants made their participation in government unlikely. Colonial officials welcomed anyone who wanted to settle, but called few non-Quakers into government. Cohort members failed to hold offices because they had not moved far enough up the economic scale. Government was in the hands of the wealthy in the decades preceding the Revolution.

Striking differences exist between the rates of mobility of seventeenth- and eighteenth-century servants. Whereas almost half of the Group I servants who could be traced through the records acquired land, less than 10 percent of Group II servants and fewer than 9 percent of Group III servants were able to do so. Only one member of Pennsylvania's first group of servants required assistance, whereas about 80 percent of Group III servants were forced to accept public aid at some point. Not one servant in Group III held a government office, whereas 25 of the 195 members of Group I worked in some official capacity.

The wholesale disappearance of former servants in the eighteenth century and variations in servant mobility are partly explained by the different experiences faced by eighteenth-century servants. First, the alterations in the institution of indentured labor had adverse affects on the servants. The nature of indentured labor changed profoundly by the mid–eighteenth

67 *Minutes of the Provincial Council* (Harrisburg, Pa., 1851), 4:669.
68 Court of Quarter Sessions Docket, December 3, 1753, to December 1760, City Archives, Philadelphia.
69 Court of Quarter Sessions Docket.
70 *Minutes of the Provincial Council*, 5:662.

Table 5.6. *Incidence of running away among selected groups of indentured servants, 1718–46*

Number of times	1718–31		1745–6	
	N	%	N	%
1	31	16.2	24	5.8
2	1	0.5	5	1.2
3+			2	0.5
Total	32	16.7	31	7.5
Total in group	191		414	

Source: Pennsylvania Gazette, American Weekly Mercury, Pennsylvania Packet and Daily Advertiser, Bucks County Court Records, Chester County Court Records.

century in response to commercial expansion and prosperity. Most of the colony's first servants were indentured in England, accompanied their owners to the New World, served relatively short terms, and labored with minimal conflict. Since newspapers did not exist in the colony when the first servants served their time, runaway advertisements are a source only during the eighteenth century. However, only three servants were called before Pennsylvania magistrates and accused of running away. And evidence of only one servant sale could be found for this early group. The men and women who traveled to Pennsylvania in the eighteenth century were indentured and labored under extremely harsh conditions. They were commodities in a business enterprise, and the level of social conflict as measured by runaways rose dramatically. Table 5.6 reports the incidence of servant runaways. Advertisements for absconding servants appeared in Philadelphia newspapers for thirty-two (17 percent) of the Group II servants and twenty-nine (7 percent) of the servants from Group III. Forty-five servants (11 percent) from Group III had their indentures transferred at least one time, and two servants (half a percent) had as many as three different owners.[71] Ethnicity changed tremendously. However, the entire burden of economic struggle cannot be placed on the Irish makeup of Group III, especially since members of Group II, who were predominantly English, did not fare well either. The Irish servants did run away at a higher rate, but their need to escape from servitude was governed by a different set of motivations than the striving for a decent competency. The reasons for emigration and the appeal of colonial Pennsylvania suggest that most servants shared similar aspirations for their postservitude lives in the New World.

71 These data are unavailable for Group II since indenture records are not extant.

Although all servants were promised freedom dues providing they served their time uneventfully, the nature of freedom dues varied considerably between Group I and Groups II and III. The servants in Group I who traveled with First Purchasers were promised fifty acres of land upon completion of their terms of indenture. Since this practice had been terminated by 1700, if not earlier, the most eighteenth-century servants could expect was clothing, one old and one new suit, and an occasional farm tool. Thus eighteenth-century servants had a number of strikes against them: Their servant experiences were less stable, the institution was far more exploitative, and when they entered society as free persons they had fewer assets for achieving success.

The general health of the economy does not appear to have been the culprit that limited mobility for Group II. The first group of eighteenth-century servants entered society as free persons during a period of economic growth. After 1728, the demand for Pennsylvania produce, primarily grain, increased and the rural sector of the colony prospered. The growth in agricultural production helped spur the Philadelphia economy as well. The city's overseas trade network expanded, which in turn stimulated the urban trades. Thus during the 1730s, when the majority of Group II entered society as free persons and the cohort members were married, the colonial economy was prospering and opportunity was ample. The decades of the 1740s and 1750s were peppered by wars which continued to encourage economic expansion. Servants were freed during a period of economic growth and the economic realities only got better.

Group III members also gained freedom during what appears to have been a favorable economic period. Except for a brief commercial downturn at midcentury, the general indicators suggest that the Pennsylvania economy was healthy and growing. During the Seven Years' War, everyone from the merchant to the seaman reaped the spoils. Provisioning contracts for one and privateering benefits for the other kept profits up and jobs plentiful.[72]

The economic benefits from war melted away after 1760, and although some Philadelphians continued to prosper, the limited economic growth did not benefit all classes equally, since prices rose faster than wages. Within a decade after the attainment of freedom for Group III servants and marriage for the cohort, opportunity was restricted and employment opportunities were reduced. Two decades into their postservitude careers, economic realities for former servants continued to worsen, as they did for the cohort. The wartime boom halted abruptly, credit contracted, and overseas trade slowed. The resumption of the Irish and German immigration compounded the problem because many new arrivals sought work in the port city. The

---

72 Nash, *Urban Crucible*, 237–9.

economic recession hit many residents hard, but the laboring classes bore the brunt of the hardship.[73] Former servants in Group III battled for twenty years to survive in a greatly restricted economy.

By 1769 the distribution of wealth and income in Philadelphia was grossly skewed, revealing that some in the city continued to prosper while others struggled. An enormous share of Philadelphia's capital wealth was owned by a very small number of Philadelphia residents. "Fewer than 9 percent [of the city's taxpayers] owned almost 65 percent of the capital wealth." The "structure of income and wealth consist[ed] primarily of a small top and a large bottom."[74]

Clearly, the limited economic growth benefited a very small proportion of the port city's taxpayers. The wealthy became wealthier, but mobility on the lower end of the economic scale was grossly restricted. This is critical because it limited the opportunities of freed servants. In addition, as the century progressed, land prices and starting costs for farms also increased. Group I had to accumulate the capital required to register their freedom land, whereas eighteenth-century servants needed capital to pay for everything – land, tools, supplies, provisions, as well as the deed registration. After Thomas Penn returned to Pennsylvania in 1732 he raised the price of land from ten pounds to fifteen pounds ten shillings and annual quitrents from one shilling to two shillings six pence per hundred acres.[75] The Penns did not alter this price until 1765 when they lowered the cost of unimproved land to five pounds for one hundred acres.[76] Land prices were reduced too late to affect the mobility of Group II and fifteen years after most of the Group III servants were released from their indentures – no doubt also too late to alter their economic position. Because of higher land prices and the general rise in the cost of necessities – firewood, bread, other foodstuffs, and taxes – individuals who began careers in the eighteenth century waged a more difficult battle than seventeenth-century servants.

The uneven growth of the economy affected the basic structure of labor in Philadelphia as well. Since some merchants and artisans prospered while others struggled, the economy facilitated a social differentiation that led to a labor surplus. The geographic distribution of freed servants is indicative of the restrictions placed on them by the economy. The majority of seventeenth-century servants, even those who had served their indentures in the city, set up for themselves in the rural areas of the colony. Freedom dues and the costs of land worked in their favor. In contrast, most of the eighteenth-century servants, those who served in the city as well as those

---

73 Ibid., 247–62.
74 Salinger and Wetherell, "Wealth and Renting," 833.
75 James T. Lemon, *The Best Poor Man's Country* (Baltimore, Md., 1972), 57.
76 Ibid.

who were indentured to rural owners, either remained in Philadelphia or sought work in the port city.

How can we account for the fact that servants remained in Philadelphia even in the face of economic adversity? If they had moved at least once previously to better their economic prospects, why did they stay rooted in the port city? First, they remained because opportunities in the rural sector were also constricting and no doubt accounted for a large number of persons moving into the city seeking work themselves. Second, servants were embedded in a city culture where a social network and a support group perhaps ironically encouraged them to remain even though they had few economic options. Their move to the colonies had been difficult and their servant experiences severe. But survival was easier for those who served in the city than it was for their rural counterparts, in part because they belonged to a distinct subculture. This network may have been the most positive aspect of their servitude. To move again, even if it was the only hope of brightening their economic prospects, may not have been worth risking the loss of their social network.

The Philadelphia economy had grown stingy and unforgiving. An economy that had once been characterized by high wages and a shortage of workers was, by the mid-eighteenth century, unable to absorb the steady stream of freed servants and immigrants. This strained economy could no longer provide ample employment opportunity. What had once been a labor shortage became a labor surplus. Artisans who had met the labor shortage by purchasing unfree laborers now struggled to find jobs for themselves. Freed servants were caught in the economic squeeze, and their career patterns reflected the limits of the urban economy. Far from a society of unlimited opportunity, eighteenth-century Pennsylvania had become a place where limits on mobility were increasing. The circumstances that limited servant mobility appear connected to the unraveling of the institution itself.

6 The decline of unfree labor

By THE LATE EIGHTEENTH CENTURY, the institutions of unfree labor in Philadelphia had reached their final phase and declined markedly. As servitude and slavery became increasingly less important for the urban work force, alterations occurred in the pattern of servant ownership, and as a result, the nature of servant and slave work changed. These changes signaled the end of the viability of unfree labor in Philadelphia and the emergence of a more consistent use of free wage earners.

In the middle of the eighteenth century, when unfree laborers accounted for almost half of the Philadelphia work force, artisan owners dominated. They relied more heavily on unfree workers than did any other occupational group. By the end of the colonial period, the artisans' share of the servant market had declined. In 1745 the city's artisans composed 48 percent of the population, but as Table 6.1 reveals, artisans purchased almost two-thirds of the indentured servants.[1] By 1769 artisans owned servants in roughly the same proportion as their number in the population. Six years later, more than 46 percent of the city's taxables were identified as artisans, but their share of the servant owners dwindled to 40 percent. The decline of artisans as servant owners dropped further through the end of the century. Artisans remained at about 50 percent of the city's taxables during the last quarter of the century, yet they accounted for only 20 percent of the servant owners in 1789 and fewer than 15 percent in 1791. In 1798 only one artisan was taxed for an indentured servant. Clearly, by the end of the century artisans were no longer dependent on the labor of indentured servants.[2]

Whereas artisans possessed fewer servants, merchants purchased more. In 1769 about one-fifth of the population worked in the merchant-retailing occupations and owned one-third of the city's servants. The relative size of this servant-owning group grew. After the Revolution, this sector owned

[1] "List of Servants and Apprentices Bound and Assigned before James Hamilton, Mayor of Philadelphia, 1745–46," manuscript, AM 3091, HSP.
[2] Philadelphia tax lists. The 1767 list is at the Van Pelt Library, University of Pennsylvania, Philadelphia; the 1789 and 1791 lists are at the Philadelphia City Archives, City Hall Annex, Philadelphia.

Table 6.1. *Distribution of merchants and artisans as servant owners, 1745 and 1769*

	Servant owners			
	1745 (1)		1769 (2)	
	N	%	N	%
Merchants and retailers	25	16.7	74	34.7
Artisans	94	62.6	90	42.3

Sources: (1) "List of Servants and Apprentices Bound and Assigned Before James Hamilton, Mayor of Philadelphia, manuscript, AM 3091" Historical Society of Pennsylvania, Philadelphia. (2) Philadelphia Tax Lists, 1769, City Archives, Philadelphia. I chose this list because the 1769 tax list has the most complete occupational information of the prerevolutionary tax lists. See Appendix B for a complete occupational breakdown, the continuation of these trends, and a comparison with the occupational structure of Philadelphia as a whole.

roughly two and one-half times as many servants as its proportion in the population. By 1791 almost three times as many servant owners were from the merchant-retailer group than would be indicated by the city's general occupational distribution.

As artisans came to own fewer servants and merchant-retailers to purchase more, the work roles of indentured servants changed. When the majority of the city's unfree laborers worked for artisans, they were involved primarily in craft production. As craftsmen relied less and less on bound workers, however, indentured servants were increasingly employed as unskilled or domestic workers. Merchants continued to buy servants to work on board their ships or to serve as clerks, but more and more often merchants purchased the time of unfree workers for domestic service. The demand for domestic labor – free as well as unfree – rose rapidly after the Revolution, when newspapers commonly carried advertisements encouraging any interested men and women, white or black, to apply for work as gentlemen's servants, waiters, or general household servants.[3]

The shifting sexual composition of Philadelphia's indentured servants provides the most striking evidence of their changing work roles. When the demand for bound labor was high, merchants implored their European agents to avoid sending women in favor of "stout laboring men and boys." The proportion of female servants increased gradually from fewer than 20

3 For example, *Pennsylvania Gazette,* June 25, August 20, November 5, 12, 1783; April 28, June 16, 30, December 22, 1784.

percent during the height of the institution to 30 percent just before the Revolution and almost 40 percent by 1795. Household servants were not exclusively women, but this sizable increase in the proportion of women suggests a dramatic rise in the importance of domestic laborers.[4]

The proportion of unfree domestic servants rose at a time when the institutions of unfree labor were disappearing in Philadelphia. An important component in the decline of unfree labor was the sharp drop in the number of slaves. The antislavery movement among the Pennsylvania Quakers was the most critical factor in the city's shrinking slave population. Before 1750 no organized antislavery effort existed. A number of individual Friends and several local meetings, especially in Chester County, demanded an end to the slave trade and at times attacked slavery itself. But the Philadelphia Yearly Meeting could only agree to caution Friends against importing or buying blacks.[5]

An antislavery policy gained momentum within the Yearly Meeting after midcentury. The new direction was signaled in 1753 with the approval and publication by the meeting of John Woolman's essay, *Some Considerations on the Keeping of Negroes*. One Year later, *An Epistle of Caution and Advice Concerning the Buying and Keeping of Slaves* appeared. It focused on the growth of slaveholding among Friends and the evil nature of the institution. For the first time in print, the Yearly Meeting argued that slaveholding itself, not just the slave trade, was un-Christian. Four years later, the Yearly Meeting went beyond simply publishing and moved forcefully against both the trade and slavery by recommending to local meetings that members who imported or purchased blacks be disciplined. If members continued their involvement in the trade, they would be unable to participate in business meetings, serve as officers or representatives, or contribute to the meeting. The meeting also appointed a committee to visit and treat with slave-owning Friends to encourage Quakers to free their slaves.[6]

In the two decades before the Revolution, antislavery policies were carried out in local meetings. Some acted vigorously and disciplined members who bought and sold slaves, whereas others continued to drag

---

4 The number of domestic workers rose dramatically through the third decade of the nineteenth century. "Mathew Carey estimated that there were in Philadelphia 9,000 households without servants, 12,000 with one, 3,000 with two, 2,000 with three, and 1,000 with four for a total of 28,000 servants." Tom W. Smith, "The Dawn of the Urban-Industrial Age: The Social Structure of Philadelphia, 1790–1830" (Ph.D. diss., University of Chicago 1980), 65–6.

5 Jean Soderlund, "Conscience, Interest, and Power: The Development of the Quaker Opposition to Slavery in the Delaware Valley, 1688–1780" (Ph.D. diss., Temple University, 1982), 53–6.

6 Ibid., 68–74; Thomas E. Drake, *Quakers and Slavery in America* (New Haven, Conn., 1950), 46.

their feet. Beginning in 1776, the Yearly Meeting, under the recommendations of the committee's report, ruled that all local meetings should disown
all slaveholders who refused to manumit their slaves and directed that
blacks of all ages were to be freed and their manumissions recorded by the
monthly meetings. By the time of Independence, the Yearly Meeting had
taken a very hard line. Since many Friends still held slaves, local meetings
were ordered to "testify their disunion" with any Friends who did not free
their slaves.[7]

Manumissions in Philadelphia were negligible before 1774. However,
after that date the floodgates opened. More than 60 percent of the
manumissions recorded by the Philadelphia meeting occurred between 1775
and 1777 and affected more than 340 slaves.[8] The Pennsylvania legislature
was caught up in the antislavery fervor too. George Bryan, a Presbyterian
legislator, with support from Anthony Benezet "planned and executed the
passage of a gradual abolition law." The law, passed in 1780, was the first
statutory action against slavery in the United States. The law stipulated that
all children born after the passage of the law would be free except those
born to slave mothers. They would be required to serve until twenty-eight
years of age. Furthermore, the act required masters to register each slave,
and if they failed to do so by November 1, 1780, they would forfeit the
slave. Finally, although "Ministers and Consuls" were allowed to have their
personal slaves for an indefinite period while in Pennsylvania, any slaves
brought into the state would be freed after six months. With periodic
assistance from the state judiciary, the Act of 1780 laid the foundation for
the eventual disappearance of slavery from Pennsylvania.[9]

In addition to the attack on the institution of slavery by Pennsylvania
Quakers, the diminished slave population in Philadelphia was related to
slave supply. The rapid shrinkage of the city's prerevolutionary slave
population was attributable in part to the inability of the slave population
to reproduce itself at a time when slave importations were declining sharply.
The rapid expansion of the slave trade during the Seven Years' War ended
as soon as importations of white indentured servants resumed. Fewer than
seventy slaves were imported into the colony from September 1764 to
September 1768. By the end of 1770 the trade had virtually ended.[10]

7 Soderlund, "Conscience, Interest, and Power," 74–6, 99; Drake, *Quakers and Slavery,*
71–2.
8 Soderlund, "Conscience, Interest, and Power," 99–100; Drake, *Quakers and Slavery,* 74,
90; Gary B. Nash, "Slaves and Slaveowners in Eighteenth-Century Philadelphia," *WMQ*
3d ser., 30 (1973), 236.
9 Paul Finkelman, *An Imperfect Union: Slavery, Federalism, and Comity* (Chapel Hill, N.C.,
1981), 47; Stanley I. Kutler, "Pennsylvania Courts, the Abolition Act, and Negro Rights,"
Pennsylvania History 30 (1963), 14.
10 Gary B. Nash, "Slaves and Slaveowners," 238.

Table 6.2. *Unfree labor in late-eighteenth-century Philadelphia*

Year	Servants (1)	Slaves (2)	Percentage of servants
1767	269	814	24.8
1769	328	770	29.9
1772	380	697	35.3
1773	467	602	43.9
1774	534	592	46.2
1775	637	405	61.1

Sources: (1) These figures include only servants and slaves of taxable ages. (2) From Gary B. Nash, "Slaves and Slaveowners in Eighteenth-Century Philadelphia," *William and Mary Quarterly*, 30 ser., 30 (1973), 327, Table 64; the number of slaves was reduced by 10 percent to exclude the township of Southwark.

Unlike slavery, indentured servitude in Philadelphia grew steadily after 1763. However, even with the increase in the number of servants the overall proportion of unfree laborers in Philadelphia declined and never again dominated the labor scene as it had from 1730 to 1750. In 1755, when Pennsylvania's participation in the Seven Years' War was already intense, indentured servants virtually disappeared from the unfree labor force in Philadelphia. Because of the disruption of the servant trade and the large number of servant enlistments into the British army, the bound labor force in the city was composed predominantly of slaves. Table 6.2 indicates that by 1767 slaves accounted for 75 percent of the city's unfree workers.

At the end of the hostilities in 1763 merchants resumed the importation of indentured servants and Philadelphia buyers, once again, turned eagerly toward white servants. The number of indentured servants in Philadelphia increased steadily from the end of the war to 1775. During the same period, the city's slave population withered to less than half.[11] The composition of the unfree labor force shifted, and by 1775 more than 60 percent of bound laborers were servants.[12] In 1767 the Philadelphia free labor force numbered about 5,330, with a total unfree labor population of approximately 1,083 (16.9 percent). By 1775, when the city's free work force had increased

11 Ibid., 236.
12 From 1763 to 1775, an average of twenty German and Irish vessels per year, transporting emigrants, deposited settlers in Philadelphia. Ralph B. Strassberger and William J. Hinke, *Pennsylvania German Pioneers, A Publication of the Original Lists of Arrivals in the Port of Philadelphia from 1727 to 1808*, Pennsylvania-German Society Proceedings (Norristown, Pa., 1934) 1:xxix; R. J. Dickson, *Ulster Emigration to Colonial America, 1718–1775 (London, 1966)*, Appendix E.

to almost 7,000, the unfree labor force had decreased to 13 percent of the workers. Philadelphia residents were purchasing servants and slaves at an insufficient rate to maintain the formerly extensive unfree labor force.

The population of unfree labor continued to shrink. Although the slave population dwindled and the number of servants increased, the proportion of unfree workers slipped from almost 10 percent of the total Philadelphia population in 1767 to not quite 7 percent by 1775. During the late colonial period, the proportion of unfree labor in the Quaker capital was in steady decline.

The Revolution caused another hiatus in the servant trade, and the institution of bound labor never recovered. The total number of bound laborers in the city continued to decline while the free population grew. At the outbreak of the war, slightly more than 17 percent of the Philadelphia labor force was unfree. After the Revolution, about 6 percent of the city's work force was unfree; by 1800 unfree workers accounted for barely 1 percent of the port city's labor force. Already in sharp decline after the start of the Seven Years' War, bound labor had become insignificant before the dawn of the new century.

The decline of European indentured servitude was not the result of any opposition leveled against the institution. No evidence suggests that servants or masters organized against indentured labor. For servants, the institution appeared to fulfill the promise of transporting poor people voluntarily to the New World. These white immigrant laborers quarreled with individual masters but made no concerted effort to change or overthrow the system.[13] And although the system of indentured servitude was fraught with difficulties throughout its colonial history, owners expressed little antagonism toward it. Masters and ship captains complained of the troublesome nature of women servants and at one time or another lambasted the Irish, German, and Scottish servants. But Pennsylvania residents continued to purchase servants, even though many absconded, especially during wartime. Indentured servitude was perpetuated even during marginal economic periods when owners were required to maintain the unfree worker or find a buyer.

Tax and other laws governing the institution of indentured servitude cannot account for the decreasing proportion of bound labor in the population. Unlike slavery, indentured servitude experienced no change in its legal structure throughout this period. No prohibitive duties were imposed to discourage investments in servants, nor were laws passed to

---

13 J. Franklin Jameson does not mention the abolition of indentured servitude as a democratic reform during the revolutionary period. *The American Revolution Considered as a Social Movement* (Boston, 1926).

make the institution less attractive to employers.[14] Furthermore, the price of an indentured servant appears to have been stable throughout the latter half of the colonial period and slightly lower, owing to declining transportation costs, in the postrevolutionary period. The average price for one year of an indentured servant's time was 3.06 pounds in 1745 and 4.45 pounds in 1775, but the gentle inflationary trend of the period largely accounts for this difference.[15] After the Revolution, the price for one year of a servant's time declined. By 1785 it cost only 4.1 pounds for a year of work.[16] Clearly, the costs of servants did not prohibit continued investment, nor can they account for the decline in the proportion of unfree labor in the city's labor force.

Finally, the proportion of unfree workers in the city after the Seven Years' War did not decline owing to problems of servant supply. In 1760, after a hiatus caused by the war, the Scots-Irish immigration resumed, and beginning in 1763, ships from the Palatinate also brought passengers to Philadelphia. The emigration from northern Ireland reached its height in the 1770s, and most of these migrants went to Philadelphia.[17] The size of the German immigration into Philadelphia did not approach its midcentury volume, but the stream was steady from 1763 to the Revolution. It is difficult to assess the ratio beween paying and nonpaying passengers among these immigrant groups, but the main sources of servant supply in previous

14 Darold D. Wax, "The Slave Trade in Colonial Pennsylvania" (Ph.D. diss., University of Washington, 1962), 42. Maldwyn Jones reports that "the only branch of the servant trade which was brought to an end by American action was convict transportation in 1788." Jones claims that Pennsylvania passed a law in the 1780s to encourage the growth of indentured servitude. In 1782 a law was passed to establish a register of all German passengers and all indentured servants along with the assignments of servants. However, it is not clear how this law encouraged emigration of servants. *American Immigration* (Chicago, 1960), p. 67. See also James T. Mitchell and Harry Flanders, comps., *The Statutes at Large of Pennsylvania from 1682 to 1801* (Harrisburg, Pa., 1906), 11:602–4.

15 Anne Bezanson reports that, except for two low points in 1765 and 1769, the prerevolutionary era was characterized by "well-sustained high prices." "Inflation and Controls, Pennsylvania, 1774–1779," *JEH*, suppl. 7 (1948), 1–2.

16 "Registry of Redemptioners, 1785–1803," manuscript, AM 3791, HSP. The cost per year was calculated by averaging the price with the length of indenture.

17 Dickson, *Ulster Emigration*, 62. Heavy emigration from Ulster was at its height in 1772 and 1773. Cited in Luther Harr, Jr., "The Status of Labor in Colonial Pennsylvania," (M.A. thesis, Temple University, 1948). Cheeseman Herrick corroborates this view. "In the five years from 1769 to 1774, an average of 8,740 persons left five Irish ports alone." Scotland appears to have sent a large number and England too sent emigrants to Pennsylvania, "but perhaps fewer in numbers." *White Servitude in Pennsylvania: Indentured Labor in the Colony and Commonwealth* (Freeport, N.Y., 1926; reprint, Freeport, N.Y., 1970), 167. Herrick's research led him to believe that the bulk of the passengers coming through the port of Philadelphia were poor and probably had to resort to selling their services in order to pay their passages.

years, northern Ireland and the German Palatinate, continued to send people into the colony.

Merchants' correspondence reveals also that servant supply was not a significant factor in the declining bound labor force during the late colonial period. In 1769 James and Drinker indicated that they were having difficulty selling their latest shipment of servants. They had sold six servants at about sixteen pounds each, they wrote, "and shall use our best endeavors to sell the remainder, though we fear we shall have but poor successer."[18] Writing to his correspondent in Liverpoole in 1772, William Pollard indicated a similar difficulty: "I have sold the blacksmith and his wife's indenture for 36 pounds, but have not been able yet to dispose of the others."[19] This report of difficulty in selling servants contrasts sharply with letters in 1765. Philadelphia merchant Benjamin Marshall explained that because of the "Cruel and Oppressive Stamp Act laid on the American Colonys," it would be impossible to carry on business as usual. However, he continued, "the chief articles that answer here from Ireland which can be bought are Linnens, Beef, Butter, Men, Women & Boys Servants."[20] Clearly, problems of demand, rather than supply, account for the decline in the bound labor force before the Revolution.[21]

The decline in the number of unfree laborers in Philadelphia after the Revolution, unlike that in the late colonial period, could have been caused both by problems of servant supply and by a movement to halt the indentured servant trade. The abrupt closure of trade between America and England, the wholesale enlistment of servants in the army and navy, and the cessation of servant importation help to explain the shrinking servant population from 869 in 1775 to only 215 in 1780. But after the Peace of

---

18 James and Drinker to Lancelot Cowper, May 19, 1769, James and Drinker Letter Book, HSP.
19 Letter Book of William Pollard, 1772–4, 79, HSP. This shipment of servants arrived with Captain William Williams on the Brig *Venus,* which entered the port of Philadelphia two weeks earlier on September 23, 1772.
20 Benjamin Marshall to Thomas Murphy, November 9, 1765, "Extracts from the Letter Book of Benjamin Marshall," *PMHB* 20 (1896), 209.
21 David Galenson argues that the disappearance of indentured servitude from the American labor force occurred in the Chesapeake toward the end of the seventeenth century with the shift to slavery. In the other regions, indentured labor died out at the end of the eighteenth century. Galenson attributes the decline to the disruptive effects the Revolution had on immigration and on the "low level of economic stimulus to immigration." The Revolution did halt the flow of immigration. However, unfree labor was on the decline before the Revolution. Galenson claims that, when immigration picked up after 1820, the low costs of transatlantic transportation limited the need for indenture. *White Servitude in Colonial America: An Economic Analysis* (New York, 1981), 179–80. Galenson is more persuasive here. However, in the case of Pennsylvania, the end of servitude resulted equally from diminished demand.

Paris, a sizable number of immigrants reached the shores of Pennsylvania.[22] Most of these arrivals were Scots-Irish, and although the volume was not as large as in the early 1770s, this wave of immigration was quite regular. The movement was short-lived, however. Beginning around 1786, immigration declined sharply, picked up in the 1790s, but did not become regular until after the War of 1812.[23]

After the Revolution, the British moved to halt the servant trade. Phineas Bond, the British consul stationed in Philadelphia, seems to have been partly responsible for the success of the anti-servant-trade movement. Bond spent considerable energy urging the government to regulate the emigrating stream of both free and bound individuals. During the 1780s, he hoped that emigration to America would be checked because of the "severity experienced by redemptioners and indentured servants."[24] He was concerned that the new American Constitution "may tempt greater numbers to follow." Controlling emigration would protect those who might leave their homes and "discover only too late the misery in which they are involved."[25] The emigration from northern Ireland was of primary concern to Bond because more servants emigrated from Ireland to the United States than from all the other parts of Europe combined. Bond feared that the lure of America would drain "the British kingdom of many useful and labourous inhabitants." Worse yet, America was deriving vast benefit from this population movement through the introduction of manufacturing while Great Britain and Ireland "suffer a severe depopulation."[26]

Two British acts were passed as a result of the movement to halt the emigrant stream. The first, in 1788, extended to Ireland the ban on the emigration of skilled artisans. The second, the British Passenger Act of 1803, limited the number of immigrants each ship could carry. This greatly reduced the profits for ships' captains, and they ceased recruiting cargoes of servants.[27] Together these acts dealt the final blow to the indentured servant trade from Great Britain, Pennsylvania's primary source of servants.

Through the last decade of the eighteenth century, Germany remained the only potential supply of servants. Redemptioners continued to trickle into

22 Jones, *American Immigration*, 65–6.
23 Marcus Lee Hanson, *The Atlantic Migration, 1607–1860* (New York, 1960), 53–4. Jones reports that the annual arrivals to America averaged about six thousand after the Peace of Paris. During the 1790s more than ten thousand arrived annually, but during the Napoleonic Wars the number of arrivals declined to only three thousand. Jones, *American Immigration*, 65.
24 J. Franklin Jameson, ed., "Letters of Phineas Bond, British Consul at Philadelphia, to the Foreign Office of Great Britian 1787, 1788, 1789," in *Annual Report of the American Historical Association 1896 and 1897* (Washington, 1897, 1898), 582.
25 Ibid., *1896*, 582.
26 Ibid., *1897*, 488.
27 Jones, *American Immigration*, 67–8.

the state until the Napoleonic Wars. When peace returned in 1815, the trade revived, but only until 1819, when Congress passed a passenger act in response to an epidemic on an overcrowded passenger ship from Rotterdam in 1818. After that, the trade in German redemptioners ceased as well.[28]

Ironically, the broad-based movement to manumit slaves in Philadelphia and the surrounding region produced a recrudescence of the system of indentured servitude as hundreds of former slaves were bound. Indenturing of blacks was slight in the years before the Revolution and from 1754 to 1775 never totaled more than three per year. From 1783 to the end of the decade, the rate of indentures jumped, due entirely to indentures from the House of Employment and averaged about 30 per year.[29]

The indenturing of blacks reached its height in the mid-1790s. From mid-1791 through 1793, waves of French planters from Santo Domingo appeared in Philadelphia, having fled "from the violence unleashed by the French National Assembly's decree granting political rights to all free-born mulatoes." Contemporaries estimated that by 1792 two hundred families had taken refuge in the port city, and by November 1793 an additional four hundred persons had arrived.[30] These planters landed in the port city with about five hundred slaves and tried unsuccessfully to persuade the Pennsylvania legislature to exempt them from the 1780 law, which stipulated freedom for any slave six months after arriving in the state. Their pleas fell on deaf ears. However, these masters managed to forestall the loss of their slaves by manumitting and then immediately indenturing them.

This practice, of indenturing recently manumitted slaves, was challenged in the courts by the Pennsylvania Abolition Society. The society argued that this practice violated the spirit of the 1780 abolition law. However, in 1794, in *Respublica v. Gaoler*, the Pennsylvania Supreme Court upheld the planters' rights to indenture their former slaves. With this flood of recently manumitted French West Indian slaves, indentures in Philadelphia escalated and from 1792 to 1796 fluctuated between 107 and 305. The rate of indentures tapered off after this but remained above 100 through 1801. From 1802 to 1810, the range of indentures fell further and vacillated between 35 and 84.[31]

---

28 Ibid., 68. The decline in unfree labor during this period was not caused by a shift in the use of unfree labor. Philadelphia residents continued to account for the overwhelming majority of the redemptioners indentured in the city after the Revolution. "Registry of Redemptioners, 1785–1803."

29 Guardians of the Poor Records, HSP. Gary B. Nash kindly made this manuscript material available to me. I worked from the microfilmed copy of the collection.

30 Catherine A. Hebert, "The French Element in Pennsylvania in the 1790's: The Francophone Immigrants' Impact," *PMHB* 108 (1984), 451–2.

31 Kutler, "Pennsylvania Courts," 23; Edward Raymond Turner, *The Negro in Pennsylvania: Slavery – Servitude – Freedom, 1639–1861* (New York, 1911; reprint, New York, 1969), 93–4. Rochefoucault Liancourt spent about four months in Philadelphia during this period

The most striking aspect of the new brand of servitude was the length of indenture. The ninety-one individuals indentured by the Philadelphia House of Employment from 1782 to 1810 owed their masters a total of 1,213 years, or an average indenture of more than 13 years. The remaining 2,454 blacks indentured by the Pennsylvania Abolition Society were to serve for an average of 10.6 years. The long indentures reflect, in part, the huge number of young blacks. For example, on September 8, 1783, two-year-old Sally was indentured for 16 years to Hester Eastburn. She was to be taught reading and housewifery, and to receive freedom dues. Betty was two years and nine months old on January 13, 1783, when she was indentured to Col. Christian Frebigeo. Betty was expected to spend the next 25 years and three months serving the Frebigeo family, and at the end of that time she, too, was to have learned to read, to have mastered the art of housewifery, and to have received freedom dues.[32]

The presence of many young people cannot account for the enormous number of years blacks owed their masters. Sampson, for example, was twenty-four in December 1783 when he was bound for seven years to Dr. Thomas Elder. On December 22, 1783, William Smith, a Philadelphia merchant, indentured eighteen-year-old Nancy for ten years.[33] A fifty-year-old female was indentured in 1793 and expected to serve seven years.[34] In 1795 two unnamed males, one eighteen and the other twenty, were indentured for twenty and eighteen years, repsectively.[35]

The laws provide some clues about the length of indenture, but even they do not explain the variations in the number of years blacks were forced to serve. The laws required that former slaves be indentured until the age of twenty-eight. If a former slave was over the age of twenty-one, she or he was to serve seven years. Clearly, masters were able, on occasion, to circumvent the laws and indenture their former slaves for longer periods. One master even went so far as to try to take his servants to New York when their term of service expired. A Philadelphia judge ordered their return.[36] It appears that masters were incapable of treating these former slaves as anything other than slaves and attempted to extract the maximum number of years. For these former slaves, servitude was an extension of slavery.

and remarked that former slaves were brought before the magistrates and indentured until the age twenty-one or twenty-eight. He claimed that the consent of blacks was required or they were declared free. *Travels Through the United States of North America . . . in the Years 1795, 1796, and 1797* (London, 1799) 2:355. See also Guardians of the Poor Records.

32 Philadelphia's House of Employment Indenture Papers in Pennsylvania Abolition Society Papers, HSP.
33 Ibid.
34 Ibid., book C.
35 Ibid., book D.
36 Finkelman, *Imperfect Union*, 56.

Both the sex ratio of black servants and the occupational profile of their owners reveal that this phase of indentured labor did not reverse the general patterns already in place in unfree labor. Black servants, like European servants, appear to have worked primarily in domestic service. Overall, males accounted for 55 percent of the indentures from 1754 to 1810. However, in many years, the sex ratio was virtually equal. And in the years 1783, 1784, 1797, and 1802, indentured females outnumbered males. Since no change occurred in the attitudes about the sexual division of labor, the large proportion of black female servants strongly suggests that they labored in domestic service.

In addition, the pattern of ownership of black servants reaffirms the declining importance of unfree labor in artisanal production during the late eighteenth century. Philadelphia's elite continued to dominate as the owners of indentured blacks. Fewer than 30 percent of the urban taxables were identified as merchant-retailers or professionals, yet almost 44 percent of the owners were from these occupational sectors. And although almost 44 percent of the city's taxables were artisans, they accounted for less than 40 percent of the owners. Even this proportion is misleadingly high because so many of the black servants were young and women and, even in the service of artisans, most likely to work as domestic laborers.

The continuing decline of the proportion of unfree labor in the post-revolutionary period, a decline that began at the end of the Seven Years' War when the supply of indentured servants was high, was primarily the result of demand. The city's employers shifted from the consistent use of bound labor to that of wage labor. In the 1760s, for the first time in the colony's history, Philadelphia did not suffer from the pressures of a labor shortage. Employers were no longer required to purchase labor in three- to four-year packages or for the life of the worker. From a growing population of poor and unemployed, Philadelphia employers could hire and fire workers as economic necessity dictated. The labor picture in Philadelphia changed. Instead of labor shortage, which had created incentives for the system of unfree labor, there was labor surplus, which began to render such a system obsolete.

The labor surplus was created by a combination of factors. The port city's population grew markedly after the end of the Seven Years' War. From about 22,000 people in 1765, the city mushroomed to nearly 32,000 ten years later.[37] However, this population spurt was accompanied by an

37 Gary B. Nash, "Up From the Bottom in Franklin's Philadelphia," *Past and Present*, no. 77 (1977), 65. For the most recent population figures for eighteenth-century Phildelphia" see John K. Alexander, "The Philadelphia Numbers Game: An Analysis of Philadelphia's Eighteenth-Century Population," *PMHB*, 98 (1974), 321; Gary B. Nash and Billy G. Smith, "The Population of Eighteenth-Century Philadelphia," *PMHB* 99 (1975), 365; Sharon V. Salinger and Charles Wetherell, "A Note on the Population of Prerevolutionary

increase in the number of poor and unemployed residents, because while the city grew, the economy developed unevenly and many laborers were affected negatively. For an increasingly large segment of the population, the economic outlook was grim. After the midcentury, prices fluctuated but followed an upward trend.[38] The war against the French accelerated the price rise. Philadelphia residents basked in economic well-being as they reaped the benefits of lucrative war contracts. But after the peace, the upward movement of prices was interrupted by severe periods of depression, with prices reaching low points in 1765 and 1769. The depression forced a number of businesses to close.[39]

When the depression hit in 1765, substantial unemployment occurred and work for many of the city's artisans dried up. For the first time since the recession of 1722–5 an undersupply of labor had become an oversupply. In 1766 the Philadelphia Grand Jury reported that "the labouring people and others in low circumstances . . . who are willing to work, cannot obtain sufficient Employ to support themselves and their Families." A report also revealed that "Employment for labouring People and Money is uncommonly scarce."[40] For the city's laborers, the economic climate had moved far away from the days of unlimited opportunity and high wages.

During the decade of the sixties, poverty hounded the city. Ten percent of Philadelphia's adult population could be counted as impoverished and another group had to send the tax collector away because of insufficient resources. Until 1760, fewer than 7 percent of the taxable population were unable to afford their tax; but in the fifteen years after 1760, this proportion climbed to more than 10 percent. More striking, by 1772 "about three-fifths of the carters, porters, breechesmakers, bricklayers, and cordwainers, and one-eighth of the gardeners, blacksmiths, barbers, and joiners were identified as poor" in the Philadelphia records.[41]

Not only were the ranks of the poor swelling, but the chances for reversing the economic hardships were dwindling. Contemporary Philadelphians reveal that the problems former servants faced in getting off the bottom of the economic ladder coincided with a growing number of poor and unemployed residents. In 1764 the "want of Employment . . . was reducing a large number of residents to great Straits." The Philadelphia Grand Jury proclaimed two years later that "many . . . People who are

---

Philadelphia," *PMHB* 109 (1985), 369–86.

38 Anne Bezanson, Robert D. Gray, and Miriam Hussey, *Prices in Colonial Pennsylvania* (Philadelphia, 1935). Chapter 1 discusses the price levels for wheat, flour, and bread in the 1760s. See especially 40–4.

39 Gary B. Nash, *The Urban Crucible: Social Change, Political Consciousness, and the Origins of the American Revolution* (Cambridge, Mass., 1979), 319.

40 Quoted in ibid.

41 Nash, "Up From the Bottom," 66.

willing to work cannot obtain sufficient Employment."[42] Thus for the first time in the Quaker city's history, labor scarcity ceased to be an issue. The city now coped with the burden of caring for a large number of poor and unemployed. Employers in need of labor had a choice. They could buy unfree workers from an ample supply of immigrant laborers that had existed since before the Revolution, or they could hire wage laborers from the growing pool of unemployed colonists.

The post–Seven Years' War economy reduced many artisans to a marginal state. Even in the brightest of economic periods, artisans could never be assured of steady employment. Seasonal shifts in demand, material shortages, and the cyclical nature of the money market were the artisans' constant companions.[43] In 1769 Benjamin Rush remarked that tradesmen had many difficulties since few were employed the "whole year around" because of the fluctuating consumer demand.[44] Thus even when the city suffered no economic setbacks, the less established artisan's existence was precarious. But in the late colonial period, the periodic depressions hit many artisans especially hard.

Changes in the labor market increasingly favored free over unfree labor. Early on, artisans purchased the time of an identured servant or bought a slave when wages for free laborers were high and workers were scarce. These unfree workers were a sound investment. At midcentury, employers paid free journeymen annual wages of about thirty-five pounds, assuming that a worker could be found.[45] In contrast, during the same period the cost of a skilled male servant averaged about seventeen pounds for a four-year indenture payable in cash but sometimes in flour, with occasional short-term credit available.[46] The price of an adult male slave averaged forty to fifty pounds.[47] Owners of bound workers had to assume the risk of illness or death and were required to provide room and board. However, room entailed no additional costs. The provision of space probably required no more than a bit of pushing and shoving of furniture to make sleeping space on the floor. Female servants often placed their mats at the foot of

42 Quoted in ibid., 71.

43 This discussion draws heavily from Nash, *Urban Crucible*, 312–38. See also Gary B. Nash, "Artisans and Politics in Eighteenth-Century Philadelphia," in *The Craftsman in Early America*, ed. Ian Quimby (Winterthur, Del., 1984), 64.

44 Quoted in Nash, *Urban Crucible*, 319.

45 Roger W. Moss, "Master Builders: A History of the Colonial Philadelphia Building Trade," (M.A. thesis, University of Delaware, 1972), 144.

46 Sharon V. Salinger, "Labor and Indentured Servants in Colonial Pennsylvania," (Ph.D. diss., University of California, Los Angeles, 1980), 177.

47 Nash, "Slaves and Slaveowners," 228, n. 12. The actual cost of slaves fluctuated greatly because varying rates of import duty were added to the purchase cost.

their mistress's bed.[48] Estimates suggest that food for an adult male laborer cost about ten pounds per year.[49] Thus barring unforeseen problems and even including the costs of provisions and bed, servants and slaves were far cheaper than free wage laborers.

By the late colonial period and especially during the years following the Revolution, bound labor lost its financial attractiveness. During the last three decades of the eighteenth century, the price for one year of a servant's time rose to an average cost of ten pounds and five shillings.[50] In addition, the costs of maintaining servants rose because food prices escalated "gradually until the outbreak of the Revolutionary War."[51] Meanwhile, wage labor became less expensive. During the same period, wages among the city's least skilled laborers actually declined, and those of other workers barely kept pace with rising prices. In 1769 the daily wage for laborers averaged a mere three shillings in Philadelphia, and in the early 1770s workers could not earn even that much.[52] Wages continued at these low levels after the Revolution. Cordwainers were paid at a stable rate during the early 1770s, but their real wages declined in 1783 and did not rise substantially until 1792. Similarly, Philadelphia's tailors experienced a decline in real wages after the war, and their income did not rise perceptibly through the more prosperous decade of the 1790s.[53] Journeymen printers suffered an even more protracted slide. Their wages remained stagnant throughout the second half of the eighteenth century.[54]

Two other incentives encouraged the shift to free labor: a decreasing amount of capital for investment in bound labor and a vacillating economy that demanded a more flexible labor system. During the late colonial period economic difficulties plagued Philadelphia, and investment in unfree labor became less feasible for a substantial portion of the artisan community as well as less economical for those still in need of and able to afford additional labor. The economic contraction after the Seven Years' War diminished the capital that city master mechanics had available to invest in labor. More important, however, along with the economic incentives for switching to wage labor was the more plentiful and reliable supply of free workers as wages decreased and mobility narrowed. The same economic constraints that limited servant mobility limited the number of Philadelphians who

48 Elizabeth Drinker Diary, August 11, 1794, HSP.
49 Billy G. Smith, "The Material Lives of Laboring Philadelphians, 1750–1800," WMQ, 3d Ser., 38 (1981), 171.
50 "Registry of Redemptioners," September 10, 1795.
51 Smith," Material Lives" 174–5.
52 Nash, *Urban Crucible*, 323.
53 Smith, "Material Lives," 194, 200.
54 Rollo G. Silver, *The American Printer, 1787–1825* (Charlottesville, Va., 1967), 14.

were able to establish themselves as independent artisans. Instead they were forced to join the ranks of permanent wage laborers, thereby swelling those ranks considerably.[55]

By the 1760s, free labor best served the needs of Philadelphia's artisans. Economic instability made it far more practical to hire short-term labor than to maintain a bound labor force. Accordingly, since wage rates had fallen below the cost of unfree labor and the uncertain economy encouraged the use of a flexible labor system at a time when the supply of wage labor was favorable, master craftsmen altered their labor practices and came to rely more consistently on free workers.

55 The split between masters and journeymen artisans was accompanied by economic stratification. Nash traces in elegant detail the impoverishment of a large portion of the Philadelphia population. "Penury was the lot of a growing segment of the community and economic insecurity hovered at the doors of many more." Nash finds many indices to support this strong statement: Poor taxes rose, the number and population of institutions for the poor grew after midcentury, forced property sales and imprisonment for debt increased, and societies were formed to administer aid to the swelling ranks of the poor. During this period, master craftsmen continued to maintain economic security and in some cases added to their assets; but by 1772, 17 percent of Philadelphia cordwainers were receiving some sort of poor relief, and 13 percent of the city's clothing workers were on the dole. Even within the better organized building trades, about one in ten workers received some sort of aid. Nash explains that this growing poverty was caused by a number of factors. After 1760, wages failed to keep pace with costs. To compound the difficulties, unemployment rose, especially in 1765–6, 1767–70, and 1774–5 during the periods of nonimportation. *Urban Crucible,* 317–26.

Epilogue: The transformation of labor

THE TRANSITION FROM UNFREE TO FREE LABOR altered labor relations in Philadelphia. As a result both the lives of workers and the organization of production changed dramatically. For workers, wage labor was often synonymous with vulnerability. During most of the colonial period, when free workers were in short supply, their wages were high and their choices great. When high employment shifted to labor surplus, wage earners suffered. A large number of workers scrambled for fewer jobs. Wages fell. Employment periods were often short, which caused incomes to be insecure. These effects of industrialization on workers' lives usually associated with industrialization were in place in Philadelphia during the late colonial period.

Former eighteenth-century servants were forced to make their way as free laborers just when this new system was forming. Their inability to succeed mirrored the difficulties of many urban wage earners. No precise dates can be attached to the process. However, after the Seven Years' War, when bound workers constituted fewer than 20 percent of the labor force, glimmerings of this new employer–employee relationship were evident.

As the paternalistic labor system was replaced by the more consistent use of wage earners, the outward unanimity of craft production collapsed. One result of this alteration in labor was that craft organizations appeared. In the prerevolutionary period, labor alliances existed but they were primarily groups of master craftsmen who organized to shore up their waning economic independence during increasingly hard times. These master mechanics sought legal controls over the prices and quality of their raw materials and occasionally over the wages of their journeymen.

The Revolution disrupted these activities. When mechanics met after the war, their societies bore little resemblance to their colonial predecessors. They articulated the increasing distance between themselves and master mechanics. Masters continued to belong to exclusive groups. However, journeymen formed their own alliances, and during the 1780s and 1790s labor disputes became endemic. Only after considerable debate were compromises reached and calm restored. Labor relations had changed perceptibly in Philadelphia.

As master craftsmen moved away from consistent use of unfree labor, their roles within their establishments changed. Prosperous Philadelphia master craftsmen donned their leather aprons and picked up their tools less often. Instead, they became primarily employers and merchant capitalists. This transformation began in the late colonial period and extended into the nineteenth century.

Colonial craftsmen tended to make their products on custom order. This bespoke product was crafted with the artisan's own tools within his work space, and production centered around household labor. As craftsmen moved away from custom work, they purchased labor either in the form of servants and slaves, or occasionally, in the form of journeymen. If the shop produced a surplus, the role of the master craftsman shifted subtly as he combined his craft skills with the jobs of retailer and employer. The productive unit remained within the household, but now combined under the workshop roof were perhaps an apprentice or two, bound servants, maybe a slave, and family members, wife, sons, and daughters. In the final stage of production before the emergence of a factory system, successful master craftsmen spent increasingly less time at the workbench and more effort buying and selling. And as the supply of free workers became more plentiful and less expensive, masters paid wages to their employees more often than they purchased the time of a servant or slave. Many master craftsmen moved to the status of employer and merchant capitalist.[1]

The careers of some successful Philadelphia artisans enable us to trace this process—the initial reliance on bound workers and the shift from bound to free labor. Peter January and Pressly Blackeston were both successful Philadelphia shoemakers. When the tax assessor made his rounds in 1767, January had not yet acquired any taxable property, although both his occupation and his possession of two apprentices suggest that he was a master shoemaker. By 1775 January's business had expanded sufficiently to enable him to purchase the indentures of six servants.[2] In addition, he hired a female servant, bringing his labor force, excluding his family, to nine—two apprentices, six bound servants, and a hired servant. January's business flourished, although five years later, after he had reaped the benefits of the wartime economy and purchased one slave, indentured servants no longer

---

1 For a complete description of this process and a review of the relevant literature see Alan Dawley, *Class and Community: The Industrial Revolution in Lynn* (Cambridge, Mass., 1976), 32.

2 Philadelphia County Provincial Tax, 1767, Rare Book Room, Van Pelt Library, University of Pennsylvania. "List of Servants and Apprentices Bound and Assigned before John Gibson, Mayor of Philadelphia, May 1771 to May 1773," manuscript, AM 3795, HSP; Constables' Returns to the Assessor, 1775, City Archives, Philadelphia.

appeared on his list of taxable property. If he used additional workers, he hired them. Moreover, January no longer considered himself a cordwainer. He gave his occupation as merchant.[3]

Blackeston followed a very similar career pattern. Like January he had achieved master status by 1772 and invested heavily in unfree labor. He owned six indentured servants before the Revolution. Blackeston was not located on the 1780 tax list, but at the end of the war his unfree labor force shrank from six to one. He too changed his occupational category from shoemaker to contractor.[4]

Francis Trumble invested heavily in bound labor before the Revolution, and his career demonstrates even more forcefully the transformation in labor systems. The 1756 tax roll listed Trumble as a joiner and a resident of Dock Ward. By 1772 he had moved to Southwark and purchased his own home; his personal property had increased to include three slaves and two servants. In that year he purchased the time of yet another servant. Thus in addition to his family, six bound workers resided in his household. At the outbreak of the Revolution, Trumble advertised the sale of three indentured servants; each had almost four years to serve. At the same time, he sought to replace these bound laborers with wage earners, for he announced that he had work available for four journeymen skilled in making spinning wheels.[5] Significantly, not only were Trumble's workers hired for wages and boarded apart from his household, but his house and shop were no longer contiguous. Although he still lived on Second Street in Southwark, his cabinet and chair store was located several blocks away on Front Street near Pine. Like January and Blackeston, Trumble had relied heavily on unfree workers during the early years of his career, but he too, in the period just before the Revolution, turned to hired labor.[6]

The transition to wage labor and the new roles assumed by master craftsmen were achieved in a far less orderly fashion than these biographical sketches would indicate. Capitalist wage labor altered productive relations in significant ways, had an enormous impact on the work environment, and exacerbated the effects of an uneven economy since a larger share of the work force labored for wages. Scattered evidence from artisan shops suggests that the postrevolutionary work place was characterized by higher turnover than its colonial counterpart. Certainly wage earners existed in the city throughout the colonial period. However, as they dominated labor,

3 Philadelphia County Provincial Tax, 1780, City Archives, Philadelphia.
4 Ibid., 1772, 1780, 1785, 1790.
5 Trumble's personal property was assessed at thirty-six pounds. Hannah Benner Roach, comp., "Taxables in the City of Philadelphia, 1756," *PGM* 22 (1961), 3–41; Philadelphia County Provincial Tax, 1772, City Archives, Philadelphia; "List of Servants and Apprentices, 1771 to 1773."
6 *Pennsylvania Gazette*, January 3, 1776.

work conditions changed. In the late colonial and early national periods, most wage earners never stayed at one job long enough to develop a close working relationship with their masters. Those who worked in Joshua Humphrey's shipyards, for example, averaged less than a few months on the job. Between 1794 and 1797, Humphrey employed more than thirty-five men. Only John Grimes, Daniel McCalla, Andrew McBride, Isaac Reilly, and Thomas Cooper were counted by the foreman for at least three years of labor and were on the job more than half the working days of the average month. The majority were typified by C. Maier, who worked half a day in October 1797, and the slightly more regular Babbit, who put in an average of seven days per month during 1796.[7] Humphrey's shipyard was hardly conducive to the building of stable relationships.

Transience characterized the journeymen's experiences in smaller work places as well. When Isaac Zane's apprentices finished their terms and he switched to wage laborers, his journeymen rotated through his shop almost by the month.[8] The turnover rates in cabinetmaker David Evans's shop were similar. He employed at least seven journeymen from the time he opened his shop in 1774 until the outbreak of the Revolution. Over the course of his career he hired no fewer than seventeen workmen.[9] From 1795 to 1803, cabinetmaker Samuel Ashton had five positions, yet forty-nine journeymen worked in his shop, averaging 145 days apiece. The variation in work days ranged from the 5 that David Fryer worked in 1801 to the 452 for which Ashton employed Pennel Beale between 1791 and 1792.[10] The records of these successful Philadelphia masters, regardless of their crafts, depict shops in which journeymen came and went with great frequency.[11]

7 Of these journeymen, only John Grimes was located in the Philadelphia directory. It is possible that he was a master craftsman, whereas the others were journeymen. Grimes was identified as a mastmaker. [Thomas Stephens], *Stevens's Philadelphia Directory, for 1796* ... [Philadelphia, 1796].

8 The apprentices inherited by Zane finished out their terms by 1752, and Zane replaced them with journeymen. First hired was Robert Miller, who was to be paid twenty-seven pounds per year plus board, but his employment with Zane lasted only one month, one week, and two days. Next, Zane signed on a former Davis apprentice, William Crage, and a year later he hired Silas Engles at four shillings per day "with the journeyman supplying his own food and lodging." Two years later Zane hired an additional five journeymen. One, Jacob Austin, stayed only "3 mo. wanting five days," and a second worker died after a few months. Roger W. Moss, "Master Builders: A History of Colonial Philadelphia Building Trades" (M.A. thesis, University of Delaware, 1972), 143.

9 David Hunter, "David Evans, Cabinet Maker, His Life and Work" (M.A. thesis, University of Delaware, 1954), 14–20.

10 Morrison H. Heckscher, "The Organization and Practice of Philadelphia Cabinetmaking Establishments, 1790–1820" (M.A. thesis, University of Delaware, 1964), 20, 24, 25.

11 Samuel Williamson ran a modest-sized silversmithing business during the first decades of the nineteenth century. Williamson employed eleven craftsmen in the year 1811 alone, and

Because of the traffic in and out of these shops, they resembled inns far more than the settings associated with the paternalistic labor system. When artisans became employers, and journeymen supplanted servants and slaves, the time each worker remained in a shop decreased. Slaves were bound for life and servants' terms were fixed at four or five years, but free workers passed through fleetingly, collected their meager wages, gathered up their tools, and moved on in search of the next job. Zane's shop was unusual for the colonial period because he relied heavily on free workers. By the dawn of the new century, this dizzying movement of workers characterized the artisan work place. Such turnover not only precluded stable work relationships but helped define labor as a commodity to be hired and fired as consumer demand dictated.

Short employment periods contributed to a high rate of geographic mobility among journeymen. Sparse records make it difficult to draw reliable conclusions, but the evidence suggests that workers shifted from shop to shop because they were forced to seek new work. Admittedly, movement itself does not imply that job possibilities were scarce – workers conceivably followed opportunity. However, other indicators reveal that the frenetic movement of workers in late-eighteenth-century Philadelphia resulted from the lack of opportunity. These circumstances were not new for journeymen, but as unfree labor died out and free laborers constituted a larger proportion of the work force, these circumstances characterized Philadelphia labor.

The ultimate obscurity of free workers suggests that, like freed servants, they could not be located because they lacked economic substance. As they switched their places of employment, they moved from residence to residence in the city. Journeymen also traveled from city to city, and they moved far and often. In the 1790s advertisements in the Northampton, Massachusetts, and Charleston, South Carolina, newspapers announced the opening of cabinetmaking shops owned and operated by individuals who had labored as journeymen in Philadelphia.[12] Also suggestive of the movement out of Philadelphia is the futility of trying to locate Philadelphia journeymen among the lists of city residents. They rarely appear on tax assessment rolls or in city directories. Only three of the seventeen journeymen employed by David Evans ever paid an occupational tax in

the number of journeymen in his shop varied from a low of six in 1807 to a high of twelve in 1810. Ellen Beasley, "Samuel Williamson, Philadelphia Silversmith, 1794–1813" (M.A. thesis, University of Delaware, 1964), 15.

12 *Hampshire Gazette* (Northampton, Mass.), April 8, 1795; *South-Carolina State-Gazette and Timothy and Mason's Daily Advertiser* (Charleston), April 23, 1796; *Charleston Gazette, 1796*, in Charles F. Montgomery, *American Furniture: The Federal Period in the Henry Francis du Pont Winterthur Museum* (New York, 1966), 16.

Philadelphia.[13] Although thirty-eight men worked in the Humphrey ship yard from 1794 to 1797, only five can be positively located in Philadelphia directories.[14] Of Samuel Ashton's forty-nine employees, twenty-six can be found in the city directories, but most of these men were listed many years after they had worked for Ashton. Perhaps these craftsmen were omitted from the directories and tax lists until they reached master status.[15] More likely, however, their elusiveness suggests that they moved often.

The boarding patterns of journeymen corroborate this picture of instability. Of those who labored for Samuel Ashton, slightly more than half (57 percent) lived with him for some period of time. However, only half of these (twenty-three of thirty-four) remained in his home for their full period of employment.[16] The rest boarded with him intermittently. Since workers averaged only 145 days in Ashton's employ, there must have been considerable movement in and out of his house. For example, between 1798 and 1802, Samuel Howell, a journeyman cabinetmaker, put in three stints of work for Ashton totaling 479 work days. He resided in Ashton's house three times, even though none of his boarding periods coincided exactly with his employment periods and he stayed for only 294 days. Thomas Nap spent two months as a carver and gilder in Ashton's shop but boarded with him for only two days. Upholsterer Samuel Davis worked for Ashton for 707 days and moved into the house four different times.[17] Similarly, during the two-year period in which Thomas Janvier did cabinetwork for Daniel Trotter, he moved in and out twice. Janvier had come to Philadelphia from Maryland just before he began his time with Trotter, and he returned to the Chesapeake region soon after he left Trotter's employ.[18] Boarding was a remnant of paternalism, but unlike the live-in arrangement typical of the servant or slave, living with one's employer did not necessarily provide security. The brevity of the stay and the constant moving about prevented journeymen from being incorporated into the shop routine, let alone the life of the family. If persistence is a measure of stability the lives of Philadelphia's peripatetic journeymen were far from stable.

In addition to promoting labor turnover and residential mobility, the transition to free labor resulted in uncertainty of income for workers. No standard form of payment existed during this early period of wage labor. Samuel Ashton paid the typical wage, but it was often completely depleted

13 Nancy Ann Goyne, "Furniture Craftsmen in Philadelphia, 1760–1780: Their Role in a Mercantile Society" (M.A. thesis, University of Delaware, 1963), 27.

14 Joshua Humphrey's Ledger, 1772–3 and Roll Book, 1794–9, HSP.

15 Heckscher, "Philadelphia Cabinetmaking," Appendix A.

16 Ibid., 27–8.

17 Ibid., Appendix A.

18 "Thomas Janvier Account Book," Down Library, Photocopy 86, Henry Francis du Pont Winterthur Museum, Wilmington, Delaware.

by boarding and other expenses. He provided workers with everything from clothes (supplied from his brother's tailoring shop) to tobacco, tools, and occasional loans. Often, at the end of a pay period very little of the wage was left to claim. The contract drawn between Ashton and Samuel Davis implies that, after everything was deducted from his pay, no cash changed hands. Davis received a fixed wage, twenty-five shillings for every six days – "Clear of board, washing and lodging . . . to be paid in cash or clothing the balance if any there to be paid." A year later, Ashton rewrote the contract and reduced the weekly wage to twenty shillings.[19] With work and boarding periods short and remuneration small, journeymen gained neither wage security nor marketplace independence with their freedom.

In addition, no standardized wage schedule existed. Philadelphia's master mechanics paid either by the piece or by time, and each rate had its own set of risks and rewards. Employers usually controlled the form of payments, often to the disadvantage and chagrin of workers. During the early 1790s, for example, master carpenters insisted on a flat wage during the long summer days but a piece rate during the winter months, when shorter days meant smaller production.[20] Typically the different payment schedules were used sequentially. Often the youngest or newest journeyman in the shop received a piece rate.[21] More than half of Ashton's journeymen were initially hired on a piecework basis, but only a third of them remained so.[22] Abel Hammer, for instance, was switched from a piece rate to work "by the month at the same rate he can earn at Bureaus."[23] Ashton apparently paid novice journeymen by the piece until he was satisfied that their productivity warranted time payment. Master silversmiths followed the same practice. Workers in Samuel Williamson's shop began by making inexpensive spoons and tongs on the piece rate and progressed through more complicated forms like tumblers and cans to such valuable pieces as sugar dishes and teapots.[24] The journeymen who accepted piecework wages were the newest employees and the least familiar with their surroundings, co-workers, and the moods of the employer; their incomes were the most vulnerable because they were

19 Heckscher, "Philadelphia Cabinetmaking," 25–6. See also the records of Thomas Janvier, who did cabinetwork for Daniel Trotter from July 1795 to September 11, 1796. Janvier boarded with Trotter for only the last three months of the work period. Janvier Account Book.

20 Ian M. G. Quimby, "The Cordwainers Protest: A Crisis in Labor Relations," *Winterthur Portfolio* 3 (1967), 90.

21 For examples of piece rate see the Ledger of Thomas Morgan (a watchmaker of Baltimore and Philadelphia), AMB 5865, HSP; Anne Castrodale, "Daniel Trotter, a Philadelphia Cabinetmaker" (M.A. thesis, University of Delaware, 1962), 25–30; Janvier Account Book; Joshua Humphrey's Ledger D, 1766–1777, HSP.

22 Humphrey's Ledger D, 27–8.

23 Heckscher, "Philadelphia Cabinetmaking," 34.

24 Beasley, "Samuel Williamson," 17.

based on the level of output, tied directly to shop demand, and subject to stopage due to inclement weather, sickness, or short supply of raw materials.

Employers made remuneration most commonly on the basis of time – by the day, month, or year.[25] Day wages were the most risky for workers because they did not provide the informal compensation afforded by the other methods. When William Crage, a yearly contract worker, lost ten days "by a lame hand," his employer, Isaac Zane, did not dock his pay. However, Zane deducted three shillings per day from the wages of Samuel Burden, a day laborer, when "he was sick 4 days and lost a day at the fair." In one instance, even the year contract did not ensure compensation time lost due to illness. Samuel Pennock was to earn twenty-five pounds per year and board, and he was to work "6 days in the week the year out, for his work and he allowing for lost time."[26] Isaac Norris, the wealthy Philadelphia merchant and urban developer, traditionally hired on a monthly basis and included subsistence. In January 1753 Benjamin Morgan agreed "to work for £3-2-5 per month on Norris's diet," and he continued to work for Norris under these terms for a year and a half.[27] At this rate he most likely earned two and one-half shillings per day and was guaranteed his wage if he lost work time due to illness or inclement weather. When building began on the Pennsylvania Hospital, Morgan signed on and altered his agreement to a daily rate of three and one-half shillings. But with this increased wage he sacrificed the security of his steady earnings. Journeymen did have some control over the style of payment, but by working for the slightly higher day wage they were vulnerable to downtime. To protect their incomes when they had to stay off the job, they often had to settle for less money.

Finally, wage labor introduced job insecurity into workers' lives. Master craftsmen could let their workmen go when demand was low, leaving them to find work where they might. Under the paternalistic system, when owners were forced to sell their bound workers during hard times, the burden rested on the master, not the servant. Besides the lack of job security, wage labor brought another disdvantage to the worker. If business was slow, the master probably paid the journeyman last. In 1767 a tradesman wrote to a Philadelphia newspaper describing how straitened economic conditions were affecting him. The nature of his trade, he explained, forced him to hire journeymen and three or four apprentices besides using the various mem-

25 See, for example, Account Book of Thomas Savery, Carpenter, Philadelphia, 1782, AM 9116, HSP; Joshua Humphrey's Ledger, 1772–3, and Roll Book, 1794–9; David Evans Account Book, 3 vols., AM 9115, HSP.

26 Moss, "Master Builders," 144–5.

27 This example is from Gary B. Nash, *The Urban Crucible: Social Change, Political Consciousness, and the Origins of the American Revolution* (Cambridge, Mass., 1979), 259.

bers of his family. The tradesman lamented that "towards the latter end of every week, I generally make a tour amongst my employers to collect a little money to pay my workmen, and answer some other immediate demands, but of late I meet with so little success, that I may as well stay at home. . . . I no sooner return home with my small collection, than my journeymen address me for their wages, whome I am obliged to compound with the same proportion as I received it."[28] When capital was scarce, labor often went uncompensated. Employers gained flexibility with the advance of the system of wage labor, but employees had to worry about their next jobs and whether and how they would be paid.

The transition brought changes in the relations between artisans and their workers even before indentured labor gave way to wage labor. The first sign was the changing contractual relationship of masters and apprentices. Although during the colonial period masters and apprentices signed formal agreements to specify the length of indenture and some of the apprentices' responsibilities, they relied for the most part on unwritten understanding of mutual obligations. As the century progressed, such items as the nature and amount of work expected from the apprentice and arrangements for education and clothing were translated into monetary values and specified in greater detail.[29]

More dramatic, as wage labor rose, were changes in the character of the colonial work place. In the colonial shop, the master craftsman labored

28 *Pennsylvania Chronicle and Universal Advertiser* (Philadelphia), May 25 to June 1, 1767.
29 David Montgomery, "The Working Classes of the Pre-Industrial American City, 1780–1830," *Labor History* 9 (1968), 6; Ian M. G. Quimby, "Apprenticeship in Colonial Philadelphia" (M.A. thesis, University of Delaware, 1963), 60. A number of studies suggest similar disintegration of master-worker relations. Charles G. Steffen finds that alterations in the work forces of wealthier Baltimore artisans resulted in considerable journeyman unrest. In the case of Baltimore, however, the innovation by the employers was to use an increasing number of "cheap" laborers, primarily apprentices and slaves. "Changes in the Organization of Artisan Production in Baltimore, 1790–1820," *WMQ*, 3d ser., 36 (1979), 101–17. For Philadelphia, John K. Alexander notes that workingmen's labor organizations were formed and political action occurred for the first time during the 1790s and that journeymen and employers clashed in economic struggles while each group pursued its own economic goals. This unrest, he claims, was the result of the continuing impoverishment of a large number of Philadelphians. He is less concerned with the alterations in worker–employer relations or in the changing relations among workers. *Render Them Submissive: Responses to Poverty in Phildaelphia, 1760–1800* (Amherst, Mass., 1980), 28. Nash relates increasing impoverishment of the colonial urban working class to its political activism before the Revolution. His impressive study ends with the Revolution, and postrevolutionary activities of the growing free wage class are not treated in *Urban Crucible*. Foner, in his excellent chapter on Philadelphia, also hints at the shift in employer-worker relations and the manifestations of these changes in the politics of the period. But he is not concerned with the specific changes in the work environment; rather, he documents the expression of these changes in prerevolutionary politics. *Tom Paine and Revolutionary America* (New York, 1976).

alongside his servants or slaves, perhaps an apprentice or two, and an occasional journeyman. Stability resulted because it took four to five years for a servant to work out his indenture term and even longer for the apprentice to learn the craft. Admittedly, servants like William Atwood, a skilled brass founder, or George Moore, a brushmaker, ran away from their owners.[30] But the servants of artisans seldom absconded. The unfree workers of the city were forced to share the workbench with their artisan owners, but the relationship was stable and, by eighteenth-century standards, long lasting.

When the master left the workbench to his employees, labor relations in Philadelphia changed markedly. The early colonial labor market encouraged the city's master craftsmen to rely heavily on skilled bound workers, both indentured servants and slaves. As the eighteenth century progressed, this coercive, paternalistic labor arrangement revealed increasing social conflict. However, relations among free workers, masters, and journeymen were based on shared goals. A mutuality existed, as Gary B. Nash writes, because for artisans, belonging to a trade carried with it more than working at a craft. It meant a sense of obligation, and masters and journeymen were bound "in service to themselves, each other, and the community." Workers did not work just to earn a living; they internalized a collective "trade identity and commitment to the community in which they labored."[31]

Only three reported exceptions marred an otherwise harmonious labor history in early-eighteenth-century Philadelphia. In 1707 journeymen complained about the general "Want of Employment, and Lowness of Wages occasioned by the Number of Negroes . . . hired out to work by the Day."[32] Twelve years later, the Common Council received several petitions from the city's carters, draymen, and porters protesting the low wages established by a recent ordinance.[33] Finally, in 1724 master carpenters separated themselves from their journeymen and combined to control labor while giving "every workman the worth of his labor."[34] Except for these minor skirmishes, Philadelphia artisans appeared united.

The traditional outlook, in which this mutuality and communal spirit dominated, began to collapse during the late colonial period. The accumu-

30 *Pennsylvania Gazette,* May 1, 15, 1776.

31 Gary B. Nash, "Artisans and Politics in Eighteenth-Century Philadelphia," in *The Craftsman in Early America,* ed. Ian M. Quimby (New York, 1984), 69.

32 Quoted in Carl Bridenbaugh, *Cities in the Wilderness: The First Century of Urban Life in America, 1625–1742* (New York, 1938), 201.

33 Luther A. Harr, "The Status of Labor in Colonial Pennsylvania" (M.A. thesis, Temple University, 1948); *Minutes of the Common Council of the City of Philadelphia, 1704–1776* (Philadelphia, 1847), June 19, 1719.

34 *The Carpenters' Company of the City and County of Philadelphia . . . Instituted 1724* (Philadelphia, 1887).

lative, entrepreneurial spirit replaced the "moral economy," and social responsibility in economic activity was lost. Individual acquisitiveness replaced the ideal of the good of the community.[35] It is impossible to say precisely when the new ethos emerged and then dominated, but it seems to have coincided with the decline of unfree and subsequent rise of wage labor and to have been tied to an economic barometer. Indeed, craft organizations appeared and demanded to be heard in the late colonial period.[36]

During the 1760s and 1770s, amidst growing economic ills and mounting tensions between Great Britain and the colonies, Philadelphia artisans organized like never before. To a degree, masters had anticipated them. In 1769 Philadelphia master cordwainers tried to convince the Pennsylvania Assembly that the cost of their raw materials should be controlled in order to protect their livelihoods. A few years later, Philadelphia carpenters, who had been loosely organized since 1724, joined together to attempt a rate fix. And the city's master tailors combined in 1771 to control the wages of their workers as well as "to fix prices at levels that would guarantee a decent subsistence."[37] But these stirrings of craft organization do not demonstrate divisions within the crafts. A possible exception was the Carpenter's Company, a virtual guild established in 1724 by wealthy builder-architects. Otherwise, journeymen had not yet identified their own interests as different from or in conflict with those of their masters.

These prerevolutionary alliances assumed the form primarily of groups of master craftsmen who desired to protect their economic independence during increasingly hard times. Master mechanics sought legal controls on the prices of their raw materials as well as on the wages of their journeymen.[38] Bakers, in a petition to the Pennsylvania Assembly, expressed their concern over the price of flour. They petitioned the Assembly to regulate the Assize of Loaf Bread and to help reduce the great discrepancy between the prices of superfine and common flour. Common flour, they claimed, was not a satisfactory product with which to bake, and they were forced to bake with the more expensive superfine flour. As a result, they

---

35 Nash, "Artisans and Politics," 69–70.

36 Ibid., 80

37 Ibid. See also Nash, *Urban Crucible,* 324.

38 Nash, *Urban Crucible,* 323. Charles S. Olton suggests that these early craft societies failed because of the nature of the colonial marketplace. *Artisans for Independence: Philadelphia Mechanics and the American Revolution* (Syracuse, N.Y., 1975), 16. Nash argues more persuasively that these organizations failed because artisans had only limited power to set prices. *Urban Crucible,* 516, n. 59.

As Eric Foner explains, even if the earlier craft organizations were exclusively for masters, this did not contradict "the belief that the interests of journeymen, as the masters of tomorrow, were embraced in the 'good of the trade.'" *Tom Paine,* 39.

argued, their profits were so inconsiderable that they were having difficulty supporting their families and needed relief.[39]

The Assembly received a petition from the city's ropemakers two years later. Their problems arose because the hemp was bound very tightly into bundles, and sellers would not allow the bundles to be opened for inspection. As a result, the ropemakers were unable to judge the quality of the hemp and thus the fair price. To make matters worse, foul hemp was often put into the middle of the bundle. Ropemakers also demanded some sort of regulation.[40]

The cordwainers were concerned over the quality of leather. In 1770 they complained to the Assembly that the leather was bad. It was insufficiently tanned; "neither [was] it in other respects well finished." The cordwainers claimed that the problems were caused by the large number of people in the business who were ill trained, the high demand for leather, and large quantities being shipped to Great Britain. The cordwainers requested that customs officers be appointed to inspect the leather.[41]

In the tanners' response to the accusations, they claimed that the cordwainers were motivated by political concerns and sought to obtain lucrative offices for themselves. They were convinced that the quality of leather had improved over the last years because a large number of tanners had served apprenticeships and were now masters. If the leather was of poor quality, it was the fault of the butchers, who, the tanners claimed, did a bad job of cutting the hides.

One month after the original petition from the cordwainers, the saddlers and harnessmakers joined forces with the cordwainers and presented to the Assembly similar grievances against the tanners. In their view, the problem was in the manufacturing, monopolizing, and exporting of leather. They echoed the request that officers be appointed to inspect leather and some method be devised to prevent the butchers from cutting the hides "in a careless manner."[42]

Aside from this attempt to protect individual crafts, the artisan community was engaged in the years before the revolution in three nonimportation movements. They called meetings, used the press to air their concerns, alerted mechanics that they needed to unite, and called upon the citizens to boycott merchants who refused to participate in nonimportation. Not only did the political struggle transcend specific craft allegiances, the movement sparked the participation by younger and poorer artisans, those who,

---

39 Votes of the Assembly, *Pa. Arch.*, ser. 8, vol. 7, May 17, 1764, 5603.
40 Ibid., January 20, 1766, 5833–4; January 21, 1766, 5839.
41 Ibid., January 5, 1770, 6457–8.
42 Ibid., February 9, 1770, 6503–5.

because they lacked property, were disenfranchised. This was their first opportunity to join the political struggles.[43]

Popular pressure finally brought the merchants into the nonimportation movement in March 1769, but artisans' suspicions of the merchants had peaked. The disillusionment was not helped by the merchants' attempt to break free from the nonimportation agreement one year later. "The partnership between different ranks was at an end." By the spring of 1770, artisans could do no more to stop the merchants from resuming importations. It became clear to the artisan community that they had to assume the leadership, since only they would work for the good of the community. Artisans emerged from the period of the nonimportation movements as a separate political entity and identified the growing class differences between themselves and merchant capitalists.[44]

The Revolution halted these activities, but the war played a pivotal role in postrevolutionary labor, for it provided the working classes with an opportunity to hone political skills and articulate the growing class differences in the city. The militia became the political school for the city's tradesmen. The politics of the militia has been thoroughly studied elsewhere. Throughout the war lower artisans fought for a return of the "moral economy," whereas upper artisans supported free trade and laissez-faire principles.[45] The results of this struggle divided the craft community forever.

When former militiamen met after the war, they formed trade societies. They called on their political know-how, and the labor organizations they formed had no colonial predecessors. Two distinct types of union emerged. Masters continued to belong to exclusive groups, but now journeymen formed their own alliances. Labor relations in Philadelphia changed perceptibly after the Revolution.

In the postrevolutionary period, cracks appeared in the once cohesive community of work. The first glimmerings of problems came at the time of the Federal Procession on the Fourth of July, 1788. All over America craftsmen joined to celebrate the new Federal Constitution by assembling demonstrations and floats and parading in shop garb. To all appearances, the Philadelphia procession was an orderly event, with apprentices, journeymen, and masters sharing the day. "Every tradesman's boy in the procession seemed to consider himself as a principal in the business," one observer recalled. "Rank for a while forgot all its claims, and Agriculture,

43 Nash, "Artisans and Politics," 80–1.
44 Ibid., 82.
45 Ibid., 87–8. See Steven Rosswurm's superb study of the militia in Philadelphia. "Arms, Country, and Class: The Philadelphia Militia and the 'Lower Sort' in the American Revolution, 1765–1783" (New Brunswick, N.J., forthcoming).

Commerce and Manufactures, together with the learned and mechanical Professions, seemed to acknowledge by their harmony and respect for each other, that they were all necesarry to each other, and all useful in cultivated society."[46]

A close inspection of these festivities, however, reveals another side to the harmony and good cheer. This same writer hoped that the different groups would "avail themselves of their late sudden and accidental association."[47] All reporters of the event seemed delighted that harmony prevailed, that masters joined with journeymen and apprentices to celebrate this national milestone. The implications are clear: Masters did not ordinarily "take counsel with journeymen or other laborers,"[48] and when they did, the gratifying convergence of these groups was cause for comment. After the festivities ended, Philadelphia residents no longer extolled the virtuous alliances between the various ranks of mechanics. On the contrary, the tenuous bonds quickly disintegrated. Journeymen organized their own groups, articulated their union with each other, and gave voice to the increasing conflicts of interest between themselves and the master artisans.

Journeyman printers organized first. In 1786 twenty-six of them banded to protest a reduction in their wages. They resolved not to work for less than six dollars per week and agreed to support any journeyman who was fired because he refused to work for less.[49] The result was Philadelphia's first labor strike, and it brought the first provision for a union strike benefit in the country.[50] The struggle lasted for some time before the terms were finally accepted by the shop owners. This labor victory set the scene for other actions to follow.

Labor relations within the carpenters' trade also reflected change. In 1791 the city's journeymen walked out in an unsuccessful strike against their masters.[51] *"Self-preservation,"* they cried, "has induced us to enter into *indissoluble union with each other."*[52] The sides were clearly drawn. The workers united to survive after their employers attempted to reduce their wages. To compound difficulties, masters paid by time in the summer and by the piece in the winter, much to their own advantage. The journeymen resented this bitterly. They demanded that the working day be fixed from 6:00 A.M. to 6:00 P.M. regardless of the season. In order to free themselves

46 "Observations on the Federal Procession on the Fourth of July 1788, in the City of Philadelphia, in a Letter from a Gentleman in This City to His Friend in a Neighboring State," *American Museum* 4 (1788), 76.
47 Ibid.
48 Olton, *Artisans for Independence,* 10.
49 Rollo G. Silver, *The American Printer, 1787–1825* (Charlottesville, Va., 1967), 14.
50 Ibid.; Richard B. Morris, *Government and Labor in Early America,* (New York, 1946), 201.
51 Quimby, "Cordwainers Protest," 90.
52 Quoted in ibid.

from their current masters, the journeymen advertised that they would work for other carpenters at 25 percent less. The masters replied with ridicule – "they will work from six to six – how absurd!" – and scoffed that for journeymen to work for less pay implied that they were unqualified to work. In order to erect the buildings of the city, the trade needed responsible workers. Underneath the bravado, however, the masters worried that the actions of journeymen carpenters would ignite Philadelphia's workers in general. "If customs productive of idleness and dissipation be introduced by journeymen carpenters," they bemoaned, "the contagion will soon be communicated to other artificers."[53] The journeymen lost, but as the masters feared, the contagion spread.

Organized journeymen emerged next from the city's cabinet- and chair-making trade. The prelude is unknown, but 1794 marked the beginning of a two-year battle between the craft's employers and employees.[54] On April 13, 1794, on behalf of the Federal Society of Chair Makers, three Philadelphia journeymen deposited a book of prices with the clerk of the district of Pennsylvania.[55] The masters stood firm against the demands and countered by announcing in the city's newspapers that they had positions for thirty or forty journeymen cabinetmakers who might need work.[56] Exactly what occurred over the next year is not clear, but the journeymen submitted a second edition of the *Journeymen Cabinet and Chair Makers' Price Book* in 1795. The city's master mechanics replied by distributing a handbill. Its precise contents are unknown, but some of its implications can be gleaned from the journeymen's rebuttal. The masters had apparently attempted to divide the journeymen by proclaiming that they "would not employ any journeymen cabinet-makers as society men, but [only] as individuals." The society of journeymen responded. They refused to work for any employer who propagated this viewpoint or alongside any journey-man "who is, or may be employed by any of the above employers, contrary to our rules."[57]

The battle raged on. In the next newspaper broadside, published on April 7, 1796, the journeymen appealed to the public for support. They argued that rapid increases in prices had left them in dire straits. Even their revised price book had been rejected, and now, they lamented, all that was left was to sever all ties with the masters. Accordingly, they announced the opening of the Ware Room on Market Street for the sale of furniture they had produced. The masters would not yield to their needs, so the journeymen struck and opened their own shop.

53 Quoted in ibid., 90–1.
54 The following discussion draws heavily from Montgomery, *American Furniture*, 21.
55 *Pennsylvania Gazette*, June 4, 1794.
56 Montgomery, *American Furniture*, 21.
57 Ibid.

At the same time, they appealed to journeymen of different crafts in Philadelphia and in other American cities. In their 1796 statement they graciously thanked the other societies in Philadelphia that had assisted them thus far in their struggle, "in particular the respectable and independent Societies of Hatters and Shoemakers whose general assistance has enabled us to answer the most extensive demands of the public." They closed with a call for a general meeting of many mechanical societies – house carpenters, carpenters, tailors, goldsmiths, saddlers, coopers, painters, and printers – "in order to digest a plan of union, for the protection of their mutual independence." Just a month before, the Philadelphia journeymen had called on their counterparts in New York. The *Argus* published an appeal "from the working Cabinet Makers of Philadelphia, to their mechanical Fellow Citizens," to "repel any attack that has or may be made on societies of this description." The Philadelphians asked their New York brethren to declare themselves ready to assist "in a cause which will determine the independence of so useful a body as the working Citizens of America."[58] Thus journeymen cabinetmakers did not perceive their struggle to be an isolated event; they were learning that workers had to organize to secure their independence.

The details of the strike's conclusion are lost, but the outcome is clear. Both the introduction to the 1796 publication of prices and the rates stipulated in the volume reveal that the workers won their demands. The introduction to the book, signed by three "employers" and three "workmen," recounts the "great deal of trouble [that] has been occasioned between the Employers and Workmen, on account of the many late improvements in our trade."[59] The publication of the final volume marked a new phase in labor relations. Both masters and journeymen agreed to the prices in this third edition and acknowledged that the new book represented the standard, guaranteed price for all work. In addition, the price book included an escalator clause for cost-of-living increases or decreases, so that wages would respond whenever the "necessaries of life, house-rent, &c. shall rise above what they are at present. . . . [I]n like manner, the Workmen do agree to reduce the prices in the same proportion as the said necessaries lower." Finally, a comparison with the prices in this edition with those rejected in the 1795 volume reveal that workmen won their price demands, since the variations are very few.[60] Thus ended the Philadelphia cabinet-makers' strike, which revealed essential differences between the visions of workers and employers. The workers' inability to support themselves on what masters were willing to pay led them to fear for their livelihoods; it

58 Quoted in ibid., 22.
59 *The Cabinet-Makers' Philadelphia and London Book of Prices* (Philadelphia, 1796); introduction quoted in ibid., 24.
60 Ibid., 23–4.

also demonstrated that their basic independence was at stake. In the course of resolving the differences, the Philadelphia journeymen found allies among other journeymen craftsmen and recognized that journeymen and masters no longer shared the same interests or goals.

The activities of the city's shoemakers brought labor conflict to a crescendo. The early history of Philadelphia shoemakers, like that of other trades, was characterized by a union between ranks and a focus on craft production. During the colonial period, the craft was organized around small shops and custom work. After Independence, the city's cordwainers produced for an expanding export market.[61] The image of the master shoemaker hunched over his workbench and surrounded by a servant or a slave faded away. Now master mechanics were more appropriately referred to as merchant capitalists, whereas the skilled journeymen became only part of the complex series of costs that affected the margin of the master's profits.

The early associations of shoemakers were reminiscent of other colonial craft organizations. In 1760 master cordwainers formed a fire company to provide members with fire insurance. Unlike the other unions of master mechanics of the period, the shoemakers' fire company made no attempt to control prices or wages.[62] The membership was neither very stable nor representative of master shoemakers generally, and, like other contemporary unions, the company was short-lived. Although master cordwainers joined together after the Revolution, masters and journeymen continued to appear allied in their support of the craft. The goals of the new masters' group were geared to the regulation of business. The central provisions of their constitution prohibited membership for any master who sold his wares in the public market or resorted to public advertising of prices. The official life of this group was also brief, but it laid an important foundation for less official coalitions of masters.

In the early skirmishes within the craft, masters and journeymen acted in concert while maintaining separate identities and distinct organizations. In 1791 Peter Gordon and Nathaniel Prentice advertised in the Philadelphia papers that they had inexpensive "new patent boots" for sale.[63] Both masters and journeymen responded to protect the craft from this encroachment. Masters opposed the sale for fear that the market would be flooded with cheap goods and that their profits would suffer. They argued that these boots were hardly new, since similar footwear had been produced for more than thirty years by London cordwainers, as well as by several local craftsmen. Journeymen worried about lower wages. When Gordon and

61 John R. Commons, David J. Saposs, Helen L. Summer, E. R. Mittelman, H. E. Hoagland, John B. Andrews, and Selig Perlman, eds., *History of Labour in the United States* (New York, 1918), 1:6–7.
62 I have drawn heavily from Quimby, "Cordwainers Protest," 86–92.
63 Ibid., 88.

Prentice offered employment to fifty cordwainers, promised to pay them one shilling six pence above any other day wage currently available in the city, and guaranteed constant employment for one year, the journeymen were not persuaded. They accused Gordon and Prentice of misleading them. Although journeymen and masters responded independently to this threat, the interests of both groups converged in defense of the craft.

The unification of craftsmen for the good of the craft was even clearer a few years later. The Philadelphia boot and shoe industry expanded steadily throughout the late eighteenth century, and by the 1790s it included a growing export business. To encourage this trade, journeymen cordwainers consented to make shoes for export at thirty-five cents per pair less than shoes to be sold from the masters' shops. Clearly, journeymen identified the growing market with their own prosperity.

After the early 1790s, however, unity within the craft broke down. Journeymen began to feel squeezed and ever more distant from the master mechanics. In 1799 at least one hundred journeymen walked out on strike to protest an attempted wage reduction. The results were inconclusive. After a time the workers returned to their benches, although as one disgruntled journeyman described it, "the settlement 'was near splitting the difference.'"[64] A relative calm resettled over the shoemakers for the next six years, but in the fall of 1805 journeymen demanded a wage increase. The masters rejected it immediately, and the workers walked out and stayed out for more than six weeks. Although they were forced to return to work at the old wage, this episode did not end the dispute.

The finale of the journeymen's actions was the well-known conspiracy trial of 1806, which manifests in eloquent detail the increasing distance between masters and journeymen. Tired of the constant sparring over wages, the masters took their cause to court. They accused the workmen of illegal collusion to control the price of labor. Philadelphia's most prestigious legal minds argued the case, and the results were far reaching. For our purposes, this trial provides one of the clearest statements about the breakdown of cohesion within the craft and the tremendous change in labor relations.

The masters and prosecutors argued that journeymen were hampering a lucrative trade. Strikes for higher wages caused business to suffer. "This is a large, encreasing, manufacturing city . . . and great sums are annually received in returns. It is then proper to support this manufacture. Will you permit men to destroy it, who have no permanent stake in the city; men who can pack up their all in a knapsack, or carry them in their pockets to New York or Baltimore?"[65] Journeymen, the prosecution declared, were "mere

64 Quoted in ibid., 92.
65 Quoted in ibid., 95–6.

birds of passage" who had only the slightest concern for the craft. Facing the prosecutors were the defendant journeymen, whose lawyers declared that "labour constitutes the real wealth of the country."[66] Caesar Rodney, a defense attorney, claimed that the battle between masters and journeymen was analogous to the clash between the rich and the poor, the powerful and the destitute. The city's master cordwainers lived in large mansions and amassed great fortunes more quickly than individuals in any other profession in the city.[67] Their employees barely earned enough to subsist. Whereas the prosecution claimed that the health of the craft was best served by the masters, Rodney argued that "the labourer [was] surely worthy of sufficient honor to enable him to live comfortably." Rodney closed his defense with the observation that, if radical inequalities were fair and right, and if "the labourer and journeymen enjoy too great a part of liberty," the jury should convict. If, however, the intent of the new Federal Constitution was to secure equality of rights without distinctions of class, the verdict should be acquittal. The jury found the journeymen guilty of "a combination to raise wages."[68]

The transition to a system of capitalist labor relations in Philadelphia was long and uneven. As the ranks of free workers swelled and unfree labor faded, labor relations changed significantly. The conflicts of the 1790s were not sudden eruptions but manifestations of fundamental difficulties. Not only did the wage labor system introduce a new set of tensions within the shop, but these tensions were exacerbated by the economic constraints on vertical mobility. Exploitation underlay the master–servant relationship, and evidence of overt conflict became more common. As the traditional labor system broke down, masters and journeymen struggled against each other to hammer out a new system of relations. The high turnover rate in the late-eighteenth-century shop may have reflected both the exploitation of labor by employers and workers' efforts to obtain more personal independence and greater resources. In either case, the social constellation of Philadelphia had changed in an unmistakable way long before the rise of industrialization in America.

---

66 Quoted in ibid., 96.
67 Ibid.
68 Leonard Bernstein, "The Working People of Philadelphia from Colonial Times to the General Strike of 1835," *PMHB* 74 (1950), 326.

Appendix A: Time series

Table A.1. *Servants indentured in colonial Philadelphia emigrating from England, Ireland, Scotland, and Wales*

Year	Ships[a]	Passengers[b]	Servants[c]	Approximate number indentured to Philadelphians[d]
1717	12 or 13			
1722	1		30	11
1723	3		216	81
1724	—			
1725	3		216	81
1726	1		72	27
1727	1		72	27
1728	10		720	274
1729	6	1,865	432	164
1730	1		72	27
1731	2	271	135	51
1732	3		216	82
1733	3	322	161	61
1734	4	755	378	144
1735	1	343	200	76
1736	7		480	182
1737	7		457	174
1738	3		216	82
1739	8		576	219
1740	1		72	27
1741	5		360	137
1742	4		288	109
1743	1		72	27
1744	1		72	27
1745	6	865	432	164
1746	2		144	55
1747	1		72	27
1748	3		216	82
1749	5		360	137
1750	6	510	432	164
1751	15		1080	410
1752	10	255	586	223
1753	5	425	360	137

Table A.1. *(cont.)*

Year	Ships[a]	Passengers[b]	Servants[c]	Approximate number indentured to Philadelphians[d]
1754	5	425	360	137
1755		170		
1756	1	85	72	27
1757		510		
1758		255		
1759		170		
1760		595		
1761		595		
1762		765		
1763	1	1,190	72	27
1764	3	808	216	82
1765	3	1,010	164	62
1766	5	1,818	215	82
1767	2	1,111	144	55
1768	5	707	100	38
1769	4	1,111	132	50
1770	6	1,212	120	46
1771	4	1,995	80	30
1772	2	1,470	172	65
1773	7	1,785	192	73
1774	8	1,575	316	120
1775	7	1,365	400	152

[a] The number of ships equals the number of different advertised shipments of servants for sale in the city of Philadelphia. These data are from the *American Weekly Mercury, Pennsylvania Gazette,* and from 1771 to 1773 the *Pennsylvania Packet and Daily Advertiser.* Neither the *Gazette* nor the *Weekly Mercury* carried a complete set of advertisements, so it was necessary to consult both newspapers for all years.

[b] Except where noted Irish immigration figures are based on the number of ship arrivals advertised in the Philadelphia newspapers. For 1717 contemporaries reported that 12 to 13 ships arrived in Philadelphia. James G. Leyburn, *The Scotch-Irish: A Social History* (Chapel Hill, N.C., 1962), 170. The figures for 1729 to 1735 are from "Passengers and Servants Imported from Ireland . . . " in Abbot E. Smith, *Colonists in Bondage: White Servitude and Convict Labor in America, 1607–1776* (Chapel Hill, N.C., 1947), 319.

The 1745 figure is calculated from the number of servants indentured in Philadelphia for that year. All these servants came from British ports, but most likely not all were Scots-Irish. "Servants and Apprentices Bound and Assigned Before the Mayor of Philadelphia, 1745," manuscript, Historical Society of Pennsylvania,

Notes to Table A.1. (*cont.*)

Philadelphia. I doubled the figures in order to estimate the number of passengers, servants and free. Finally, I reduced the total by 13.5 percent to account for non-Irish servants.

R. J. Dickson supplies the number of ships per year beginning with 1750 and ending in 1775. Dickson estimates that from 1750 to 1763, 6,000 persons arrived in Philadelphia from Ireland. On the basis of this number and the number of ships, I calculated an average of 85 persons per ship. R. J. Dickson, *Ulster Emigration to Colonial America, 1718–1775* (London, 1966), Appendix E.

During the years from 1764 to 1770, Dickson estimates that 1,300 passengers per year arrived in Philadelphia from the north of Ireland. This totals approximately 7,800 persons for the six-year-period, an average of 101 passengers per ship. Ibid.

The years from 1771 to 1775 were the climax of northern Irish immigration into Philadelphia. Dickson estimates that 8,000 Irish arrived from 1771 to 1775. I calculated an average of 105 passengers per ship. Ibid.

a If the actual number of servants was unspecified in the advertisements, I calculated that a parcel consisted of 72 servants. In order to arrive at this figure, I checked the number of ship advertisements against the passenger and servant lists provided by Abbot Smith. Smith reports that 322 Irish arrived in the port of Philadelphia in 1733. I found advertisements for three separate servant parcels in that year. If half of these passengers were servants (161) and they arrived on three ships, that would average out to about 54 servants per ship. For the years 1731, 1733, and 1734, the average was 72 per ship. Smith, *Colonists in Bondage,* 319.

d In order to determine how many servants were indentured to Philadelphia owners, I analyzed the residences in the "List of Servants and Apprentices Bound and Assigned Before the Mayor of Philadelphia" in 1745 and 1772. Both manuscripts are at the Historical Society of Pennsylvania, Philadelphia. In 1745, more than 58% of the servants were bound to Philadelphians, and in 1772, 38% of the servants were purchased by city residents. I assumed that 38% of the servants for sale remained in the city.

Occasionally, the advertisement specified either the number of servants for sale or the total number of passengers. If the latter, I calculated that 50% of the passengers were indentured.

The figures for 1731, 1733, and 1734 are from Smith, *Colonists in Bondage,* 319. I reduced his figures by half to estimate the number of immigrants who were indentured.

On September 4, 1735, the *American Weekly Mercury* reported "An Account of Passengers and Servants imported since 1st May last":

	Passengers	Servants	Total
Ireland	195	177	372
Carolina	185	—	185
London and Bristol	75	99	174
West Indies	51	43	94
Total	506	319	825

Smith reported that 343 passengers and servants arrived from Ireland in that same year. *Colonists in Bondage,* 319. In order to determine how many servants arrived

Notes to Table A.1. *(cont.)*
in 1735, I excluded the West Indies figures and used only those from the British Isles. However, I found only one advertisement for a servant parcel, and I concluded that some of the London and Bristol shiploads may have been redemptioners from the Palatinate. In May 1735 Palatines were transported on the ship *Mercury* of London. In June Palatines arrived on the Philadelphia brig *Mary*, James Marshall, Master, also from London. In August, Palatines were brought into Philadelphia from South Carolina. Thus I reduced the London and Bristol figures to avoid counting immigrating servants twice. Eighty-five Palatines were indentured in 1735 (see Table A.2). Nine of these were on the South Carolina vessels; thus 76 were subtracted from the London–Bristol figures. Ralph B. Strassberger and William J. Hinke, *Pennsylvania German Pioneers: A Publication of the Original Lists of Arrivals in the Port of Philadelphia from 1727 to 1808*, Pennsylvania-German Society Proceedings (Norristown, Pa., 1934). 1:146–54.

From 1765 to 1775, advertisements revealed that each servant shipment was not a parcel but often "a number" or "a few." Parcels continued to be counted as 72 servants, but when a number or a few was indicated I calculated 20 servants. This was an average figure as well as the most common number requested by merchants. See, for example, Willing and Sons to Juhn Perks, October 1754, Willing and Sons Letter Book, Historical Society of Pennsylvania, Philadelphia. Also, Grace Larsen, "The Profile of a Colonial Merchant: Thomas Clifford of Pre-Revolutionary Philadelphia" (Ph.D. diss., Columbia University, 1955), 120–1, 123.

Table A.2. *Servants indentured in colonial Philadelphia emigrating from Germany*

Year	Ships[a]	German passengers[b]	Adult males[c]	Approximate number indentured to Philadelphians[d]
1717		363		
1721	1		84	16
1722	2		172	33
1727	5	970	331	63
1728	3	390	152	29
1729	2	306	134	25
1730	3	442	147	28
1731	4	629	235	45
1732	11	2,071	775	147
1733	7	1,295	401	76
1734	2	388	138	26
1735	3	260	85	16
1736	3	828	300	57
1737	7	1,506	608	116
1738	16	2,748	1,205	229
1739	8	1,343	575	109

Table A.2. *(cont.)*

Year	Ships[a]	German passengers[b]	Adult males[c]	Approximate number indentured to Philadelphians[d]
1740	6	870	375	71
1741	10	2,120	668	127
1742	5	1,440	297	56
1743	9	2,170	609	116
1744	9	1,609	375	71
1745	—			
1746	2	676	157	30
1747	5	1,300	343	65
1748	7	2,561	544	103
1749	25	8,778	3,511	675
1750	15	3,869	1,463	278
1751	16	4,134	1,869	355
1752	19	5,135	2,034	386
1753	19	4,086	1,889	359
1754	19	5,006	1,967	374
1755	2	260	110	21
1756	1	110	43	8
1757				
1758				
1759				
1760				
1761		75		
1762				
1763	4	587	261	50
1764	11	1,815	1,030	196
1765	5	684	320	61
1766	5	495	281	53
1767	7	828	450	86
1768	4	771	338	64
1769	4	167	141	27
1770	7	465	224	43
1771	9	821	374	71
1772	8	928	409	78
1773	15	1,717	854	162
1774	6	625	253	96
1775	2	85	79	30

[a] The data for 1721 to 1726 are from the advertisements in the *American Weekly Mercury* that announced the arrival of vessels with German servants for sale. Three ships arrived from 1721 to 1722, and each advertisement provided the number of passengers on board or the number of servants for sale. The brig *Ceasar* arrived with

Notes to Table A.2 (*cont.*)

140 Palatines. The notice appeared on September 21, 1721. On October 18, 1722, an advertisement announced the arrival of the ship *Globe* with 120 Palatines. On December 18, 1722, 100 Palatines were advertised for sale. The name of the ship was not given. In order to determine the number of servants for sale from the *Ceasar* and the *Globe*, I calculated the number of adult males per ship based on the assumption that this was the population most likely to be indentured. Ralph B. Strassberger and William J. Hinke found a ratio of five males to every seven passengers. *Pennsylvania German Pioneers: A Publication of the Original Lists of Arrivals in the Port of Philadelphia from 1727 to 1808*, Pennsylvania-German Society Proceedings (Norristown, Pa., 1934), 1:xxxi. I calculated that 84 adult males traveled to Philadelphia on the *Ceasar* and the *Globe*.

[b] Except where noted German immigration figures are from a count of the number of individuals on the ship lists in Strassberger and William, *Pennsylvania German Pioneers*, 1:7–776. If the ship lists did not include all passengers, I counted the number of adult males and assumed a ratio of five males to two passengers (p. xxxi).

For 1717 see Strassberger and Hinke, *Pennsylvania German Pioneers*, 1:xvii–xviii. The 1719 data are from ibid., xix.

Abbott Smith amended the 1749 German immigration figures. He concluded that Strassberger and Hinke undercounted the number of vessels as well as the number of passengers for that year. I have used Smith's figures for the number of Germans arriving in Philadelphia from 1740 to 1750. *Colonists in Bondage: White Servitude and Convict Labor in America, 1607–1776* (Chapel Hill, N.C., 1947), 320–3; see also *Pennsylvania German Pioneers*, 1:xxx–xxxi.

No ships entered the port of Philadelphia from Germany in the period from 1757 to 1760. Strassberger and Hinke, *Pennsylvania German Pioneers*, 1:xxx.

[c] From 1727 to 1775 the number of adult males was calculated by counting the number of male signers published in Strassberger and Hinke, *Pennsylvania German Pioneers*.

[d] In order to determine how many of these newly arrived Palatines were indentured to city residents, I assumed that 50 percent of the adult males signed indentures. By analyzing the residences of the servant purchasers named in the "List of Servants Bound and Assigned before James Hamilton, Mayor of Philadelphia, 1745 and 1746" manuscripts Historical Society of Pennsylvania, Philadelphia, and the comparable list for 1772, I found that 58.6% in 1745 and 38% in 1772 were indentured to city owners. To ensure that my figures leaned toward the conservative side, I calculated that half the adult males arriving from Germany were indentured and 38% of these were purchased by Philadelphians.

Table A.3. *Philadelphia labor force*

Year	Servant immigration British Isles[a]	Germany[b]	Total[c]	Servant work force[d]	Slave population[e]	Slave work force[f]	Total unfree work force[g]	Philadelphia population[h]	Philadelphia work force[i]	% Unfree work force[j]
1685				86	150	105	191	1,250	433	30.6
1721		16								
1722	11	33			701			5,077		
1723	81		141							
1724			125							
1725	81		162							
1726	27		108							
1727	27	63	198							
1728	274	29	420							
1729	164	25	582	582	1,059	741	1,323	6,540	2,254	37.0
1730	27	28	547							
1731	51	45	340	340	1,406	984	1,324	6,958	2,398	35.6
1732	82	147	380	380	1,628	1,140	1,520	7,170	2,469	38.1
1733	61	76	462							
1734	144	26	536							
1735	76	16	399							
1736	182	57	501							
1737	174	116	621							
1738	82	229	840		988			8,440		
1739	219	109	929	929	1,014	692	1,621	8,653		
1740	27	71	737	737	1,011	710	1,447	8,866	2,979	35.2
1741	137	127	690	690	1,031	708	1,398	9,078	3,052	32.5
1742	109	56	497	497	1,140	722	1,219	9,443	3,125	30.9

1743	27	116	542	542	1,142		798	1,340	9,808	3,251	27.2
1744	27	71	376	376	1,103		800	1,176	10,173	3,376	28.4
1745	253	—	494	494	1,115		772	1,266	10,538	3,501	25.1
1746	55	30	436	436	1,202		781	1,217	10,903	3,627	25.9
1747	27	65	430	430	1,235		841	1,271	11,268	3,752	24.5
1748	82	103	362	362	1,204		864	1,226	11,633	3,878	24.7
1749	137	675	1,089	1,089	1,125		842	1,931	11,998	4,003	23.4
1750	164	278	1,429	1,429	1,017		787	2,226	12,363	4,129	31.9
1751	410	355	2,019	2,019	998		712	2,731	12,723	4,254	34.4
1752	223	386	1,816	1,816	803		699	2,515	12,805	4,379	38.4
1753	137	359	1,870	1,870	952		562	2,432	12,887	4,409	36.3
1754	137	374	1,616	1,616	952		666	2,282	12,968	4,437	35.4
1755	55	21	1,083	1,083	985		689	1,772	13,050	4,466	33.8
1756	27	8	622	622	1,214		809	1,431	13,132	4,495	28.3
1757			111		1,293		900	1,011	13,537	4,523	24.0
1758					1,409				13,941	4,672	17.8
1759					1,340				14,346		
1760					1,417				14,750		
1761					1,629				14,910		
1762					2,097				15,070		
1763	27	50			2,366				15,230		
1764	82	196			2,099				15,390		
1765	62	61	478	478	1,796				15,550		
1766	82	53	536	536	1,392				15,710		
1767	55	86	399	269	1,452		814	1,083	15,870	5,334	16.9
1768	38	64	378	378	1,337				16,106		
1769	50	27	320	328	1,321		770	1,098	16,341	5,626	16.3
1770	46	43	268	268	1,331				17,004		
1771	30	71	267	267	1,401				17,666		
1772	65	78	333	380	1,566		697	1,077	18,329	6,311	14.6

Table A.3. *(cont.)*

Year	Servant immigration			Servant work force[d]	Slave population[e]	Slave work force[f]	Total unfree work force[g]	Philadelphia population[h]	Philadelphia work force[i]	% Unfree work force[j]
	British Isles[a]	Germany[b]	Total[c]							
1773	73	162	479	467	1,606	602	1,069	18,499	6,347	14.4
1774	120	96	594	534	1,287	592	1,126	18,670	6,428	14.9
1775	152	30	633	637	1,112	405	1,042	20,300	6,989	13.0
1783				362		304	666		9,687	6.4
1785				266		223	489		9,493	4.9
1789				223		181	404		9,112	4.2
1791				192		162	354		10,164	3.4
1793				298		143	441		11,245	3.8
1795				422		105	527		12,116	4.3
1797				434		86	585		12,569	4.7
1798				258		67	501		13,012	3.9
1799				97		31	108		13,895	1.0
1800				114		12	126		14,336	1.0

[a] The number of servants indentured from the British Isles is from Table A.1.

[b] The number of servants indentured from Germany is from Table A.2.

[c] The servant population was calculated by assuming that servants served an average three-year indenture. By combining the number of servants indentured in 1721, 1722, and 1723, I estimated the servant population of Philadelphia for 1723. In order to determine the number of servants in the city for 1724, I added the number of servants indentured in 1722, 1723, and 1724, and so on.

The lists of servants indentured before the mayor of Philadelphia reveal that the majority served four years or longer. In 1745, of 208 servants, 120 (58%) were indentured for four years. In addition, 44 servants were to serve longer than four years. Thus in 1745, 79% of the servants were to serve four years or longer. In 1772, four years was also the average length of indenture. However, using four years to derive the servant population inflated the figures. This was checked against years in which the servant lists as derived from advertisement and immigration statistics could be compared with the servant populations included in the tax lists. Perhaps the attrition rate for servants was high and some servants did not serve their full terms. Because of death, transfer of owners, or running away, the average time served may have been about three years.

The 1745 figure is from the "List of Servants and Apprentices Bound and Assigned before James Hamilton, Mayor of Philadelphia, 1745," manuscript, Historical Society of Pennsylvania, Philadelphia.

In cases where the total number of servants differs from the size of the servant work force, work force figures are from actual counts of the tax lists. These instances provide a few points at which comparisons can be made to determine the accuracy of the estimating technique.

[d] For the prerevolutionary period, data are from Tables A.1 and A.2. I saw no reason to alter the figures of the servant population to fit them into the work force. The figures for the German population include only males 16 years and older. The servants emigrating from the British Isles included very few under the age of 15 years.

For the years from 1783 to 1793, servant data are from a count of servants listed on the Philadelphia Tax Assessors' Reports, City Archives, City Hall Annex, Philadelphia.

For the years from 1795 to the end of the century, servant population is from the Registry of Redemptioners, 1785–1803, Historical Society of Pennsylvania, Philadelphia. These figures represent the total number of servants indentured to owners in Philadelphia for three-year periods.

During the first three years of settlement, 195 servants arrived in Pennsylvania. It was possible to identify the residences of 117 of these servants. Fourty-four percent were indentured to Philadelphia residents. Of the total arrivals in the first three years, I estimated that 44.4%, or 86, resided in Philadelphia.

[e] I calculated the slave population by comparing white and black burial data from bills of mortality and by assuming that white and black mortality was comparable. In order to even out the data, I used a three-year moving average.

Bills of mortality include the number of white and black burials for the year. The burial data are replete with difficulties and were used with extreme caution. Problems of miscounting were always present. A number of considerations, however, suggest that the white and black death rates are comparable. First, although a high black mortality may have been related to immigration, the white population experienced high mortality from the same cause. See Billy G. Smith, "Death and Life in a Colonial Immigrant City: A Demographic Analysis of Philadelphia," *Journal of Economic History*, 37 (1977), 874–5. Also, the populations most at risk were those in the age range of zero to four years. Most likely few Pennsylvania slaves fell into this bracket. Moreover, the white immigrant population during years of high German immigration had more individuals in the susceptible age range. Slaves of 19 and 20 were preferred. See Darold D. Wax, "Negro Imports into Pennsylvania, 1720–1766," *Pennsylvania History*, 32 (1965), 261–87; also see the age distribution calculated by Gary B. Nash for the Philadelphia slave population in "Slave and Slaveowners in Colonial Philadelphia," *William and Mary Quarterly*,

Year	Servant immigration			Servant work force[d]	Slave population[e]	Slave work force[f]	Total unfree work force[g]	Philadelphia population[h]	Philadelphia work force[i]	% Unfree work force[j]
	British Isles[a]	Germany[b]	Total[c]							

3d ser., 30 (1973), 237. Edgar McManus found similar mortality figures for the black and white populations of New York in *A History of Negro Slavery in New York* (Syracuse, N.Y., 1966), 62–3.

Bills of mortality for 1722, 1729, 1731–2, and 1742 were published in the *American Weekly Mercury*. Benjamin Franklin printed bills for 1738 to 1744 in the *Pennsylvania Gazette*. The Anglican church published the bills annually from 1747 to 1775 except for 1749 and 1750. These bills included the number of burials in each Philadelphia church burial ground, the "Negroes Ground," and the "Strangers Ground." The bills are available on microcard in the collection of Charles Evans, *American Bibliography: A Chronological Dictionary of All Book, Pamphlets and Periodical Publications Printed in the United States . . . 1639–1800* (Chicago and Worcester, Mass., 1903–59). Mortality data are unavailable for 1730, 1733–7, and 1745–6. For 1745 and 1746, I calculated the black population by using the average mortality figure for the period. See Smith, "Death and Life," Table 2.

Unlike the information on servant parcels for sale, the number of slave parcels has no apparent relation to the size of the black population. During the early period, slaves were purchased on consignment and were not advertised in the papers. During the later period, slaves that were brought into the colony through Maryland may have also been sold on consignment. There is reason to believe that a considerable number of Pennsylvania slaves were delivered from other colonies rather than through the port of Philadelphia. See Thomas E. Drake, *Quakers and Slavery in America* (New Haven, Conn., 1950), 75; Wax, "Negro Imports," 261–87.

[f] Except for the year 1685, data are adjusted figures. In 1685, "150 slaves were incorporated into the town's social structure." Nash, "Slaves and Slaveowners," 226.

I have adjusted the total slave population so that the slave labor force includes slaves 12 years and older. Slaves were considered taxable property at age 12 presumably because they were income producing. Nash provides an age structure for slaves and I have reduced the pre-1767 figures, those years not based on the tax lists by 30%. "Slaves and Slaveowners," 237, n. 32.

The slave population in the postrevolutionary period, 1783–93, is from a count of the Philadelphia Tax Assessors' Reports, City Archives, City Hall Annex, Philadelphia.

For the years 1795–1800, the slave population was derived by assuming steady decline at about 19 per year from 143 slaves on the 1793 tax list to the 50 slaves on the 1798 tax list.

g The total number of unfree workers combines the number of servants with the number of slaves in the work force.

h Philadelphia population figures are from Gary B. Nash and Billy G. Smith, "The Population of Eighteenth-Century Philadelphia," *Pennsylvania Magazine of History and Biography*, 99 (1975), 366. For years when population figures were not provided, I assumed steady growth.

i Calculated from the number of taxables taken from Nash and Smith, "Population of Philadelphia," 366. I made two adjustments in the figures. Since taxables are persons 21 years and older, I added 13% of the population to the taxables to include males and females 16 years and older. This estimate is based on the assumption that Smith's mortality figures can be used to fit a model population. See Ansley J. Coale and Paul Demeny, *Regional Model Life Tables and Stable Population* (Princeton, N.J., 1966), 126 and 132. In order to select the population model I used Smith, "Death and Life," Tables 4 and 6.

I also corrected the city's taxables to include women who were in the work force but were not listed as heads of household. Only 5 to 6% of the city's taxables in the late colonial period were women. This figure cannot be an accurate reflection of the women who labored outside the home, since it represents only women heads of household, and most likely not even all of those. If women worked as hired servants and were married, they would not appear on the tax lists. See Sharon V. Salinger and Charles Wetherell, "Wealth and Renting in Prerevolutionary Philadelphia," *Journal of American History*, 71 (1985), 826–840.

For 1767, 1769, 1772, 1773, 1774, and 1775, the number of servants in the city is taken from a count of the city's tax lists and includes only servants of taxable ages. Slave populations for this period are from Nash, "Slaves and Slaveowners," 237, Table 4. I reduced this figures by 10% to exclude Southwark. Estimates for city population are based on the years 1782 and 1789 at steady decline. See Nash and Smith, "Population of Philadelphia," 366. They report that the population declined from 28,414 in 1782 to 16,466 in 1789. No population figures could be found for 1791 and 1793. The population was computed by assuming steady growth from the 1790 census to the 1800 census at 1,270 per year.

j Philadelphia work force (ninth column) divided by total unfree work force (seventh column).

Appendix B: Occupational structure of servant masters, 1745–75, and Philadelphia taxpayers, 1772 and 1774

Appendix B: *Occupational structure of servant masters, 1745–75, and Philadelphia taxpayers, 1772 and 1774*

Occupational category	Servant owners												Philadelphia			
	1745		1767		1769		1772		1774		1775		1772		1774	
	N	%	N	%	N	%	N	%	N	%	N	%	N	%	N	%
Government	1	0.7	1	0.5	3	1.4	5	1.8	6	1.7	3	0.5	46	1.5	59	1.3
Professionals	4	2.7	6	3.2	9	4.2	19	6.8	14	4.0	27	4.9	87	2.8	125	2.7
Merchants and retailers	25	16.7	63	33.3	74	34.7	98	35.1	133	37.6	211	38.0	503	16.1	653	13.9
Clerical	—	—	2	1.1	3	1.4	1	0.4	5	1.4	6	1.1	35	1.1	38	0.8
Artisans	94	62.6	88	46.6	90	42.3	110	39.4	144	40.7	221	39.8	1,485	47.4	2,192	46.6
Building crafts	15	10.0	2	1.1	2	0.9	1	0.4	11	3.1	18	3.2	100	3.2	159	3.4
Cloth	35	23.3	35	18.5	36	16.9	33	11.8	49	13.8	67	12.1	415	13.3	660	14.0
Food	17	11.3	27	14.3	25	11.7	32	11.5	33	9.3	49	8.8	187	6.0	322	6.8
Marine	9	6.0	—	—	4	1.9	7	2.5	4	1.1	10	1.8	123	3.9	187	4.0
Metal	7	4.7	11	5.8	5	2.3	9	3.2	18	5.1	27	4.9	141	4.5	215	4.6
Wood	6	4.0	7	3.7	8	3.8	18	6.5	18	5.1	29	5.2	364	11.6	450	9.6
Miscellaneous	5	3.3	6	3.2	10	4.7	10	3.6	11	3.1	27	4.9	155	5.0	199	4.2
Service	6	4.0	23	12.2	28	13.1	30	10.8	37	10.5	44	7.9	192	6.1	339	7.2
Mariners	15	10.0	6	3.2	6	2.8	8	2.9	10	2.9	19	3.4	345	11.0	366	7.8
Unskilled	5	3.3	—	—	—	—	5	1.8	2	.6	2	0.4	325	10.4	829	7.6
Widows	—	—	—	—	—	—	3	1.1	3	.8	22	4.0	112	3.6	105	2.2
Total	150		189		213		279		354		355		3,130		4,706	

Sources: "List of Servants and Apprentices Bound and Assigned before Mayor James Hamilton, Philadelphia, 1745," manuscript, Historical Society of Pennsylvania, Philadelphia; Philadelphia tax lists, 1767, 1769, 1772, and 1774; Constables' Returns to the Assessor, Philadelphia, 1775.

Index

Index

Scottish emigrants, 84
Scottish emigration, 85
Scottish servants, 142; indentured as
 felons, 10
servant owners: occupations, 24, 62–7,
 72, 74, 99, 137–8, 148; relationship
 to servants, 10, 25–8, 80–1, 102–4;
 see also master artisans; runaway
 servants
servants: in British army, 107, 141;
 conditions, 108; cost, 73–4, 143;
 ethnicity, 132; supply, 143–4, 145–
 6, 148–9
servant trade, 8, 11, 59, 85–6, 88,
 144–6; convict, 77–8; death rate,
 91–2; disease, 89; effect of war, 141;
 morality of, 76–7; profit, 76–7, 93;
 regulation in 1720, 89; regulation in
 1741, 90; regulation in 1750, 94–5;
 regulation in 1765, 95–6 (*see also*
 English Board of Trade, Provincial
 Assembly); sale, 96–8;
 transportation costs, 13
Seven Years' War: effect on economy,
 134, 150, 151; effect of immigration,
 54, 140–3, 148; effect on labor
 supply, 60; enlistment of servants in,
 106–7; *see also* colonial wars
Sewell, Samuel, 5
skilled servants, 14, 145, 150; clauses
 in indenture, 10; demand, 62–3; as
 freemen, 31, 42, 151–2; status, 29
slave labor: benefit, 73; demand, 23,
 60; preferred during war, 57
slavery, 14; antislavery movement,
 139; model, 17; opposition to, 71–2;

as paternalistic, 25; system, 6; in
 Virginia, 14–15, 17; *see also*
 Gradual Abolition Law
slaves: from Barbados, 19; cost, 73–4;
 demand, 75–6; manumission, 140,
 146; population, 22, 61, 139, 140,
 141; tax, 74; *see also* black servants
slave trade, 83; mortality, 71–2; profits
 from, 74–6; Quakers, 73; supply,
 140
Smith, Abbot E., 8
Smith, Adam, 12n24, 14n28
spirits, *see* emigrant agents
staple crop economies: models, 12–13,
 16–17, 23; and unfree labor, 15–16
Statute of Artificers, 7
Sutton Air Pipes, 92–3
Swiss emigration: hazards, 11

taverns: and urban servants, 102
Thomas, Gabriel, 5
Thomas, George (governor of
 Pennsylvania), 18, 89, 90

unskilled labor, 14
urban labor, 16; demand, 69; duties,
 28; in New England, 15; in
 Philadelphia, 15, 24–5
urban servants: duties, 98–101;
 subculture, 101–2, 136

Virginia: indentured servants, 8;
 tobacco economy, 14–15
Virginia Company of London, 8, 14

Wallerstein, Immanuel, 14n29
Willing, Thomas, 60, 62
Winthrop, John, 5

Index to servant names

Index